Human Rights in Eastern Europe

Law in its Social Setting

Human Rights in Eastern Europe

Edited by
Istvan Pogany
School of Law, University of Warwick

Edward Elgar

© Legal Research Institute 1995.

Published by
Edward Elgar Publishing Limited
Gower House
Croft Road
Aldershot
Hants GU11 3HR
England

Edward Elgar Publishing Company
Old Post Road
Brookfield
Vermont 05036
USA

British Library Cataloguing in Publication Data

Human Rights in Eastern Europe. - (Law in
Its Social Setting Series)
  I. Pogany, Istvan S. II. Series
  323.0947

Library of Congress Cataloguing in Publication Data

Human rights in Eastern Europe / edited by Istvan Pogany.
    272p. 23cm. — (Law in its social setting)
    Includes bibliographical references and index.
    1. Civil rights—Europe, Eastern. 2. Civil rights—Former Soviet
republics. 3. Human rights—Europe, Eastern. 4. Human rights–
–Former Soviet republics. I. Pogany, Istvan S. II. Series.
JC599.E92H85   1995   95–19496
323'.094'0901717—dc20   CIP

ISBN 1 85898 333 9

Printed and Bound in Great Britain by
Hartnolls Limited, Bodmin, Cornwall.

Contents

List of Figures and Tables

Figures

Tables

List of Contributors

Vernon Bogdanor is Reader in Government at the University of Oxford and Fellow of Brasenose College. He has served as an adviser to the governments of the Czech Republic, Hungary and Slovakia under the auspices of the American Bar Council and the Council of Europe. His most recent books are *Comparing Constitutions* (with Bernard Rudden, 1995) and *The Monarchy and the Constitution* (1995).

Bill Bowring is a barrister practising in the fields of public law and human rights. He is an Executive Committee Member of the Bar Human Rights Committee and has undertaken numerous human rights missions, including missions to Russia, Belarus and Latvia. He teaches constitutional law, civil liberties and international human rights law at the University of East London and has published widely on questions of human rights and Russian law.

Pál Dunay, is Associate Professor in the Department of International Law at the Eötvös Loránd University, Budapest. During 1991–92, he was Director of the Department of Security Policy and Disarmament in the Hungarian Ministry of Foreign Affairs; since November 1994, he has been Deputy Director of the Hungarian Institute of Foreign Affairs. His recent publications include *The CFE Treaty: History, Achievements and Shortcomings* (1991) and *Verifying Conventional Arms Limitations* (1991).

Gábor Halmai has been Chief Counsellor to the President of the Hungarian Constitutional Court since 1990. His most recent books include *Az egyesülés szabadsága* (*Freedom of Association* (1990)) and *A véleményszabadság határai* (*The Limits of Free Speech* (1994)).

Gábor Kardos is Associate Professor in the Department of International Law at the Eötvös Loránd University, Budapest. He has published numerous articles on the international protection of human rights, on the law of international organisations and on non-military aspects of international security. His forthcoming books include *Emberi jogok – egy* *új korszak határán* (*Human Rights – at the Beginning of a New Age* (1995)) and *New Forms of Security* (co-edited with Pál Dunay and Andrew T. Williams, 1995).

Jacek Kurczewski is Dean of the Faculty of Social Problems in the University of Warsaw. He served formerly as Deputy Speaker of the Polish Seym and was a long-standing adviser to Solidarity, of which he was an early member. His recent publications include *The Resurrection of Rights in Poland* (1993).

Rein Müllerson is Professor of International Law at King's College, London. From 1992–94 he was Visiting Centennial Professor at the London School of Economics. Between 1988 and 1992 he was a member of the UN Human Rights Committee, and in 1991–92 he was Deputy Foreign Minister of Estonia. His recent publications include *International Law, Rights and Politics* (1994).

Boldizsár Nagy is Associate Professor in the Department of International Law at the Eötvös Loránd University and also teaches at the Central European University in Budapest. He has published widely on international refugee law, international environmental law and on other international law topics. He is on the Editorial Board of the *International Journal of Refugee Law*.

Istvan Pogany is Senior Lecturer in Law at the University of Warwick. His publications include *The Security Council and the Arab-Israeli Conflict* (1984); *The Arab League and Peacekeeping in the Lebanon* (1987); *Nuclear Weapons and International Law* (edited, 1987); *Current Issues in International Business Law* (co-edited, 1988) and *Righting Wrongs in Eastern Europe* (1996, forthcoming).

Jirí Pribán is Lecturer in the Department of the Theory of Law and Legal Philosophy at the Charles University, Prague. He has published widely on aspects of legal theory and on the transition process in East Central Europe.

General Editor's Preface

Law in its Social Setting aims to foster the established commitment of Warwick to the contextual study of law. The series will bring together authors from other research centres in Britain and abroad to enrich debates on issues of contemporary importance in the area of socio-legal studies.

This collection of essays examines some of the key issues to arise from the effort to secure the recognition of human rights and the rule of law in the post-Communist states of Central and Eastern Europe. The book makes a welcome and original contribution to the literature, combining the complementary perspectives of political science, the sociology of law, constitutional and international law. At a time when the transition to democracy and respect for human rights has shown signs of faltering in some of the post-Communist states (the brutal conflict in Chechnia is merely one of the most flagrant examples), this timely collection of essays provides valuable insights into the problems and prospects of human rights protection in Central and Eastern Europe.

Mike McConville
University of Warwick
February 1995

Editor's Preface

The collapse of Communism throughout Central and Eastern Europe was widely acclaimed as a moral triumph; a victory of the values of liberalism, human rights and market economics over an alien, imposed and collectivist ideology. Most famously, Francis Fukuyama proclaimed the end of history itself:[1]

> As mankind approaches the end of the millennium, the twin crises of authoritarianism and socialist central planning have left only one competitor standing in the ring as an ideology of potentially universal validity: liberal democracy, the doctrine of individual freedom and popular sovereignty. Two hundred years after they first animated the French and American revolutions, the principles of liberty and equality have proven not just durable but resurgent.

However, the euphoria which greeted the dismantling of the Berlin Wall and the ousting of Communist regimes possessing neither ideological legitimacy nor economic credibility, has been replaced by a new realism. The removal of unpopular and nominally Communist administrations has not been, in itself, a guarantor of human rights (let alone of economic advancement). Moreover, the historical experience of many (indeed most) of the post-Communist states offers very uncertain foundations for the construction of pluralist democracies of the Western type. Many commentators have been alarmed by the spectre of nationalism apparently replacing Communism as the dominant ideology in parts of Central and Eastern Europe (see for example the chapter by Vernon Bogdanor). Certainly, the stirrings of nationalism and of xenophobia, generally suppressed and denied during the socialist era, have caused disquiet in almost every post-Communist state.

However, there are also grounds for optimism. The political, institutional and legal landscape of Central and Eastern Europe is being fundamentally (perhaps irrevocably) transformed by regional and international mechanisms. In particular, the European Convention on Human Rights and the texts adopted by the Organization on Security and Co-operation in Europe (formerly the CSCE) provide a normative and institutional framework for the recognition and protection of individual and minority

---

[1] (Fukuyama, 1992 p. 42).

rights. As of 18 July 1994, Bulgaria, Hungary, the Czech Republic, Slovakia, Poland, Romania and Slovenia had ratified the European Convention and had accepted the right of individual petition to the European Commission of Human Rights in accordance with Article 25 of the Convention. In addition, eight post-Communist states – Albania, Belarus, Croatia, Latvia, Macedonia, Moldova, Russia and the Ukraine have applied for membership of the Council of Europe, a preliminary to ratification of the European Convention. Thus, as Jacek Kurczewski notes in his chapter in this volume, the constitutional process is being *internationalized*, a phenomenon which can only promote (if not guarantee) the consolidation of human rights protection in Eastern Europe (see also the chapters by Pál Dunay and Gábor Kardos).

At the domestic level, one of the most important elements in the constitutionalization of the post-Communist states has been the establishment of constitutional courts, invested with significant powers of review. In political cultures which are still in the process of democratic development and where human rights are frequently politicized, such courts can play a crucial role in asserting and elaborating fundamental rights and freedoms. To that extent, the Constitutional Courts have an historic opportunity to help define and shape the essential character of the post-Communist states (see for example the chapters in this volume by Bill Bowring, Gábor Halmai and Jirí Pribán).

Of course, generalisations about Eastern Europe are not sustainable. This is, perhaps, one of the truths which the West is only just beginning to grasp. Eastern Europe *appeared* homogeneous and undifferentiated because of the straight-jacket of socialism. The appearance of 'likeness' was also compounded by the unabashed ignorance of many people in the West for whom Budapest and Bucharest were readily interchangeable, and whose knowledge of the history of the region was, at best, superficial.

The differences *within* Eastern Europe are now evident and accelerating. Legal and institutional mechanisms for the protection of human rights in the Czech Republic, Poland or Hungary, for example, are no longer very different to those in many West European states.[2] By contrast, the recognition and enforcement of human rights in many of the post-Soviet states remains, at best, precarious (see for example the Chapters in this

---

2 This is not exactly fortuitous. Western institutions such as constitutional courts or ombudsmen, for example, have been studied and emulated by numerous post-Communist states. Perhaps a more telling difference between East and West can be found in the way in which these institutions function as the political and constitutional systems of the post-Communist states have not yet, for the most part, stabilized into patterns of predictable behaviour.

volume by Rein Müllerson and Bill Bowring). 'Eastern Europe' is, in fact, a political rather than a geographical concept, whose continuing relevance has greatly diminished in the post-bipolar world. Rather than aiding our understanding of the political, legal and cultural realities of the societies beyond the eastern frontiers of the European Union, it is now little more than a reminder of a vanished era.

As will be readily apparent, the contributors to this book do not subscribe to a single view of the dangers of nationalism or of the underlying prospects of constitutionalism and of human rights protection in Central and Eastern Europe. Rather, the authors examine these and related issues, including the role of the newly-established constitutional courts and the problems arising from refugees and minorities from a variety of perspectives, reflecting the diversity of views on these subjects.

I am grateful to the editors and publishers of the *Political Quarterly* for permission to include a revised version of Vernon Bogdanor's article, 'Overcoming the Twentieth Century: Democracy and Nationalism in Central and Eastern Europe', which was originally delivered as the Mishcon lecture at University College, London in May 1994. Rein Müllerson's chapter is a revised and expanded version of Chapter 6 of his book, *International Law, Rights and Politics*, published by Routledge and the LSE in 1994. I should like to express my thanks to the Nuffield Foundation for a grant which enabled me to undertake research for my own Chapter in the stimulating surroundings of the National Library in Budapest, Hungary.

The bulk of the contributions to this book are based on papers given at a Conference on Human Rights in Eastern Europe, held at the University of Warwick on 21 May 1994 under the auspices of the University's Legal Research Institute. I am grateful to the British Council, the Foreign and Commonwealth Office and the University of Warwick for their generous financial contributions towards the costs of the Conference and to the Director of the Legal Research Institute, Mike McConville, for his unwavering support and encouragement. Lastly, I should like to record my debt to Bernadette Royall, without whose efficiency, commitment and cheerfulness neither the Conference, nor the book, would have been possible and to my wife, Ruth, who found the time to prepare the index despite numerous other commitments.

Istvan Pogany
Stratford-upon-Avon

1. Overcoming the Twentieth Century: Democracy and Nationalism in Central and Eastern Europe.

Vernon Bogdanor[1]

I

The 20th century began in 1914 when the outbreak of the First World War showed that nationalism was to be the dominant political force of the era superseding the class war and the conflict between capitalism and socialism.

The forces of capital, as Norman Angell had pointed out in his book 'The Great Illusion' published in 1910, had nothing to gain from war, since international capital had created a Europe so economically interdependent that war was bound to disrupt it. War could not benefit the aggressor state economically, and it was precisely because war would not prove profitable that Angell succeeded in persuading many that it would prove to be a thing of the past.

Socialists, whether social democrats or Marxists, also held that war was unlikely since the working classes of different nations had more in common with each other than with their rulers. Socialists believed that the working classes would therefore resist any attempt by their leaders to fight each other.

Both the representatives of capital and those of labour were proved wrong. In 1914, the City of London and financial centres everywhere were terrified of war, while there was immense popular enthusiasm for it. Capital proved to be international, while labour was patriotic.

Poland's inter-war leader, Jozef Pilsudski, once observed that he had got onto a train whose destination was socialism, but had left it at the station

1 This paper was delivered as the Mishcon lecture at University College, London in May 1994. I am grateful to Professor Archie Brown for his comments on the first draft.

marked nationalism. Pilsudski's journey symbolises the 20th century. In the 19th century, Karl Marx had predicted a future of class war and revolution. Instead, the 20th century has been one in which the classes have collaborated but the nations fought. This was recognised by the Kaiser in 1914 as, for the first time, he received the German Social Democrats, who had abandoned their internationalism and voted for war credits. 'I no longer recognise parties', he declared, 'I recognise only Germans' (Craig 1978 p. 340). In Britain the Labour Party, after some initial hesitations, came out in favour of the war to the dismay of Keir Hardie who never recovered from the shock. Everywhere the masses, whom Marx saw as revolutionary, found that they had more in common with the ruling classes of their own country, than with the workers of another.

It was during the war that a young Italian journalist, Benito Mussolini, abandoned his youthful socialism and became an Italian nationalist; while at the end of it, Hitler came to find his vocation in National Socialism. They ensured that the First World War, far from proving to be 'the war that will end war' as so many hoped, was but the prelude to the advance of yet more extreme forms of popular nationalism, dignified with the titles of Fascism and National Socialism. The new nation-states of Central and Eastern Europe, formed after the break-up of the three great empires in 1918, the Austro-Hungarian, the German and the Russian, proved to be not model democracies, but unstable and on the whole ill-governed. By the mid-1930s all of them except Czechoslovakia had abandoned parliamentary democracy. When, in southern Europe in 1931, one country, Spain adopted – for a brief period so it was to prove – liberal institutions, Mussolini declared that 'this was going back to oil lamps in the age of electricity'.[2] In Europe east of the Rhine, the people were voluntarily embracing dictatorship, most obviously in Germany where Hitler was the product of a democratic and liberal constitutional order, put into power by the votes of the German people and sustained by their enthusiasm. 'The principle of the sovereignty of the people', the French reactionary De Maistre had declared at the end of the 18th century, 'is so dangerous that even if it were true it would be necessary to conceal it.'

The war of 1914 led also to another form of dictatorship, ideologically distinct from Fascism and National Socialism, yet in reality bearing more than a few similarities with these movements – namely Communism. For Communism too, in its Stalinist form, was a nationalist movement, designed to show that socialism could be created in one country and that Russia

---

2   Cited in Lukacs 1993 p. 153.

could, by overcoming her congenital backwardness, become a light unto the nations. For the Bolsheviks represented an indigenous form of socialism against their cosmopolitan opponents. The young Trotsky once called them slavophilising Marxists.

In the 19th century, nationalism had been seen as essentially a liberal force. This was most apparent in the thought of Mazzini, for whom nationalism was the analogue on the political level to individual freedom. Mazzini hoped to see a Europe of independent nation-states, freely co-operating together for the good of their peoples. But the 20th century has proved inhospitable to such hopes, and nationalism has become not a liberal force, but a radical one, the most powerful radical force indeed in Europe in the 20th century. In his diaries, François Mitterrand remarked that de Gaulle 'was the last of the wide-ranging political minds of the 19th century' (Mitterrand 1982 p. 6), for he too, like Mazzini, saw nationalism as a liberating force. In the 20th century, by contrast, the combination of nationalism and democracy has proved an explosive force which almost destroyed European civilisation. This combination was given legitimacy by the American president Woodrow Wilson in his Fourteen Points, and it became the basis for the treaty settlements after the First World War. The doctrine of the American scholar-president has swept all before it – in Central and Eastern Europe the sentiments which he legitimised have outlived those inspired by Marx and Lenin.

For today, popular nationalism in Central and Eastern Europe, long suppressed by Communism, is proving the dominant force in the new democracies of the region. Not only has it destroyed the empire created by the Czars and restored by Lenin and Stalin, but it has destroyed the two multinational states created by the peace treaties of 1919 – Czechoslovakia and Yugoslavia. Nor is Western Europe immune to the depredations of radical nationalism. For there are a number of signs of a revival of the radical right in Austria, Belgium and France, while in Italy a party which openly admits to admiration for Mussolini has just taken its place in government. In Central and Eastern Europe, there is growing nostalgia in new states such as Croatia and Slovakia for wartime nationalist leaders, while in Hungary, Horthy has been given an honourable reburial and in Rumania, streets are being renamed in honour of the wartime dictator, Marshal Antonescu.

The central challenge facing the new democracies is not economic, but political. It is the challenge of nationalism. The new democracies have overcome the legacy of Lenin. Can they now overcome the much deeper legacy of Woodrow Wilson? If they are to overcome the twentieth century, the new democracies will have to overcome nationalism, the most powerful political force of the mid twentieth century.

II

Many people have spoken of events in Europe since 1989 as the creation of a new political order. But it would be more accurate to think of what is happening as the restoration of an old order, an order which the peace-makers at the end of the First World War sought to create to fill the vacuum left by the decay of empire. The slogan of the peace-makers was national self-determination. Unfortunately, however, that slogan is not only incomplete as a guide to democratic rule, it also contains within itself an internal contradiction which can render democratic government unworkable. This contradiction is replicated in the Charter of the United Nations which, on the one hand, declares in Article 1 that there should be 'respect for the principle of ... self-determination of peoples', while Article 2(4) defends the 'territorial integrity or political independence of any state'. To what extent are these aims compatible?

In every one of the new democracies, there are large national minorities. Even Poland, normally thought of as a homogeneous state, contains around 250,000 Germans, while roughly the same number of Poles live in Lithuania. In every state bordering Hungary, except for Austria, there is a large Hungarian minority, amounting to two million in Rumanian Transylvania. Indeed, almost 30 per cent of the Hungarian-speaking population of central Europe live outside Hungary. Similarly, 1.8 million Albanians live in Kosovo, a region of Yugoslavia, while Bulgaria contains around one million Turkish speaking Muslims, amounting to 10 per cent of the population. The Baltic states contain large Russian minorities, and indeed there are 25 million Russians living outside Russia, while Bulgaria, the Czech Republic, Hungary, Rumania and Slovakia contain large gypsy populations, and Hungary has a substantial Jewish minority. The internal divisions within the states formed from the former Yugoslavia are too painfully obvious to need recital.

These ethnic divisions create two problems for democratic stability. The first is internal. Democracy presupposes that all groups can, in principle, participate in government. In a homogeneous state, this principle can be given effect through the possibility of alternation in government, or potential alternation in government. Party allegiance is likely to depend largely on socio-economic factors, and opposition parties can hope, through the swing of the pendulum, to replace the government of the day.

Where, however, there are ethnic, religious or linguistic differences within the state, and where party lines are determined by ethnic allegiance, then, as the experience of Northern Ireland has shown, the possibility of alternation will be absent. Where political cleavages are based on fundamental loyalties, the ethnic minority will be a permanent political minority. It will be permanently out of power.

The second danger posed by ethnic divisions is that of irredentism. Where a minority in one country looks to a majority in another, that majority may regard itself as responsible for its brothers and sisters, and make political claims upon the country in which the minority live. The late Hungarian Prime Minister, József Antall, declared that he was the representative of all Hungarians while nearer home, the constitution of the Irish Republic lays claim to the whole territory of the island of Ireland. In the last resort, such claims can easily lead to demands for territorial revision. It was demands of this kind which made Central and Eastern Europe so unstable an area during the inter-war period, and which gave Hitler the excuse he needed to destroy first the Czech and then the Polish state.

There is often no method of resolving these complex problems through application of the principle of self-determination. Partition or secession may be an appropriate solution when a particular ethnic group is territorially concentrated. But it is of little use where, as in Northern Ireland, or in much of Central and Eastern Europe, minorities and majorities are inextricably intermingled. There is simply no way of creating homogeneous national communities by drawing lines on a map. Wherever the line is drawn in Lithuania, in Rumania, in Croatia or in Bosnia, significant minorities will be left on the wrong side. Thus, if democracy depends upon the creation of a homogeneous national community, it would seem to be paralysed. That indeed was the conclusion drawn by a great 19th century student of democracy, Sir Henry Maine, who in his book Popular Government published in 1885, the year before the first Irish Home Rule bill, declared, 'democracies are quite paralysed by the plea of Nationality. There is no more effective way of attacking them than by admitting the right of the majority to govern, but denying that the majority so entitled is the particular majority which claims the right.' (Maine 1897 p. 28.)

Was Sir Henry Maine right? Does democracy depend upon national homogeneity, or at the very least upon national minorities being willing to suppress their nationality in the interests of the greater good of the country as a whole ? If so, then it has to be admitted that the prospects for the new democracies of Central and Eastern Europe may not be as bright as most of us now tend to assume.

III

It would be premature, however, to conclude that ethnicity will inevitably undermine the nascent democracies. What is needed is to think more carefully about the different ways in which democratic government can operate. There is a desperate need for fresh thinking, for escaping from the presuppositions of Anglo-American democracy, based as they are upon the Westminster Model of alternating majorities, a model which is not applicable to most of the new democracies.

Under the Westminster Model, democracy comes to be identified with majority rule. That model, as we have seen, can only work in homogeneous societies. It cannot work successfully, as history has shown, in a society such as Northern Ireland, and it cannot work in many of the new democracies, divided like Northern Ireland between permanent majorities and minorities on an ethnic basis.

There is indeed no divided society, whether the division is one of ethnicity, language or religion – which has succeeded in preserving democratic stability for any length of time without departing from the Westminster Model of government. If the central theme of the Westminster Model is that of alternating majorities, the *leitmotif* of democratic stability in plural societies, such as Belgium or Switzerland, the Netherlands and South Tyrol, divided as they are by ethnicity, language or religion, is, by contrast, the acceptance of power sharing. The essence of such an arrangement is that 'the different segments of the population share power roughly in proportion to their numerical strength so that no segment feels permanently left out in the cold'.[3] Power-sharing is indeed the basis upon which successive British governments have, since 1972, sought to govern Northern Ireland. They have tried to secure a structure of government which enables both the Nationalist minority as well as the Unionist majority to share in power. Apart from a brief experiment in 1974, such efforts have, so far, proved unsuccessful. Yet, they remain at the root of all attempts to resolve the Northern Ireland problem.

Such an approach differs considerably from the Anglo-American approach to the protection of minorities which relies upon legal safeguards for minorities, but is suspicious of the positive recognition of group rights. Yet, where legal safeguards do not touch the essence of the political process, their practical value may be smaller than their advocates hope. It

---

[3] Professor J.H. Whyte, Letter to Clerk Assistant to the Northern Ireland Assembly, 16th September 1984, reproduced in Second Report from the Devolution Report Committee, Vol. II (Northern Ireland Assembly, 19th February 1985).

is worth remembering, perhaps, that the emancipation of the black population in the United States owes less to the Constitution and the Bill of Rights, or even to the landmark Brown decision of 1954, than it does to the Voting Rights Act of 1965, by which blacks were enabled to exercise their political rights, a measure which led to very rapid change, especially in the South, so allowing blacks to assume their proper place in the American political process.

The international community has, quite rightly, taken a considerable interest in the problems raised by minorities in the new democracies. The CSCE has recently established a Commissioner on Minorities. Yet, while this is a valuable initiative, its effect is likely to be limited. Nor does the fate of the minorities treaties sponsored by the League of Nations between the wars constitute an inspiring precedent. In the last resort, the solutions to the problems posed by minorities must be found in the political and not the legal kingdom. European experience seems to show that the best protection for minorities lies not so much in statutory provisions as in institutional instruments which assist in the sharing of power. There are two main routes through which power-sharing can be achieved – the electoral route and the governmental route.

Some ethnically divided societies employ devices such as separate electoral rolls for different groups. In India, for example, until 1985, 15 per cent of the seats in the federal lower house were reserved for the so-called Scheduled tribes and Scheduled castes (Untouchables). The short-lived 1960 Cyprus constitution used a similar device. Other countries, while employing a common voting roll, have provided for a fixed number of national seats for each community.

Devices of this kind, however, can easily institutionalise ethnic differences. The danger is that all issues take on an ethnic form. Methods of separate representation, therefore, may actually worsen ethnic relations by concentrating too much attention upon them to the exclusion of other political issues. Moreover, these methods of separate representation do have connotations, even if faint, of apartheid. Modern democratic practice generally requires there to be some concept of political equality according to which electors are to be represented as individuals and not merely as members of ethnic groups. Democratic states, therefore, generally choose to be governed under a common electoral roll.

There are, even so, a number of ways in which the electoral system can play an important part in protecting minorities without departing from the principle of a common roll. Most of the new democracies have adopted one of the proportional electoral methods to elect their legislatures. Indeed none of them have adopted the British first past the post system.

Proportional representation, however, is not the name of a single electoral system, but a generic term covering a wide range of different systems, all with different political consequences. There are some proportional systems which can do a great deal to help accommodate minorities. Of course, systems based on party lists such as those used in the Netherlands or Israel entail tight party control of candidates. But there are systems, such as those in Finland or the Irish Republic, which allow voters to choose between different candidates of the same party: they build in a kind of primary election to be combined with the legislative election.

Proportional systems of this kind are much more likely to allow for minority representation since they allow voters from minority communities to select those representing their community. Indeed, it will be to the advantage of political parties to put up candidates from minority communities in areas where such minorities are concentrated. Thus, such systems of proportional representation will enable minorities to be represented within existing party systems without needing to form separate ethnic minority parties which could do damage to the internal cohesion of the state. In addition, devices used in Switzerland such as *panachage*, whereby electors can vote across party lists, and cumulation, whereby in multi-member systems voters can cast two votes for a single candidate, can also do much to assist minority representation within the framework of a national party system. For they allow voters from minority communities to concentrate their votes on the candidates from their communities.

Proportional representation cannot, however, of itself do anything to ensure that minorities have a say in government. Indeed, it is not designed to do so. What is achieved is the fair representation of minorities. But a minority in the population will still remain a minority in the legislature; and, under the Westminster Model of democracy, it will remain without a share in government. It will still be at the mercy of a determined majority which gains control of government and is prepared to use its powers to the full. So it is that the introduction of proportional representation for local and European elections in Northern Ireland has not altered the basic fact that the Catholic population is a minority there. Proportional representation cannot convert a minority into a majority. All it can do is to ensure that majority and minority are accurately represented. It cannot ensure that minorities are treated fairly, only that their voice is heard.

IV

Yet minorities require more than fair representation if their rights are to be effectively secured.   We need, therefore, to look at machinery at governmental as well as at the electoral level.   A federal structure of government may do much to protect minorities where minorities are territorially concentrated; for a minority at national level may well be a majority at provincial level.   But power-sharing can also be introduced at the level of the federal executive.   In Switzerland, for example, the Federal Council, by convention, always contains a minimum of two out of seven seats for the French-speaking cantons, and ensures that there is a balanced representation of religious and linguistic communities.   In Belgium, Article 86b of the new constitution requires that 'With the possible exception of the Prime Minister, the Cabinet comprises an equal number of French-speaking and Dutch-speaking ministers', thus over-representing the Francophone minority.   In Canada, convention rather than any constitutional rule ensures that cabinets balance Anglophones and Francophones.   In the Austrian Laender, with the exception of Vorarlberg, power-sharing at executive level is secured in a novel way.   The Land parliaments, elected by proportional representation, choose Land executives by proportional representation also, thus ensuring that minorities are represented in government.   That is similar to the model of the ill fated Northern Ireland assembly of 1974, designed to ensure that the minority community as well as the majority were able to participate in government in a divided society.

The emphasis on power-sharing at executive level can be strengthened by requiring weighted majorities on issues which affect the interests of particular groups.   In Belgium, for example, each chamber is divided into two linguistic groups, one Flemish and one Francophone.   Article 107d of the Constitution requires that certain laws 'be passed with a majority vote within each linguistic group of both Houses, providing the majority of the members of each are present and on condition that the total votes in favour of the two linguistic groups attain two thirds of the votes cast'.   In addition, the Constitution provides for an 'alarm bell' procedure (Article 38b) for those laws, excluding the budget, not requiring a special majority.   In the case of such laws, three-quarters of the members of one of the linguistic groups 'may declare that the provisions of a draft or proposed bill which it specifies are of such a nature as to have a serious effect on relations between the communities'.   In such cases the Cabinet, in which, as we have seen, each linguistic group enjoys parity of representation, reconsiders the bill and parliamentary consideration of it is suspended for thirty days.   A suspensive veto of this kind has the virtue of protecting the interests of particular groups while avoiding the dangers of inflexibility to which an absolute veto can give rise, for frequent recourse to the veto can make government immobiliste so that no decisions at all can be taken. In Cyprus after 1960, for example, overuse of the veto by the representatives of the Turkish minority on tax bills was a major reason for the failure of the Cypriot constitution by 1963. Thus the scope of the veto should be as narrow as is consistent with the provision of a feeling of security for the various groups. 'The veto power', it has been said, 'must be regarded as a kind of emergency brake', and not as part of the normal machinery of government (Lijphart 1982 p. 177).

Such methods of power-sharing at executive level require, if they are to be successful, modification of the constitutional convention characteristic of the Westminster Model, of collective responsibility. For members of the executive will tend to see themselves as brokers for their ethnic groups as well as ministers in a cohesive government. Such a brokerage role may also prove incompatible with strong political leadership on the part of the prime minister. Decision making under a power-sharing government may be slower and more difficult than it is under a more cohesive form of government; yet the decisions made may be more lasting and more legitimate if care is taken to ensure that the main ethnic groups in a country are all committed to them.

But, in most of the new democracies, minorities are not territorially concentrated, and federalism will be of little help. There are likely to be territorially dispersed minorities which do not constitute a majority even in very small local constituencies. How can the participation of minorities be assisted in such situations?

The problem of securing communal autonomy in multinational states was one which exercised many in the last years of the Hapsburg Empire, and in particular the Austrian Social Democrats. They sought to adapt the idea of federalism to a situation of territorially dispersed minorities by means of a highly original idea known as 'personal federalism'.

According to the concept of personal federalism, the state was to be divided into non-territorial associations, each of which was to comprise members of a given ethnic community. Membership of the associations was, however, to be voluntary. These non-territorial associations were to be entrusted with the administration of educational and cultural affairs, while political and economic questions would continue to be dealt with by the authorities of the empire. In their Brunn programme of 1899, the Austrian Social Democrats proposed that the associations be known as 'National Universities' and that citizens would have the right to register with them regardless of their place of residence. This was indeed an adaptation of the millet system under the Ottoman empire by which the affairs of cultural and religious minorities were regulated through autonomous communities of their own (Lieven 1994 pp. 217, 226).

The Hapsburg Empire never succeeded in resolving its nationality problems, but the methods advocated by the Social Democrats have continued to be applied in other countries. In modern Belgium, for example, the new constitution combines territorial federalism with personal federalism. There are three regional authorities – in Flanders, Wallonia and Brussels, and also three linguistic communities defined partly in non-territorial terms, Flemish, French and German-speaking. The Flemish region and the Flemish community have one common executive and legislature, but the Walloon region and the French community are not coterminous, for the French community includes the French-speaking population of Brussels, while the German speaking population has a community authority but no region. Community powers comprise what is known as 'matters linked to the person', and include cultural affairs, social affairs, health and welfare; while the regional powers concern matters linked to territory – environmental protection, physical planning, housing, regional economic policy and energy policy.

Amongst the countries of Central and Eastern Europe, Estonia stands out as having sought to adopt this method of providing for the self-expression of minorities, both between the wars and also more recently. The Estonian Law of Cultural Autonomy of 1925 provided for the right of ethnic minorities numbering over three thousand people to create their own self-governing cultural councils, through separate elections among their members. These councils received state support and were, in addition, allowed to tax their members to support minority language schools and other elements of minority cultural life. The cultural autonomy law was particularly beneficial to Estonia's German and Jewish communities which were territorially dispersed and would otherwise have faced considerable difficulties in organising their educational and cultural life.

In the 1990s, Estonia's minority problems have assumed greater magnitude. In 1934, her minorities constituted 11 per cent of the population. Today, they constitute around 38 per cent of the population. Moreover, their composition has altered. In place of the Germans who have either emigrated or been expelled, and the Jews, most of whom were killed by the Nazis, the main minorities are Russians, who constitute over three-quarters of the minority population, Ukrainians and Byelorussians.

In 1993, the new democratic government in Estonia passed a law on Cultural Autonomy for National Minorities drawing inspiration from the law of 1925 on the same subject, once again granting to members of minorities rights not linked to territory, but which can, in principle, be exercised anywhere in the country.

It is, of course, far too early to be able to judge how successful this new law will be; and, in any case, the introduction of personal cultural autonomy can only be successful if it is seen as one element – however important – in a broader pattern of minority protection, which must include legal provisions guaranteeing the use of minority languages outside the cultural sphere – in, for example, the courts and in administrative procedures. Moreover, since, in Estonia, a high percentage of the Russian-speaking population are not at present Estonian citizens, there must be a rapid programme of integration of the Russian minority within the state. They must be allowed to exercise their rights to establish their own institutions, and to vote in elections for them.

A system of personal federalism can only work where there is full confidence in the practical application of the rule of law. Anyone who fears direct or indirect discrimination as a result of public affiliation to a given national minority will hesitate to apply for registration. That is particularly important if official enrolment in a particular ethnic group is to be the only means of obtaining certain educational or cultural benefits.

There are many other difficulties with the Estonian model – difficulties involving the appropriate demarcation of responsibilities, especially financial responsibilities, between the government and the councils, and means of ensuring that the councils are representative and also that they are accountable. Nevertheless, the Estonian Law on Cultural Autonomy for National Minorities constitutes a revival of an original and sophisticated approach to minority protection. It is an approach well worth consideration by other democracies in the area, for it allows minorities to unite with fellow-members of their community without disrupting the state.

V

It would, of course, be wrong to suggest that there is just one method by which the participation of minorities can be secured, and that this one method should constitute a paradigm for all of the new democracies. The argument is only that there is a wide range of institutional devices, a number of which have been adopted in the plural societies of Western Europe, which may be of value to the new democracies. It is not the adoption of a specific institution which is crucial, but rather the spirit with which minority problems are approached. What is needed is to assimilate to the democratic logic of one person one vote, a second democratic logic of co-operation between different groups. Once that second logic is accepted, the question of the appropriate institutional devices becomes merely a question of what means is best adapted to secure an agreed end. The answer will legitimately vary from country to country.

But the problems of minorities cannot be resolved by internal reforms alone, however sophisticated these may be. For, as we have already seen, they give rise to problems of irredentism when a minority in one state is of the same ethnic composition as the majority in another. Irredentist claims can only be conciliated by establishing links between peoples such that minorities can realise their identity without compromising established boundaries. There must be power-sharing *between* countries as well as *within* them. An example of an attempt to create such links is the Anglo-Irish Agreement of 1985, one of whose aims was to enable the nationalist population of Northern Ireland to express its identity through establishing institutional links between Britain and the Irish Republic.

Similar ideas have been advocated for the new democracies without yet having won acceptance. In January 1990, shortly after Poland and Czechoslovakia had returned to democracy, the American strategist, Zbigniew Brzezinski, proposed that a Polish/Czech federation be established, mirroring proposals during the inter-war years for a Danubian confederation, a form of regional unity which might well have succeeded in containing Nazi Germany.

The need for inter-regional co-operation in Central and Eastern Europe is at least as important as the integration of the new democracies into the European Union. Yet such co-operation has remained underdeveloped for two reasons. The first is the fear, felt particularly by Hungary's neighbours, that the establishment of such institutions will be used as a basis for territorial revision. Therefore a precondition for successful co-operation across borders must be that existing borders are accepted as inviolable, to be altered only by the free consent of all parties. This means that states must renounce border changes and irredentist claims in the interest of establishing a relationship with their kinsmen and women in other countries.

A second reason for the comparatively slow progress made by schemes for inter-regional co-operation is the fear that it would be used to delay their integration into the European Union, and that in consequence, the new democracies would have only second class status in Europe. It is up to the members of the European Union, surely, to dispel such fears, and to encourage the creation of institutional links between countries, analogous perhaps to those in Western Europe, so that the identities of minority groups can be effectively expressed. The challenge surely is to create

institutions which can achieve the dual aim of encouraging the self-
expression of different nationalities, and creating a genuine union between
peoples so that the underlying unity of the region of Central Europe can be
displayed.   Such a challenge is of course primarily one for the new
democracies themselves. But it ought to be possible for those living in
Western Europe to give practical effect to their generosity of spirit by
helping their neighbours to devise institutional structures. What better way
could there be of showing by deeds as well as by words that Europe is a
single Continent, a single civilisation, something which, until 1914, hardly
anyone doubted.

<h1 style="text-align:center">VI</h1>

Shortly after Woodrow Wilson produced his Fourteen Points, his Secretary
of State, Robert Lansing, declared with some prescience:

> The more I think about the President's declaration as to the right of 'self-determination',
> the more convinced I am of the danger of putting such ideas into the minds of certain
> races. It is bound to be the basis of impossible demands. What effect will it have on the
> Irish, the Indians, the Egyptians, and the nationalists among the Boers? Will it not breed
> – rebellion? The phrase is simply loaded with dynamite,. It will raise hopes which can
> never be realised. It will, I fear cost thousands of lives. In the end it is bound to be
> discredited, to be called the dream of an idealist – What a calamity that the phrase was
> ever uttered. (Lansing, as quoted in Mansergh 1975 pp. 302–3.)

Woodrow Wilson's notion of self determination was founded upon the 19th
century liberal idea that humanity was naturally divided into nations and
that every nation should have its own state. Such an ideal, as we have seen,
is not capable of realisation in Central and Eastern Europe where minorities
are territorially dispersed, and there is no way in which they can be united
by means of territorial revision. This means that there is an urgent need for
new thinking as to how the national identities of peoples can be made
compatible with democratic stability.

The answer to the problem lies in de-emphasising the concept of
sovereignty, whether the sovereignty of the majority within the state, or the
sovereignty of the state *vis-á-vis* other states, and instead emphasising the
concept of power-sharing. But how likely is it that such a new approach
will in fact be adopted ?

The answer to this question, of course, remains open. It is in no sense
predetermined. Indeed, as Spain's first post-war democratic leader Adolfo

Suarez, once said, '[t]he future is not written because only the people can write it'.[4]

Yet democracy depends not only upon the people, but also upon those who lead the people. For democracy is not perhaps a 'natural' form of government. It depends, more than any other form of government, upon skilful leadership, upon the recognition by elites that it is in their interest to transcend nationalism and to be sensitive to the demands and challenges posed by minorities. It is not yet possible to tell whether the leaders of the new democracies will be able successfully to defuse the tensions aroused by minority and irredentist claims. It is only possible to hope that, having overcome the legacy of Lenin, they are also able to overcome the legacy of Woodrow Wilson. For the need to transcend nationalism is the fundamental challenge facing the emergent democracies of Central and Eastern Europe. Upon their success in achieving this, in overcoming the 20th century, the democratic stability of the region and perhaps also the peace of the Continent depend.

---

[4] Cited in Pzreworski 1986 p. 60.

2. Nationalism and Ethnic Conflicts in Eastern Europe: Imposed, Induced or (Simply) Reemerged

Pál Dunay

I INTRODUCTION

It has become a major challenge for conflict resolution studies to devise dispute settlement methods that can help resolve violent and protracted ethnic conflicts. The decades of the Cold War were characterized by the dominance of a bipolar world order in two senses of the word. On the one hand, there was a conflict between two different social systems organized in accordance with fundamentally different values, *inter alia* as far as democracy and respect for human rights were concerned. On the other, there was a conflict between two superpowers, leaders of their respective blocs. The latter conflict was of a global nature as the Soviet Union and the United States played a global zero-sum game in every corner of the world. The dominant conflict overshadowed every other one and hence neither theories nor political practice paid sufficient attention to ethnic conflicts and means for resolving them. It resulted in a situation where '[t]heories concerned with social conflicts or group conflicts have managed to accumulate a body of studies on mediation, arbitration, the role of third party bargaining, negotiations and problem solving. Further, there has been a cumulative growth in studies concerned with inter-state conflicts within the international system' (Rupeshinge 1987 p. 527). It is the opinion of scholars that hardly any attention was paid to theory building on ethnic conflict resolution during the period of the East–West conflict. In sum, research, just as the attention of political decision-making, focused on the dominant conflict type. It would be easy to conclude now that the nearly exclusive emphasis on inter-state conflicts was inadequate in the period 1949–89. First of all because this emphasis was a reflection of the fact that the world political agenda was dominated by the conflicts at the centre of international relations; though the rivalry of the superpowers had a great influence in the Third World, inter-ethnic rivalry has never been taken off the agenda there. It was also a somewhat inappropriate perception that ethnic conflicts had no role to play in the first and the second world. But the situation was remarkably different from that in the Third World. In the industrialized countries, the so-called first world, such conflicts were tackled, largely successfully, by means of democracy domestically and by means of integration internationally. In the socialist countries, the so-called second world, they were declared non-existent on the basis of 'socialist internationalism'. Ethnicity, and conflicts induced by ethnicity that have persisted for decades, have not been resolved but oppressed in the socialist countries. Thus, there was no reason to assume that they will not reemerge when oppression eases or ceases altogether. In some countries of Eastern Europe (e.g. in Poland and Hungary) this process has come about gradually, though the change from some type of dictatorship to a commitment to democracy came abruptly, in a matter of months rather than years.

There are three principal arrangements of power possible among states: hegemony, bipolarity and multipolarity. Hegemony means that one country exercises a decisive role in the international system. There is one country that can aspire to such a role nowadays, the United States. Although it has a leading role, there are several reasons why it cannot dominate world policy. First of all, military potential and preparedness, where the U.S. has the most convincing performance, are not the only determinants of power; economic performance and technological innovation have acquired increasing importance. Therefore other power centres, like the European Union or Japan, are at least competitive in these fields. Secondly, the U.S. does not wish to take full responsibility for being the ultimate guarantor of peace in the world. This is reflected in the burden-sharing debate between the U.S. and its allies and in its reliance on decisions of multilateral fora. The U.S. can influence the course of world events by blocking the adoption of those decisions with which it disagrees. One can conclude that the future international system will certainly not be unequivocally unipolar based on the hegemony of one state. In this respect it has to be emphasized that the privileged role of the U.S. in world affairs has costs and benefits as far as ethnic conflicts are concerned. On the one hand, the U.S. has been a democracy since the inception of independent statehood. This carries with it the promise that it will not tolerate suppression of the rights of ethnic groups as the means of 'resolving' ethnic conflicts. On the other hand, however, the U.S., due to its special history with ethnic groups, has little empathy towards ethnic conflicts that may complicate its involvement in their management and resolution.

The bipolar world order has come to an end and no nation that experienced its influence East of the Elbe (and not many in other parts of the world) want it back. The Russian leadership is of a different opinion: 'The United States does not have the capability to rule alone. Russia, while in a period of transitional difficulties, retains the inherent characteristics of a great power... And other rising power centers of influence strive for a greater role in world affairs' (Kozyrev 1994 p. 63). There is no reason to dwell on the interpretation of 'transitional difficulties' here. It has to be mentioned, however, that Russia is a country that has never experienced democracy in its history, its treatment of minority conflicts is deplorably intolerant both domestically and in its neighbourhood, and its culture of conflict resolution has too frequently been based on violence to permit us to believe that its reemergence as a world power could help resolve and not only suppress many conflicts. Even though the 'lonely' superpower, the U.S., has a tendency, for certain reasons (nuclear weapons, similar interests in some parts of the world, e.g., in Asia), to show understanding towards Russia's quest to regain its status in world affairs, these attempts are not viewed sympathetically in Europe, in spite of the fact that a bipolar system is considered to be more peaceful than a multipolar one.

This preference for bipolarity is due to three reasons: 1. '[T]he number of conflict dyads is fewer, leaving fewer possibilities of war;' 2. '[D]eterrence is easier, because imbalances of power are fewer and more easily averted;' 3. '[T]he prospects for deterrence are greater because miscalculations of relative power and of opponents' resolve are fewer and less likely' (Mearsheimer 1990 p. 14). Bipolarity, similarly to hegemony, restrains democracy in the international system, leaving the most important decisions to two decisive powers. Even if it can be an effective means of suppressing emerging conflicts, it has proven its unfitness as a means of resolving them in the sense of eliminating their sources in the long run.

Certain elements of hegemony and bipolarity are present in the post-Cold War international system. This fact notwithstanding, it has been increasingly recognized during the process of transition that the new world order will be predominantly multipolar. It has to be taken into account that the elimination of the former Soviet threat and of the communist political system in Central and Eastern Europe does not guarantee the shape of the region's future. Building viable new economic and political systems, incorporating the free market and democracy, is now the challenge. The continuation of the transformation process is a precondition of managing conflicts, both domestic and international alike. It requires that no force put constraints on the free interaction of states, which is the precondition of any kind of long-term conflict resolution. Unless multipolarity dominates international affairs conflict sources cannot be eliminated through the consolidation of democracy in Central and Eastern Europe, nor can international institutions help manage such conflicts. Every other system of international relations would make the countries of the region, which are small or medium size, dependent on the decisions and conflict management of some great powers. In such a case their short-term interests would probably give priority to the suppression of conflicts.

II ETHNICITY AND THE SOURCES OF NATIONALISM

It is not easy to draw a line between ethnic communities and nations, as can be seen from numerous definitions. For example, an ethnic community or *ethnie* is meant to be 'a named human population with a myth of common ancestry, shared historical memories, elements of shared culture, an association with a specific "homeland" and a measure of solidarity', whereas the concept of nation has been defined as 'a named human population inhabiting an historic territory and sharing common myths and historical memories, a mass public culture, a common economy and common legal rights and duties for all members'. According to this author, the 'nation shifts the emphasis of community away from kinship and cultural dimensions to territorial, educational and legal aspects, while retaining links with older cultural myths and memories of the *ethnie*' (Smith 1993 p. 130; emphasis in the original). It is clear there is only a minor difference between ethnie and nation according to the above quotation. Moreover, the introduction of 'a common economy and common legal rights and duties', two notions closely related to statehood, further complicates the situation. It is obvious that peoples belonging to the same nation, living in different states, neither enjoy common legal rights and duties nor share a common economy. It is also clear that many problems of multi-ethnic societies stem from the fact that certain groups of citizens are deprived of some rights which others enjoy. Consequently, the above concept of nation would be applicable to states which consist of one nation only.

In order to avoid international conflicts, people belonging to the nation forming a state should 'ideally' not live in any other state. The Swiss international lawyer Johann Caspar Bluntschli more than a century ago expressed his desire that '[t]he world should be split into as many states as humanity is divided into nations. ... Each nation a state, each state a national being.'[1] Nations and states do overlap and there are only a few states that can be regarded as a 'nation state' in the sense that the territory of the country is inhabited only by people belonging to one ethnic group. However, one has to cope with the fact that approximately 5,000 ethnic groups live in 200 states. In Central and Eastern Europe the situation is particularly colourful given the fact that, of the 28 states of the region, only six (Albania, Armenia, the Czech Republic, Hungary, Poland and Slovenia) can be regarded as relatively homogeneous ethnically. Homogeneity is meant to mean that the ratio of minorities in the whole population is below ten per cent (Miall 1994 p. 1). Not even each of these countries can regard itself as 'happily freed of ethnicity related problems', given the fact that their majority nations form a minority in one country or another and thus they may appear in the capacity of 'demandeur' to guarantee the rights of their ethnic brethrens in the respective neighbouring countries. This is the case for instance with Albania and Hungary, both having significant Albanian and Hungarian national minorities respectively in neighbouring countries.

There is some uncertainty concerning the question which (ethnic) communities form nations. The answer is the ones which have had 'a substantial ethnic community with its own memories, symbols, myths and traditions and whose populations share common sentiments and aspirations' (Smith 1993 p. 130). That is why ethnicity is the core of the problem and has a global relevance for the study of international relations.

The nation as a political phenomenon is a product of the modern age. Nation and nationalism came into being in already established and largely integrated dynastic states. In Eastern Europe, where state formation was often interrupted, nationalism served in the disintegration of empires and the liberation of nations from, in many cases, foreign hegemony, for example in the Ottoman and the Habsburg empires.[2]

In the revolutions of 1989, nationalism served two purposes in Eastern Europe. It was used against foreign political and military domination, virtually against an empire, the Soviet Union, even though by that time the Soviet empire did not resist the striving for independence of the East Central European nations. Nationalism can also be regarded as a reaction to the internationalist ideology of the communist movement. If one does not share the internationalist 'values' of the communist movement and the form it was given in Eastern Europe, one can conclude that nationalism served positive aims in the 1989 revolutions. It is well-known that nationalism has

---

[1] Quoted by Lind 1994 p. 87.
[2] For a more detailed analysis see Gerrits 1992 pp. 6–7.

a mobilizing role that can aid the new leaderships in Eastern Europe which have begun to build parliamentary democracies under very severe economic conditions. As an ideological vacuum came to the fore following the end of socialism, there was a need for an ideology that was easy to understand by a broad strata of the populace and around which a consensus could be built. Nationalism and nothing else could meet these requirements.

If one can assume that nationalism served such positive aims in Eastern Europe, why is the world at large so concerned about the reemergence of nationalism in the region? Of course, nationalism can take different forms, from benign patriotism to malign chauvinism. In light of the above; ethnicity and nation are fairly difficult categories to separate, at least in Eastern Europe. Nevertheless, some analysts argue that ethnic nationality is a rather dangerous source of conflict, in contrast to civic nationality. 'Ethnic nationality is based on the consciousness of a shared identity within a group, rooted in a shared culture and a belief in common ancestry. Civic nationality, by contrast, is inclusive within a territory. Membership in the national group is generally open to everyone who is born or permanently resident within the national territory, regardless of language, culture or ancestry' (Snyder 1993 p. 7). Consequently, it is civic nationality which has no ethnic roots.[3] One has to differentiate between *nationality*, which has more to do with citizenship, and *nationalism*.

It may be correct to state that those nations whose historic development was 'harmonious', free of major interruptions, resulting in the creation of nation-states in the 18th and 19th centuries, achieved some type of 'civic nationalism'. Such non-ethnic nationalism is the exception, however; nationalism is still overwhelmingly related to ethnicity. According to Snyder, civic nationalism is also present in the Eastern European region, as the Russian and the Ukrainian leaderships advocate it. It is understandable that President Yeltsin favours civic nationalism in Russia, since his country is a multinational state that should be kept together without discriminating against the numerous minorities and without endangering the integrity of the Russian Federation. This approach only seemingly contradicts the ethnic nationalism of Russia, when it supports the minority rights of the more than twenty million ethnic Russians who reside in other republics of the former Soviet Union.

Beyond this fundamental differentiation, nationalism can be categorized several ways; the terminology used is far from uniform. For the purpose of analysing Eastern European security politics, two typologies deserve special

---

3 Other authors differentiate between ethnic and constitutional nationhood. It seems, however, they attribute a similar meaning to these notions as Jack Snyder with the introduction of 'civic' and 'ethnic' nationality. See Hassner 1993 p. 50.

attention. According to a Polish expert, the following types can be discerned currently in Eastern Europe: 1. The nationalism of stronger, more powerful nations against the nationalism of weaker nations; 2. The nationalism mobilised by the ruling elite (from above) and one developed by groups not in power (from below); 3. The nationalism which is induced from outside the national society and the nationalism which originates from inside; 4. The nationalism which manifests itself in aggression against other states or nations and one which refers to legitimate self-defence; 5. The nationalism which is motivated by special interests and one which is value-oriented. This value can be a common tradition, a political ideology or religious fundamentalism which helps determine the enemy of the nation; 6. The nationalism of a majority and that of a minority.[4]

According to another expert, there are the following categories: 1. Ethnic nationalism. 2. Protective nationalism. 3. Territorial nationalism. (Interestingly, this category is not similar to 'civic nationalism' which would be a logical assumption. It is regarded as identical with irredentism which is 'almost universally abjured – at least officially'.) 4. Separatist nationalism 'describes a situation in which ethnic communities reject the authority of the state in which they reside'. 5. Emotive nationalism. 6. Religious nationalism. (Brown 1992 pp. 7–8.)

It is obvious that certain types of nationalism carry the risk of destabilisation and can influence security and military policies of individual Eastern European countries. Those states which pursue aggressive or territorial nationalist policies are more prone to conflicts than those which reject such policies.

'Hypernationalism' is used by some American political scientists for the most dangerous type of nationalism which has emerged in Eastern Europe. This is 'the belief that other nations or nation-states are both inferior and threatening and must therefore be dealt with harshly' (Mearsheimer 1990 p. 21). The perception of inferiority or superiority is regularly present in group-to-group relations.[5]

It is naive to 'promote moderation' by structuring 'the electoral system of the state so that most political parties and mainstream politicians cannot perceive a political advantage in adopting extremist positions on ethnic issues' in Eastern Europe (de Nevers 1993 p. 33). Although I do not believe that those nationalistic policies which cannot be kept under some control by political means are always bad, the recommendation above does not provide an adequate response to the problem. As many East European

---

[4] See Lamentowicz 1993 p. 32.
[5] For more details see Horowitz 1985 pp. 167–71.

countries are emerging parliamentary democracies, some politicians will take extremist positions on ethnic issues if this can increase their popularity. The maturity of the electorate and the composition of the political spectrum will be factors in determining whether intolerant nationalism will fade away gradually in Eastern Europe or whether it will gain new momentum.

A deeper understanding of the double role of nationalism in the region leads to the conclusion that '[i]t would ... be inappropriate to advise the East Europeans to "overcome their nationalism". In the wake of the denationalizing repression of the Soviet era, they are now experiencing an overpowering need to recover their national identities; and besides, in many countries of Eastern Europe there are no other political awareness focusses that could take the place of national values to form the basis of the forthcoming reconstruction' (Wettig 1992 p. 21). Even though it is an exaggeration to state that 'democracy is next to impossible in a country with a multi-ethnic population' (Maynes 1993 p. 12), it is certainly true that multi-ethnicity and the accompanying nationalism are complicating factors when parliamentary democracy is introduced in any country. One can assume that nationalism contributes to the cohesion of societies in Eastern Europe to a certain extent, but it also has the potential to get out of control. Therefore, the most important question is not whether or not it can be eliminated in the short term, but how it can be effectively influenced 'in the right direction' so that it could contribute to the consolidation of democracy. That is why one can agree with the view that when the West fights against 'small nationalisms' in the region, it indirectly defends and strengthens the 'great power chauvinism' of certain leading imperial nations, e.g. those of Russia and Serbia (Wettig 1992 p. 6).

A distinction can be drawn between three types of ethnic conflicts: 1. The most common one is the irredentist, like the Arab-Israeli dispute or the conflict over Cyprus. The primary actors of this conflict type are states. 2. The secessionist type has its origins within state settings, but spills over into the international arena by drawing in third parties. 3. Ethnic conflicts can involve the processes of decolonization between colonial powers and nationalist groups.

Empirical evidence shows that '[e]thnic conflicts result in higher levels of violence than non-ethnic conflicts'. Furthermore there 'is a rank order of ethnic conflicts such that anti-colonial ethnic conflicts are the least violent, secessionist ethnic conflicts the second most violent and irredentist conflicts the most violent' (Carment 1993 pp. 139–40). Consequently, given the ethnic composition and the presence of intolerant nationalism in Eastern Europe, there is cause for concern, since existing conflicts and the ones which may emerge in the future will most likely be the most violent sort. The situation is further aggravated by two supplementary factors. Evidence shows that new state involvement in ethnic conflicts will increase their level of violence and that economically weak and dependent regions are more prone to violent ethnic conflicts than regions without these features (Carment 1993 pp. 143–4).   Consequently, it seems clear unfortunately that violent ethnic conflicts will be present in Eastern Europe in the years to come.

III THE REEMERGENCE OF NATIONALISM IN EASTERN EUROPE AND ITS DANGERS

One of the most important reasons for the reemergence of ethnic conflicts in Eastern Europe is the fact that the four decades of the East–West conflict was not accompanied by integration in the region. What we could witness was a kind of integration of the communist elites in the name of internationalism that left the population of Eastern Europe totally unaffected. Consequently, no feeling of solidarity has developed among the nations of the region and, as a side-effect of certain developments,[6] the situation has worsened. The ideological basis of politics in the socialist countries vanished together with the system itself in a matter of months leaving nothing else behind but a longing for some of its slogans, like social justice and full employment.[7] The internationalist ideology had no effect whatsoever on the population. Hence, when the system collapsed a kind of ideological vacuum could be perceived in the region. It could be filled only by an ideology that met certain criteria. These were that it had historic roots, that it could contribute to the cohesion of the society, that it was fairly easy to understand by a broad strata of the population, and that it had a certain anti-hegemonial thrust. No ideology other than nationalism could meet these criteria. As the history of the years since the collapse of the 'socialist world system' has demonstrated, very different political forces have recognized that nationalism can be used for their political purposes. The fact that a potentially dangerous type of nationalism has emerged can

---

6 Apart from the anti-Soviet feelings prevalent in many Eastern and Central European countries one can particularly refer to the invasion of Czechoslovakia in 1968 that spoiled the relations between the population of that country and of the five invaders.

7 I do not in any manner want to give the impression that I regard social justice as nothing but a slogan. What I mean is that due to the inherent constraints of the socialist system, resulting in very low economic efficiency, social justice could not be put into practice except as 'poverty for everyone'.

be explained by the simultaneous appearance of several catalytic factors. 1. The diminution of Soviet influence that suppressed intra- and interstate violence has disappeared and thus an important restraint on the manifestation of violent nationalism within and between these states has been removed. 2. The search for a new ideology was manifestly present in the period of system change. 3. With the rejection of the left there was a turn to the political right which is more sympathetic to nationalism than socialist and liberal forces. This does not mean that other forces were not willing to rely on nationalism in their rhetoric, simply that their attitude was somewhat more restrained than that of the conservatives.[8] 4. The unrealistic hopes invested in swift and substantial improvements in living standards and the emerging socio-economic hardships have resulted in widespread pessimism about the future and quick disappointment with the new governments that came to power following the collapse of the socialist system. Many dissatisfied people turned their envy and resentment toward those who were able to adjust quickly and profit from the emerging market conditions, especially if these new entrepreneurs happened to be members of different ethnic groups or nationalities.[9] 5. The countries of the region, irrespective of the significant differences between their development patterns, have experienced political liberalization, particularly freedom of expression; however this has given way to increased discord rather than to mutual understanding.[10]

When one takes a closer look at these factors it is clear there is no one single reason for the emergence of nationalism in Central and Eastern Europe. As the nature of conflicts stemming from the treatment of minorities and nationalism varies from country to country, it is necessary to analyse each case closely in order to develop the appropriate dispute-resolution methods. The conclusion that nationalism was induced by external forces is not provable. No unequivocal answer can be given to the question whether its reemergence was primarily due to the activity of the new political elites in countries east of the Elbe or to the desire of masses to find an ideology that answers certain problems coherently. Its emergence has probably been due to the coincidence of the 'top down' and the 'bottom up' approach. Given the fact that nationalism has not resolved practically

---

[8] It is interesting to note that five years after the revolutions in Central and Eastern Europe there is a tendency in a number of countries from Hungary to Lithuania and Poland that non-conservative forces gain power. This demonstrates that the voting pattern of the electorate is more effectively influenced by promises concerning the satisfaction of daily needs than by any kind of nationalistic overtone.

[9] On this point see Huntington 1990 p. 43.

[10] For two somewhat similar, though by no means identical, viewpoints with that expressed above see Barány 1994 pp. 168–70; and Schoch 1992 p. ii.

any of the pending problems of the region there has developed a certain disillusionment with nationalistic ideas in some countries.

The danger of nationalism has been recognized early on by the West as a source of conflict that could destabilize the whole region. It was the assumption of western institutions that '[r]isks are less likely to result from calculated aggression against the territory of the Allies, but rather from the adverse consequences of instabilities that may arise from the serious economic, social and political difficulties, including *ethnic rivalries and territorial disputes*, which are faced by many countries in Central and Eastern Europe'.[11] The new NATO strategy seems to have misunderstood the post-Cold War European environment. The Alliance made a false assessment of the potential threats to the old continent. As a German analyst, Philipp Borinski, wrote: 'NATO analysed the sources of crises in Central and South-Eastern Europe and on the periphery of the CIS as potential threats of a classical type ... the same type as those in Northern Africa or Western Asia' (Borinski 1993 p. 29). According to Borinski the threat assessment was unrealistic, since it was highly unlikely that the crises in the above areas would spill over to any member-state of NATO. The war in the former Yugoslavia, for example, has continued for more than three years. None of the neighbouring countries have got involved in this conflict and there was no sign whatsoever that the conflict there might pose a direct threat to any West European state. In sum, one can conclude that for the time being no development in Central and Eastern Europe has threatened the West directly. It has either posed no threat internationally or it has been limited to the neighbours of the conflict area.

Beyond this general assessment one has to differentiate between nationalisms carrying different risks and threats. The most important one is its intensity, ranging from benign patriotism to malign chauvinism, which has already been mentioned. Three other differences must also be taken into account.

1. The nationalism of ethnic minority groups which form the majority in another country carries more severe risks than the nationalism of groups which cannot count on the effective support of a nation represented by a state. Hence, ethnic conflicts e.g. involving the gypsy population of a country, do not pose a direct threat to stability and security and may remain the concern of NGOs like Amnesty International. They certainly do not go beyond the scope of 'traditional' human rights concerns. However, nationalistic conflicts which involve, for instance, the 'ethnic' Russians in

---

11 'The Alliance's New Strategic Concept Agreed by the Heads of State and Government participating in the meeting of the North Atlantic Council in Rome on 7–8 November 1991' (1991), *NATO Review,* 6 (39), p. 26. (Emphasis added.)

other CIS countries, or Hungarians in Transylvania, do have implications in terms of political security and can endanger the fragile stability of the region.

2. There is a significant difference between minorities dispersed in a large geographic area, mixed with (an)other, in most cases majority, group(s), and ones which are settled in separable entities in the vicinity of the mother nation. Whereas the former category is not prone to territorial solution by means of secession, the latter may give rise to such dreams amongst nationalist politicians. That is why an increasing number of analysts, including the author of this chapter, are of the opinion that the risks associated with e.g. the approximately two million Hungarians in Transylvania have been largely overestimated. George Schöpflin's views, while certainly not shared by many in Hungary, nevertheless highlight the impossibility of a territorial solution for the problem of ethnic Hungarians in neighbouring countries. Thus, Schöpflin has suggested that 'Trianon was the best thing that ever happened to Hungary and any idea of frontier revision would be a major disaster. If Hungary's enemies wanted to destroy Hungary forever, they would get together and return to the 1941 frontiers. Hungary would then have 6 million Romanians, nearly 1 million Slovaks, and as many Serbs; if democratic institutions were maintained, Budapest would have to be a totally multilingual city, not to mention the necessary economic, political, and cultural reintegration.'[12] Thus, while international legal experts concerned with the rights of minorities may express concern over their maltreatment, political analysts have to limit their attention to those cases which threaten to undermine stability. Such a danger is present primarily in cases when conflicts over minorities are overlaid with territorial disputes.

3. Even though the five years that have passed since the fall of the Berlin wall have clearly been insufficient to draw conclusions of unquestionably lasting validity about the pattern of historical development of Europe, one can state the following provisionally. It seems that post-Cold War Europe is divided not into two but rather into three parts as far as conflict management and resolution are concerned. These are, respectively, Western Europe, which is dominated by the rule of law and democracy and the states of which are tied together by an extensive web of international conventions and institutions. This makes conflict management both domestically and internationally possible. However, the former Eastern bloc

---

[12] Comments of George Schöpflin in Shafir and Reisch 1993 p. 32. By late 1941, following two arbitration awards and the invasion of both Yugoslavia and the Soviet Union, Hungary temporarily gained back much of the territory it had lost after World War 1 as a result of the Trianon Peace Treaty.

has not remained united since the end of the East–West conflict. It can therefore be divided into two parts as far as conflict potential and the means of their resolution are concerned. Such a differentiation between different zones of Eastern Europe has a long history which seems to have regained the relevance which it lost long ago.[13] What we have experienced since the end of the Cold War is that, though ethnic conflicts characterize both the so-called former non-Soviet Warsaw Pact area and the former Soviet Union and dominate their security agendas, there is a fundamental difference between their management in these two areas. Despite the frequently intolerant rhetoric in Central Europe concerning minorities and ethnic issues, conflicts have remained exclusively political in the former non-Soviet Warsaw Pact area; there has been no danger of military escalation.[14] In the former Soviet Union, on the other hand, ethnic conflicts nearly automatically escalate into military ones. With the exception of the decisive conflict in that area, the one between Russia and the Ukraine, there is violence from Moldova to Tajikistan through Armenia, Georgia and Azerbaijan. On this basis one can state that the differentiation between the three regions of Europe has reacquired its relevance.

IV THE TREATMENT OF ETHNIC CONFLICTS

The difficulty of managing ethnic conflicts stems from several factors, including the fact that they are conditional on different elements in the development of societies. Consequently, such conflicts are produced by a variety of factors such as the historical development of a society, its traditions, economic conditions etc. Hence effective conflict resolution, in the sense of the elimination of conflict causes, requires changing deep-rooted development patterns in a lasting manner. Complexity is only one problem, however. A further one, as mentioned above, is the fact that, in many cases, the causes of ethnic conflicts are not exclusively dependent on the activities of rational state actors. Thus, influencing the behaviour of state organs may not be sufficient to ease ethnic tension.

These considerations notwithstanding, it is necessary to get involved in the resolution of ethnic conflicts on the assumption that they cannot be managed in Eastern and Central Europe without external support and

---

[13] For an excellent historical analysis see Szücs 1993 pp. 291–332. The study was first published in Hungarian in 1981 and in English in 1988.

[14] It should be noted that Yugoslavia, a non-aligned country, which has witnessed the bloodiest ethnic conflict since 1991, never belonged to the non-Soviet Warsaw Pact group.

influence. One may raise the objection that it would entail interference in
the domestic affairs of states. A narrow interpretation of the UN Charter
would not permit this, as it declares that '[n]othing in the ... Charter shall
authorize the United Nations to intervene in matters which are essentially
within the domestic jurisdiction of any state.'[15] The meaning of non-
interference was not so unambiguous when the Charter was drafted in San
Francisco as one might otherwise conclude from the above-stated rule. As
stated at the San Francisco Conference, 'if the fundamental freedoms of
individuals were grievously outraged so as to create conditions which
threaten peace or obstruct the application of the Charter, then they cease to
be the sole concern of each state'.[16] The development of international law
during the last five decades has taken a direction which has permitted the
former Secretary-General of the UN to argue with reason: 'Has not a
balance been established between the right of States, as confirmed by the
Charter, and the rights of the individual, as confirmed by the Universal
Declaration? We are clearly witnessing what is probably an irresistible shift
in public attitudes towards the belief that the defence of the oppressed in
the name of morality should prevail over frontiers and legal documents.'[17]
Interference should serve limited goals only, namely to prevent or eliminate
violent ethnic clashes, and to hinder the emergence of extremist tendencies.
Two issues require particular caution, namely secession and assimilation.

   Secession would further destabilise Central and Eastern Europe as it
would result in territorial disputes since no state is willing to give up
territory in order to 'promote' the rights of a minority. It is a popular
argument nowadays that border changes are no longer taboo in the region.
One has to note, however, that only unification of states and the dissolution
of federations, but no border change between two existing state entities, has
taken place. Even though border revision may be tempting to terminate 'a
civil war between communal groups with irreconcilable differences'
(Shehadi 1993 p. 72), stability should be guaranteed throughout the process.
This does not seem realistically possible under current conditions. There are
some important arguments against border changes: 1. It may result in a
domino effect; 2. Opening up the possibility of border changes will revive
dormant conflicts and trigger the use of force; 3. Allowing for such changes

---

[15] Charter of the United Nations, Article 2, para. 7.
[16] United Nations Conference on the International Organization. Selected Documents.
   Quoted by Boles 1988 p. 5.
[17] 'Secretary General's Address at University of Bordeaux', SG/SM/4560, 24 April
   1991, p. 6. (Statement of Javier Perez de Cuellar delivered at the University of
   Bordeaux on April 22, 1991.)

will lead to the proliferation of states, with detrimental effects on regional stability and economic development. (Similarly Shehadi 1993 pp. 73–4.)

Secessionist tendencies can be discouraged by influencing states not to support secessionist movements. This is one of the ways of easing security risks involved in ethnic conflicts. It is certain, however, that if tendencies towards coerced assimilation do not gain the upper hand in a country, there is less interest in secession. Consequently, it is necessary to work for guaranteeing minority rights, while at the same time discouraging secessionist tendencies that would strain ethnic relations.

4.1 Arrangements for Guaranteeing Minority Rights and Preventing Ethnic Conflicts

a) The United Nations

Despite the widespread violations of human rights during World War 2, the UN Charter does not provide any international guarantees for the protection of minorities, nor does it even mention the principle. This fact does not mean, however, that the UN was virtually immobilized on this issue. For example, by virtue of the rules governing the pacific settlement of disputes (Chapter VI), the Security Council may investigate any dispute, or any situation which might lead to international friction or give rise to a dispute, in order to determine whether the continuance of the dispute or situation is likely to endanger the maintenance of international peace and security (Article 34). Moreover, any member of the United Nations may bring any dispute or situation of this kind to the attention of the Security Council or the General Assembly (Article 35, para. 1); the Security Council is entitled to recommend appropriate procedures or methods of adjustment (Article 36, para. 1); and the General Assembly can make recommendations with regard to any such question (Article 11, para. 2). These rules can also be applied to disputes arising between states over the protection of minorities. A word of caution seems necessary here. First of all, Europe was a condominium of the superpowers for more than four decades during the years of the East–West conflict. Europe thus remained a sanctuary where no international institution could contribute to the settlement of conflicts. Since 1990 the Security Council has become involved in conflict management, since 1991 primarily in the former Yugoslavia, though the old continent seems to have largely remained *terra incognita* for the UN. Secondly, many Third World countries have been of the view that priority should be given to state sovereignty and non-interference rather than to human rights and self-determination. There are frightening examples concerning the treatment of minority conflicts under UN auspices. It is sufficient to mention here that the Council declined to declare that the events in Rwanda, the most flagrant violation of human rights, amount to genocide. Hence, there is reason to doubt that the world organization is the most appropriate forum to tackle minority issues and ethnic conflicts in Eastern Europe.

Despite the inherent link between the purposes and principles of the UN Charter and minority rights, no specific international system for protecting minorities has been created under the UN Charter. This fact is certainly due to a new understanding of the minority problem prevailing after World War 2 and could also be attributable to the unfavourable experiences of minority protection in the framework of the League of Nations, as well as the territorial settlements and population exchanges made after the War. Accordingly, the question of minorities was supplanted by a comprehensive framework of human rights, and an effective system of human rights protection replaced the special provisions and methods of minorities protection. This has been a doubtful endeavour in light of the fact that only a tiny minority of states has an ethnically homogeneous population. Unsurprisingly, a massive amount of evidence shows that inter-ethnic tensions can and do evolve repeatedly in different regions.

One cannot conclude by stating that no major step has been taken in this field by the United Nations. The Economic and Social Council of the UN has been authorized to set up commissions for the promotion of human rights (Article 68). In 1946 the Commission on Human Rights and in 1947, within its framework, the Sub-Commission on the Prevention of Discrimination and Protection of Minorities were established to assist ECOSOC in fulfilling its task to make recommendations for, and ensure observance of, human rights and fundamental freedoms for all (Article 62, para. 2). The tasks of the Sub-Commission include contributing to international legislation on minorities protection and the implementation of regular investigations into concrete cases.[18] Nowadays, contrary to the early period of its activity which was dominated by contributing to international legislation, the examination of concrete cases constitutes virtually the whole workload of the Sub-Commission.

The Universal Declaration on Human Rights, adopted by the UN General Assembly on December 10, 1948, does not contain any reference to minorities as such. In order to avoid the impression of having neglected the minorities issue the General Assembly, in its resolution 217C (III), stated that the UN could not remain indifferent to the fate of minorities, but added that it was difficult to adopt a uniform solution to this complex and delicate

---

[18] *Study on the Rights of Persons Belonging to Ethnic, Religious and Linguistic Minorities* (1991), New York: United Nations, pp. 28–9.

question that could be applied in all states. It seems this difficulty was one of the principal reasons for the decision not to mention the problem of minorities in the Universal Declaration.

Whereas the Declaration does not contain any rules on the protection of minorities, the Covenant on Civil and Political Rights, opened for signature nearly two decades after the former document had been adopted, regulates the protection of ethnic, religious and linguistic minorities. Article 27 provides that '[I]n those states in which ethnic, religious or linguistic minorities exist, persons belonging to such minorities shall not be denied the right, in community with other members of their group, to enjoy their own culture, to profess and practise their own religion, or to use their own language.' The text of the article calls for interpretation in several respects. It is open to question whether the article ensures minority rights for individuals constituting the minority (individual approach) or for the minority as a group (collectivist approach).[19] Nor is it clear how the negative formulation of this provision should be interpreted with respect to the preservation of the ethnic, religious and linguistic identity of minority groups. Most importantly, what steps can be taken in order to suppress assimilationist efforts of the state representing the interests of the majority nation? Also, what exactly does the prohibition of discrimination mean? What kind of choice is open to an individual to free himself from a minority situation or to remain in it? To what extent can the state be forced to act, i.e. to go beyond the mere tolerance of the existence of a minority? What is more, the Covenant provides a guarantee for minority protection inasmuch as the states which are parties to it assume the obligation to report to the UN on the realization of the stipulations contained in the convention (Article 40). Despite the significant step forward made by the Covenant, and beyond such problems of interpretation, the Covenant does not contain an extensive enumeration of minority rights, it does not distinguish between rights and duties, and it does not establish effective guarantees for the protection of minority rights.

The profound changes that have taken place since the mid-1980s, primarily in the Soviet Union, made the revision of the previous attitude of the UN towards the minority problems possible. The Sub-Commission assumed responsibility for studying the practice of minority protection under the relevant provision of the Covenant. Its initial findings were summarized in the Capotorti Report (Capotorti 1988 p. 41). The study undertook to define the notion of a minority, to outline the basic principles of the international protection of minorities, and to draft some proposals for

---

[19] For more details on this problem see the contribution of Dr. Gábor Kardos in this volume.

the procedures to be used in this sphere. The definition of a minority as 'a group numerically inferior to the rest of the population of the state in a non-dominant position, whose members being nationals of the state possess ethnic, religious or linguistic characteristics differing from those of the rest of the population, and show, if only implicitly, the sense of solidarity, directed towards preserving their culture, traditions, religion or language' (Capotorti 1988 p. 44) – leaves the question of an 'individualist' or 'collectivist' approach open.

In 1992, the General Assembly passed a Declaration on the Rights of Persons Belonging to National or Ethnic, Religious and Linguistic Minorities, a document that is more assertive than previous UN instruments. It does not contain a definition of minorities and leaves some room for ambiguity. It calls upon states not only to prevent discrimination against minorities, but to protect and promote their identity and rights. This is certainly an important change of 'ideological' approach from the negative (non-discrimination) to the positive (protection and promotion). As with other comparable UN human rights instruments (the Declaration is a resolution of the General Assembly, not a treaty), there are no enforcement or implementation measures attached to the Declaration. It seems that the UN, having emerged from four decades of paralysis caused by the bipolar world order, may in future take a more active role in the monitoring and protection of minority rights. It was a significant achievement in this respect that the General Assembly, in late 1993, appointed a diplomat from Ecuador to be the first UN High Commissioner for Human Rights. He will have to rely mostly on moral and political persuasion and preventive diplomacy. Nevertheless, this development demonstrates that the UN, having recognized the conflict potential of ethnic rivalry, has understood that monitoring and preventive diplomacy might contribute more effectively to avoiding a worsening of the situation than adopting further rules. It would be premature to state, however, that the UN has found an adequate response to one of the major conflict sources of the post-East–West conflict environment.

b) The CSCE
The countries which signed the legally non-binding Final Act of the Conference on Security and Cooperation (CSCE) in Helsinki, in 1975, took responsibility for the rights of persons belonging to national minorities on their territories. In particular, Principle VII of the Declaration on Principles Guiding Relations between Participating States, provides that '[t]he participating States on whose territories national minorities exist will respect the right of persons belonging to such minorities to equality before

the law, will afford them the full opportunity for the actual enjoyment of human rights and fundamental freedoms and will, in this manner, protect their legitimate interests in this sphere'.[20] Principle VIII asserts that '[t]he participating states will respect the equal rights of peoples and their right to self-determination'.[21] As the participating states, who became signatories to the Final Act, assumed responsibility for the appropriate treatment of national minorities, complaints related to minority affairs could no longer be rejected by referring to the principle of the prohibition of intervention in the domestic jurisdiction of states. In any event, the acceptance of the international character of the protection of minorities, provided for in treaties and in other documents, would not imply the renunciation of state sovereignty, because the right of states to conclude international agreements is derived from their sovereignty. Consequently, a request that a state respect obligations of an international character cannot amount to an infringement of either the principle of sovereign equality or of non-intervention.

The concluding documents of the first two follow-up meetings did not bring any improvements concerning minorities. At the third follow-up meeting, held in Vienna (1986–89), the issue of human rights became an increasingly important element in the evolving definition of European security. In February 1987 the member states of the European Community and NATO proposed the insertion into the Helsinki process of a human dimension mechanism that would facilitate the endorsement of human rights (see Lehne 1991 p. 72). Three stages were envisaged: first, upon request, governments would be required to supply information about suspected violations, then, if the response proved unsatisfactory, bilateral consultations would be held and, as a last resort, a special CSCE meeting could be convened to address the situation. The Soviet delegation blocked the proposal for several months. In the end the concluding document included elaborate provisions on human rights and fundamental freedoms for all 'without distinction of any kind such as race, colour, sex, language, religion' (*CSCE Final Act* p. 106). It should be stressed that during the meeting the absence of unity of the East, *inter alia* on human and minority rights, became apparent. 'To protest Romania's treatment of their Hungarian minority, the Hungarian delegation co-sponsored a strongly worded Canadian proposal on minority rights, the first time in Helsinki history an Eastern country has 'crossed-over' to co-sponsor a major

---

[20] *CSCE Final Act of Helsinki* (1975) and the Concluding Documents of the Follow-up Meetings at Belgrade (1978), Madrid (1983), Vienna (1989) of the Conference on Security and Cooperation in Europe (1989), Malta: Department of Information, p. 12.
[21] Ibid., p. 13.

Western human rights proposal' (Fry 1993 p. 123). Despite the development of the Helsinki commitments at the three follow-up conferences, the results remained cosmetic as long as the bipolar world order remained.

The first sign of a fundamental shift in the climate of opinion was evident at the second conference on the Human Dimension that met in Copenhagen in June 1990. The concluding document, enshrined the conditions necessary for elections to be considered free and fair and enumerated principles for a sound legal system. The document also extended CSCE undertakings on freedom of expression, association, peaceful assembly and movement. It reaffirmed respect for the rights of national and ethnic minorities. Disputes erupted at the conference concerning the 'new Europe's' security problem, the treatment of national minorities, which the CSCE was ill-equipped to handle. The most deplorable shortcoming of the document, however, was its neglect of what was rapidly becoming Europe's preeminent security problem – managing the likely separation or secession of different components of existing multiethnic states.

The Charter of Paris for a New Europe, adopted a few months later in November 1990, marked the end of the East–West conflict. However, it did not introduce anything novel concerning the rights of minorities. Later on, recognition grew that the attempts of the CSCE to resolve ethnic conflicts were 'too little, too late'. Prevention had been abandoned in many instances for management, not even for resolution. It was of great importance, however, that the process of institutionalization had begun. Among the first institutions of the CSCE to be established was the Office for Free Elections, later transformed into the Office for Democratic Institutions and Human Rights.

The July 1991 meeting of experts on national minorities, held in Geneva, further contributed to the monitoring of national minority issues by the CSCE. The meeting stated unequivocally that these issues were of 'legitimate international concern and consequently do not constitute exclusively an internal affair of the respective state'.[22] In Geneva, the main issue was not the division between the proponents and opponents of minority rights. Rather, the issue was reverse discrimination; the notion that a minority sometimes has to be favoured at the expense of the majority if such groups are to achieve genuine equality. The debates created strange divisions. Romania and the U.S. found reasons to critcize the idea, while France joined Hungary in sponsoring the proposal which advocated elaborate solutions that would take 'particular circumstances' into account.

---

22 *Report of the CSCE Meeting of Experts on National Minorities* (1991), Chapter 2.

During 1991 an emphasis was put on consolidating the conflict management potential of the CSCE. At the first June 1991 Council meeting of CSCE foreign ministers the emergency mechanism, which had not been adopted by the preparatory committee preparing the Paris Charter due to the reluctance of the U.S., got adopted. According to this text, upon the request of at least 13 CSCE participating states an emergency meeting of the CSCE Committee of Senior Officials shall be convened in order to consider whether the underlying concerns of the participating states are well-founded or not. The meeting is to open a maximum of 72 hours after the request was made and shall last up to a maximum of two days. The only agenda item to be discussed at the meeting is the issue in response to which the emergency mechanism was invoked.[23] With the exception of the mechanism on unusual military activities, established by the 1990 document on confidence- and security-building measures, this was the first occasion when the consensus rule was not observed. Nevertheless, the Council's decision remained ambiguous insofar as the grounds for invoking the mechanism are concerned; hence it may be argued that it also extends to domestic affairs which adversely affect the international situation. However, this conclusion would be wrong given the fact that three countries made the adoption of the document conditional on the insertion in the text of a reference to non-interference in domestic affairs. One of these, Turkey, was worried about Cyprus, whereas the other two, Yugoslavia and the Soviet Union, as recent history demonstrates, could have been worried about the future development of their countries. This was the first mechanism that could also be invoked in the event of a massive violation of minority rights. A few month later, in October 1991, the CSCE, without referring expressly to the emergency mechanism, supported the proposal of the EC to investigate the status of human and minority rights in Yugoslavia. The delegation of the Belgrade government insisted that, according to the consensus rule, the mission could only come to Yugoslavia with its approval.[24]

The conflict management potential of the CSCE has been further developed in the document of the Moscow meeting on the human dimension.[25] The establishment of a human dimension mechanism was a clear recognition of the fact that the massive violation of human rights may trigger conflicts threatening peace and security. The process is fairly

---

[23] *Berlin Meeting of the CSCE Council 19–20 June 1991* Annex 2: Mechanism for Consultation and Co-operation with regard to Emergency Situations, point 2.

[24] For further details see Weitz 1992 pp. 24–6.

[25] *Document of the Moscow Meeting of the Conference on the Human Dimension of the CSCE* paras 1–14.

complex encompassing several phases. It is most important to emphasize that several means are available to the CSCE participating states in order to keep the human rights record of another country on the agenda, even if the country in question is opposed to such international scrutiny. A state may ask for information from another state and, if it is dissatisfied with the answer, a bilateral meeting can be held. It is also possible for an expert mission to be sent to the country in question. Last, but by no means least, observers can also be sent. Basically, there are three possibilities for invoking this last mechanism. A state can invite observers, for instance as Albania did before becoming a participant in the CSCE process. The CSCE can also send observers without the invitation of the state. The worst case is when a country consistently rejects cooperation. In that eventuality, ten participating states can decide to send observers to the country where the human rights record gives ground for concern. The human dimension mechanism which, as a last resort, can be invoked without the consent of the 'other side' and without the consensus of all the CSCE participating states, provides the parties with an effective mechanism *in abstracto* for investigating alleged human rights violations.

The consensus rule – the most important decision-making principle of the CSCE since 1975 – has been questioned in different fields. Exceptions were adopted in 1990–91 on certain issues without weakening its application on most substantive questions. Meetings in case of unusual military activity could be convened, the emergency mechanism could be invoked, and observer missions under the human dimension mechanism could be sent to a country without the consent of each CSCE participating state. For a number of reasons, several participating states were of the opinion that the time was ripe for breaking with the consensus rule with respect to substantive issues as well. At the January 1992 meeting of the CSCE Council a decision was adopted according to which, in cases of 'gross and uncorrected violations of ... CSCE commitments', the 'consensus minus one' formula will be applied, which means that the state directly involved will not be in a position to veto the decision. However, the traditional principle of state sovereignty will continue to apply as '[s]uch actions would consist of political declarations or other political steps to apply outside the territory of the state concerned'.[26] Even though I share the view that the consensus rule proved to be a major stumbling-block to increasing the CSCE's efficiency, each case should be thoroughly examined to

---

[26] *Prague Document on Further Development of CSCE Institutions and Structures,* Section IV, para. 16.

determine whether reaching agreement without consensus is unavoidable or whether there is a chance of reaching consensus through tough bargaining.

The 9–10 July, 1992 Helsinki summit developed the conflict management potential of the CSCE further. The new 'institution' which was established then by the participating states, the CSCE High Commissioner on National Minorities, is to play a monitoring and early warning role. It was the expectation of the participating states that the function of the High Commissioner will primarily be that of conflict prevention rather than management. Thus, the mandate of the High Commissioner is to serve 'as an instrument of conflict prevention at the earliest possible stage' through the provision of 'early warning' and of 'early action'.[27] The latter concept is elaborated in a somewhat ambiguous provision which indicates that the High Commissioner may be authorised to go beyond its role of observer and mediator: 'The High Commissioner may recommend that he/she be authorized to enter into further contact and closer consultations with the parties concerned with a view to possible solutions, according to a mandate to be decided by the CSO (Committee of Senior Officials). The CSO may decide accordingly'.[28] This involves a departure from mediation in favour of conciliation, which presupposes a more active role for the High Commissioner extending also to the recommendation of solutions for the resolution of the potential conflict. The practice followed by the High Commissioner since the beginning of 1993 has demonstrated that his focus has been on fact finding in potential trouble spots. He has been involved in the following situations: 1. Latvia and Estonia, with regard to the Russians living there; 2. Slovakia (the Hungarian minority) and Hungary (the Slovak minority); 3. Romania, in particular concerning the Hungarian minority; 4. The former Yugoslav Republic of Macedonia and its Albanian population; 5. Albania, with regard to the Greek population in the south of the country; 6. Ukraine, in particular the situation on the Crimea; and 7. Inter-ethnic relations in Kazakhstan and Kyrgyzstan (Van der Stoel 1994 p. 11). The activities of the High Commissioner have helped to foster an understanding of the realistic options available concerning the management of minority conflicts. One of the important conclusions, which should serve as a warning signal to political forces involved in upcoming ethnic conflicts, is that 'it is clear that territorial arrangements and in particular secession are not realistic options because they are not viable and are unacceptable to almost all states' (Zaagman 1994 p. 222).

---

[27] *CSCE Helsinki Document 1992: The Challenges of Change: Helsinki Decisions* Section II. CSCE High Commissioner on National Minorities, paras. 2, 3.
[28] Ibid., para. 16.

The whole activity of the CSCE in building institutions and in preventing and managing ethnic conflicts is an experiment of unprecedented proportions in the process of adaptation to the post-East–West conflict scenario. It would be premature to state whether it has been successful or not. It is a fact, however, that the CSCE has gone a long way towards becoming an effective mechanism for tackling current conflict types. The development of CSCE monitoring and dispute settlement capacities seems more important than its continuing norm creating activity.

c) The European Convention for the Protection of Human Rights and Fundamental Freedoms

The European Convention system is the most fully developed of the regional human rights structures in existence. The European Convention for the Protection of Human Rights and Fundamental Freedoms was signed by member states of the Council of Europe on 4 November 1950, and entered into force three years later. It created two bodies for the implementation of human rights: the European Commission of Human Rights and the European Court of Human Rights. The Convention contains a rather long and detailed catalogue of rights and freedoms, entitlement to which is secured without discrimination on any grounds such as sex, race, colour, language, religion, political or other opinion, national or social origin, association with a national minority, property, birth or other status (Article 14). Thus, the Convention stipulates that the rights of minorities in the contracting states shall be protected and, in addition, it establishes special organs to ensure the observance of the commitments undertaken in the Convention (Article 19).

The rights and freedoms contained in the Convention were based, generally, on the provisions of the Universal Declaration of Human Rights. However, the Convention made a significant step forward by including, in Article 14, a reference to possible discrimination on the grounds of association with a national minority. Both the European Commission and the Court of Human Rights have had to deal repeatedly with concrete cases which concern this provision. Those of us in Central and Eastern Europe who followed the reports of the Commission and the judgments of the Court over the past decades frequently envied the human rights record of the member countries of the Council of Europe. Most of the disputes referred to the Commission and Court reflected minor, individual violations lacking political relevance. The situation is about to change. The Central European countries have already joined the Council of Europe and have become parties to the Convention. Even though their human rights record has improved significantly, some of them face political conflicts over their treatment of minorities which may lead to references to the organs established under the Convention. If these bodies continue to focus on individual violations they may become politically irrelevant.[29] If they react to the challenge posed by political conflicts they may well become over-politicized. The choice is not easy, particularly in light of the possible further extension of the membership of the Council of Europe to include countries facing even more severe minority conflicts. It would be highly desirable to combine the two approaches i.e. to continue to deal with individual human rights cases without losing sight of the significant threat potential posed by minority conflicts in current and future member countries of the Council and parties to the Convention.

In October 1993, the declaration issued at the first (failed) summit meeting of the member states of the Council of Europe recognised the importance of the proper treatment of minorities and indirectly expressed the necessity of focusing on groups as well, rather than exclusively on individuals. This was reflected in the summit declaration which expressed the intention to 'pursue the close co-operation engaged between the Council of Europe and the CSCE High Commissioner for National Minorities'.[30] It is clear that the CSCE High Commissioner places emphasis on the treatment of minorities and on the politically relevant, large scale i.e. not individual, violation of their rights in his monitoring activity. As the summit was unable to adopt a Convention on minority rights it instructed the Committee of Ministers, as a fall-back position, 'to draft with minimum delay a framework convention specifying the principles which contracting States commit themselves to respect, in order to assure the protection of national minorities'.[31] It does not mean that the Council has abandoned its former focus on individual rights, as may be illustrated by the fact that the Council has also instructed the Committee of Ministers 'to begin work on drafting a protocol complementing the European Convention on Human Rights in the cultural field with provisions guaranteeing individual rights, in particular *for persons belonging to national minorities*'.[32] It does mean, however, that the member states are aware that if the Council is to maintain its political relevance in a period of ethnic turmoil, following the extension of its membership to states which are embroiled in political conflicts over minorities, it cannot but adapt to the new conditions.

---

[29] In any event, the present Convention organs will be replaced by a single Court when Protocol No. 11 enters into force. For the text of Protocol 11 see e.g. (1994) International Legal Materials Vol. XXXIII, No. 4, p. 960.

[30] Council of Europe Summit, Vienna Declaration, SUM (93)2, 7 October 1993.

[31] Ibid.

[32] Ibid. Emphasis added.

d) De Lege Ferenda: Pact on Stability in Europe

As it gradually came to be recognized that latent and existent ethnic conflicts will dominate the security agenda of Central and Eastern Europe, and that the current practice of European conflict resolution has not been sufficiently effective, there was a tendency to try to find new means and methods to keep potential ethnic conflicts, arising in the vicinity of the West, under control. One of these, which has attracted significant attention in the media, is the so-called Balladur plan (named after the prime minister of France), which envisages the conclusion of a pact on stability in Europe. The original initiative met with mixed reactions in Central Europe as it explicitly referred to the possibility of 'minor border modifications' and to 'collective minority rights', two ideas disliked by many countries that have significant minorities and which gained additional territory under the terms of peace treaties (by contrast Hungary was a 'loser' in both respects after both World Wars). Those who had liked the original idea became disappointed and disillusioned after it was picked up and 'digested' by the EU. The proposal of the 12 emphasized the stability of borders and the importance of respect for the rights of minorities. The EU initiative aimed at stabilizing the extended Central European region (the six former non-Soviet Warsaw Pact countries and the three Baltic states) by backing the conclusion of bilateral treaties between states experiencing tensions related to minority or ethnic issues. Because the plan has been endorsed by the EU, all the nine countries have pledged themselves to participate in the conference – but without enthusiasm.

Even though some Eastern European countries wanted to leave the process the EU left no doubt that such a step would jeopardize the eventual integration of the respective states in the EU. As integration is the declared priority of the nine countries, Bulgaria, the Czech Republic, Estonia, Hungary, Latvia, Lithuania, Poland, Romania and Slovakia remain in the process. Following the inaugural Conference for a Pact on Stability in Europe, held in late May 1994, the nine participating states are expected, within a period of one year, to conclude bilateral or regional treaties regulating *inter alia* good neighbourly relations 'including questions related to frontiers and minorities'.[33] The EU expressed 'its readiness to play the role of moderator in the bilateral talks at the request of the interested parties'.[34] Two regional round tables were formed in accordance with the Document, one for the Baltic region and one for the other Central and Eastern European countries. The most important purpose of the whole

---

[33] *Concluding Document of the Inaugural Conference for a Pact on Stability in Europe*, point 1.5.
[34] Ibid., point 2.4.

exercise, however, is to regulate pending minority and border problems bilaterally. Those states which are not interested in having high profile talks on these issues have already announced their unwillingness to conclude the so-called basic treaties in this framework. Hungary, by contrast, would actually favour the involvement of the EU in such bilateral talks in the hope that it could thereby achieve a more satisfactory arrangement concerning the rights of the Hungarian minorities, particularly in Romania and Slovakia. This has been clear from the interpretative statement attached to the concluding document by Hungary: 'The initiative of the European Union is designed to initiate a process in which bilateral talks will take place between two neighbouring countries, with an EU presence and with its contribution as a mediator, and as a result of these, good-neighbourly agreements will be reached taking fully into account the minorities' interests and views. An important and indispensable factor in these negotiations is that a continuous dialogue commences between the minority and government concerned in the presence of an EU mediator, with the purpose of settling the questions in dispute, in order that the agreements are satisfactory to both sides. The Hungarian government cannot formally represent the citizens of other countries who belong to a Hungarian national minority, but it considers it an essential requirement that the representatives of the minorities concerned should be able to present their views during the process and on the agreements reached.'[35]

It seems increasingly clear that the purpose of the exercise is nothing else than to demonstrate the 'final resolution' of pending minority problems and to confirm existing borders. The latter, contrary to the former, can be regarded as useful. Given the direct involvement of non-state actors, i.e. ethnic groups and NGOs in minority conflicts, it is doubtful whether measures monitoring state activity could be considered as guaranteeing respect for minorities. In the light of this, one can be confident there will be no breakthrough with regard to the most sensitive problem of European stability, that of minorities. There is every reason to believe that the conference will end with a final document far from meeting the original expectations and ambitions of its initiator. The high profile interest towards the stability pact in certain cases may even have been counter-productive. It merely highlights once again the gap between some neighbouring states concerning their treatment of minorities.

---

[35] Ibid. Interpretative statement.

V CONCLUSIONS: OR WHERE DO WE GO FROM HERE?

Nationalism and ethnic conflicts are lasting phenomena of post-Cold War European security. Nationalism has played a double role in Central and Eastern Europe since the end of the East–West conflict. On the one hand, it contributed to the cohesion of societies in the period of transition and, on the other, it increased tension between states and ethnic groups. Thus, it has contributed to stability and instability simultaneously.

The complexity of minority conflicts is due to a number of factors. It is not exclusively influenced by state actors; group-to-group relations at the grass-root level are of similar importance. They are dependent on a broad range of societal phenomena ranging from historic traditions to economic development patterns and the culture of conflict settlement in the society.

There is every reason to assume that three historic regions of the continent have reemerged in this respect; Western, Central, and Eastern Europe. It is a widespread conviction that democracy and integration guarantee that the emergence of minority conflicts will not destabilize societies or result in interstate violence in Western Europe. On the other hand, it is the concern of many that ethnic conflicts may easily result in interstate tension and political instability in Central Europe. Even though no evidence underlying this assumption has been available since the end of the East–West conflict, the concern diminishes very slowly and with difficulty, if at all. The desire of these countries to integrate is an important impediment to violent conflict resolution on the state level. For this reason there is a certain exaggeration in the picture presented to the western public. 'It is particularly difficult to understand the attempts made by some analysts or politicians to reduce the strategic problems of Central and Eastern Europe to the question of nationalism or tensions resulting from the position of national minorities. They frequently mistake cause for effect and – focusing their attention on the superficial – are unable to grasp the heart of the matter, the essence of the actual problems with which the nations and states ridding themselves of the heritage of communism and Soviet domination in this part of Europe have to cope.' (Skubiszewski 1993 pp. 18–9). The third region, comprising the 12 republics of the former Soviet Union, is full of ethnic violence and instability. The respect for minority rights there is dependent on the termination of violence.

The traditional difference between conflict resolution and respect for persons belonging to national minorities has been maintained and hence there is fairly little coordination between efforts to eliminate conflict causes and measures for the improvement of the situation of minorities. The huge interest of the international community concerning the resolution of ethnic conflicts is encouraging nevertheless.

It is necessary to develop programs fitting specific needs and based on an in-depth knowledge of the situation in individual countries and regions. The general means and methods presented in this chapter, whether of a global or a regional character, are necessary though insufficient. The adoption of further specific legal regulations on the protection of minorities might be useful. However, it is even more important to improve the continuing monitoring activity of international institutions in potential conflict areas.

In the long run, the resolution of ethnic conflicts may come about through the consolidation of democracy and the integration of conflict-torn countries in international institutions. And till then?

3. Perspectives on Human Rights and Democracy in the Former Soviet Republics

Rein Müllerson[1]

It is not an easy task to reflect on human rights and democracy in countries in transition. The situation is volatile and positive developments (if there are any) are more often than not counter-balanced by immediate backlashes. Another problem stems from the intensive legislative process which is difficult even to follow. A legal act which may seem extremely important today is often overshadowed by subsequent developments. As one famous Russian artist put it: you produce a film about the absence of sausages, but next day the cheese is gone. Or, what is even more realistic in many places in the former USSR, everything is available in the shops but there are few who can afford to buy.

To avoid the danger of writing a paper which will be outdated before publication one needs a perspective which is a bit more detached from everyday events. It is more important to try to discover tendencies than to report mere facts. Such an approach should include a look at the historical roots of current developments and problems as well as some theoretical reflections on what is happening in the newly-born states in the territories of the former Soviet Union.

One more preliminary remark needs to be made. The situation with respect to human rights is different in each of the former Soviet republics, although there are certainly some common features as well. But the limits of the paper, as well as of my knowledge of the situation in the different former Soviet republics, does not allow me to deal with the situation in each of these newly-born states. Therefore I have chosen to concentrate on the human rights situation in Russia, which is by far the biggest of the new

---

[1] This is an expanded and revised version of R. Mullerson (1994), *International Law, Rights and Politics*, London & New York: Routledge/LSE, Chapter 6.

states. I shall also deal with some specific issues in some of the other former republics, while skipping over some states altogether.

I FROM TOTALITARIANISM TO PERESTROIKA AND GLASNOST

In a totalitarian state, and the USSR was undoubtedly an exemplary one, it is hardly possible to speak of human rights at all. Human rights, which are often rights of the individual versus the state, presuppose the existence of a civil society and the autonomy of the individual *vis-à-vis* the state. This was not the case in the Soviet Union. The state and the Communist Party were omnipresent. Even when, for example, a Soviet citizen travelled abroad he or she was not exercising his or her liberty of movement. Rather, the state or the Communist Party had allowed him or her to travel as a special favour. Neither could there be any freedom of press, for example, as all mass media was not only state- or Party-owned but was also controlled by them.

Absence of an independent judiciary meant that declared rights could not be guaranteed. Though executive and judicial branches might have had some independence from each other, they were both completely subordinated to the Communist Party. In the early 1970s Professor Piotr Galanza, in his lectures on the history of law at the Moscow University, used to emphasize that courts were most independent in the Soviet Union because they were subordinated to nobody but Party committees. He could probably afford such jokes, which were especially dangerous as they corresponded to reality, because of his age and, more importantly, because he had been a member of the Communist Party since March 1917.

Certainly, one could speak of violations of human rights in the Soviet Union from the point of view of international human rights standards. In the international arena the Soviet Government was rightly accused of violating these standards, which did not penetrate 'the Iron Curtain', though the USSR had ratified most UN instruments on human rights. Under the Soviet legal system there were no human rights. There were privileges for proper and good behaviour and deprivations for bad or politically incorrect behaviour.

After March 1985 when Mikhail Gorbachev became the Secretary-General of the CPSU new winds started to blow, though very slowly. For example, it took several years for newspapers to start publishing material which cautiously referred to the possibilities of introducing a multiparty system in the USSR. The mass media began to criticize, though such criticisms were directed only at distortions of socialist ideas; they did not dare to question the foundations of these ideas. Gorbachev himself and the Soviet mass media spoke only of a 'socialist democracy' and of a 'socialist rule of law state' as the aims of these reforms.

It is interesting to note that when Gorbachev for the first time, and I think unwillingly, cast doubt on one of the pillars of Marxism–Leninism, namely the subordination of common human values to the interests of class struggle (or could one even say, the complete negation of the possibility of the existence of such values), he had to quote Lenin (Gorbachev 1987 p. 149). However, there is probably only one and rather vague reference in Lenin's works to the priority of common human values over the interests of the working class. On the other hand, one can find tens or maybe even hundreds of very clear remarks by Lenin and by the other founding fathers of Marxism–Leninism where they expressed contempt for democracy as such and derided common values because, according to them, every social class had its own values, morals and interests. But Gorbachev, both because of his background and especially because of the conditions prevailing at that time in Soviet society, simply had to refer to Lenin, though he was in essence undermining the very foundations of Marxism–Leninism – the class approach to all social issues.

However, notwithstanding the fact that the processes unleashed by Gorbachev in 1985 were very slow to gain momentum, by 1991, the year of the demise of the USSR, the country had already undergone substantial changes. I think that it is necessary to pay tribute to the first and the last President of the Soviet Union for unleashing and leading these processes. One has to be courageous to start processes of democratization in a totalitarian society and one has to be committed to democratization in order not to turn back and revert to the use of methods which were only too familiar to every Soviet leader in order to safeguard the power of the Communist Party and its Secretary-General.[2]

Of course, Gorbachev did not foresee what kind of forces he had unleashed. The developments and events had their own inner dynamic. What he wanted to reform had, ultimately, to be completely dismantled, and

---

2   Of course, force was used in clear violation of international human rights standards in Tbilisi (1989), in Baku (1990) and in Vilnius (1991) and Gorbachev bears his share of responsibility for that. But, as a whole, Gorbachev's policy of gradually introducing reforms and balancing the different political forces, which may have been seen as demonstrating a lack of decisiveness (and to a certain extent it clearly was), nevertheless prepared Soviet society for the support of democratic reforms, helped to change the balance of political forces within Soviet society, awakened the population from social hibernation and was necessary for the rejection, in August 1991, of the coup.

this dismantling involved not only communist ideology and policy, but also the country itself. The ideology on which the communist regime was based was utopian. However, the composition of the USSR was artificial as well. Gorbachev wanted to reform the state, to make it, according to his own words, a genuine federation, because, notwithstanding its official title, it had always been a very strong unitary state. Later, the idea of a federation with some confederative elements was proposed but here, as often happened, Gorbachev was too late.

All drafts of the Treaty of Union elaborated under Gorbachev's leadership were not only late but they also had one fundamental deficiency – they tried to combine the incompatible in various domains. In the political field such incompatible elements were, for example, the maintenance of the leading role of the Communist Party in society, while at the same time seeking the democratization of society and of the state. In the reform of the state structures, such contradictions could be found in the sovereignty of the constituent republics *and* in the sovereignty of the USSR itself.

But now, looking retrospectively at these events, it seems that these inconsistencies were almost inevitable. They reflected the struggle which was going on between the new and the old, and they also reflected the level of development of the society at that moment, as well as the correlation of the different political forces. Compromises, though short-lived, were, at the time, very often inevitable.

By the end of 1991, when the Soviet Union collapsed, some democratic changes had already been introduced. The main and one of the few tangible achievements of *perestroika* was *glasnost*, which may be described as tantamount to the freedom of the press or to freedom of expression except that it existed in a chaotic and uncertain social environment and was therefore often without any limits but at the same time also without guarantees.

Laws on mass media, on freedom of conscience and religious organizations, on non-governmental associations and on the right to leave the country, though far from corresponding in all aspects to the respective international standards (especially concerning the right to leave one's country), were passed by the Supreme Soviet of the USSR.[3] The Soviet Union also adhered to the Optional Protocol to the International Covenant on Civil and Political Rights.[4] Adoption of all of these measures was

---

3 *Vedomosti Siezda Narodnih Deputatov SSSR i Verhivnogo Sovieta SSSR*, 27 June 1990, No. 26; 10 October 1990, No. 41; 17 October 1990, No. 42; 12 June 1991, No. 24.
4 *Vedomosti Siezda Narodnih Deputatov SSSR i Verhovnogo Sovieta SSSR*, 17 July 1991, No. 29.

achieved as a result of hard struggle between, on the one hand, democratic forces and, on the other, conservatives in the Central Committee of the Communist Party, in the military industrial complex and in the KGB.

In 1989, the two most odious articles of the Criminal Code of Russia (Articles 70 and 190) and the corresponding articles in the codes of the other republics, under which most dissidents had been sentenced, were repealed (*Pravda* 11 April 1989 p. 1). But, even here, the law repealing these articles contained new provisions intended to maintain at least some elements of the old articles. Only under the pressure of public opinion and influenced by articles published by some well-known academic lawyers, which were highly critical of these provisions, did the Supreme Soviet change the law which had just been passed.

This shows, on the one hand, that glasnost had already played a positive role but, on the other hand, it also indicates how difficult it was for the seeds of democracy and human rights to germinate.

II COLLECTIVISM, INDIVIDUALISM AND HUMAN RIGHTS

In order to better understand current problems and future prospects in the field of human rights in the new states which emerged after the dissolution of the USSR, a short excursion of a theoretical nature is needed into the history of socialist ideas and Soviet practice concerning human rights. I think that such an excursion may reveal something useful regarding some other countries as well.

Now there is probably no doubt that the most important ideas of Karl Marx, especially those concerning communism, were as utopian as the ideas of those whom Marx, Engels and Lenin had called the 'utopian socialists' (Campanella, More, Owen) and which were considered by them to be the precursors of 'scientific socialism', i.e. Marxism–Leninism. Such basic ideas of Marxism as the elimination of market relations, socialism as the first stage of communism (communism being considered to be a completely new social formation), the role of the proletariat and its dictatorship etc. all proved to be utopian.

It is interesting that Marks and Engels themselves warned that a massive growth of the productive forces, and a high degree of development were absolutely essential practical preconditions for the success of a socialist revolution. Without them only widespread poverty would result and, in cases of extreme need, the struggle for essential objects would have to start all over again, which would mean that all the old abominations would have to return (Marx and Engels *Politizdat* vol 3, p. 33).

In offering this warning Marx and Engels were both right and wrong at the same time. They were right (although probably they did not have this in mind at all) in thinking that the acceptance of really viable socialist ideas entailed certain economic, cultural and intellectual preconditions which were clearly absent at that time (and not only in Russia). They were right also in foreseeing what would happen in the case of a successful socialist revolution (successful in the sense of the seizure of power) in an under-developed and poor country. But they were wrong in believing that such a revolution could be successful in a highly developed society.

It was only in underdeveloped countries that there was a chance for the violent planting of the utopian ideas of Marxist teaching. In these countries there were no economic, social, or spiritual foundations for realising the positive sides of socialist teachings. They therefore, at best, remained slogans only, or were frequently perversely used for the suppression of the individual and his rights and freedoms. But at the same time only under these conditions could a socialist revolution become a reality.

The record of many countries has shown that socialist ideas were perceived rather superficially and put into practice in countries which were economically and socially underdeveloped. Thus it was in Russia in 1917, and thus it was in the so-called 'countries of socialist orientation' in the Third World. Is this a coincidence? It seems not. As Lenin himself noted: 'for Russia in the concrete, historically extremely original situation of 1917, it was easy to launch the socialist revolution; but to continue it to the end in Russia will be far more difficult than in the European countries' (Lenin *Politizdat* vol. 41, pp. 47–8).

But those difficulties which Lenin probably had in mind were really insurmountable, because the aims themselves were utopian. And in order to implement utopian ideas in Russia after 1917 violence was widely used (and how could one put into practice utopian ideas without violence?) not only against the overthrown, so-called exploitative classes, who naturally desperately resisted the new power, but also against the peasants, the intelligentsia, as well as against the representatives of the new ruling, i.e. the working, class itself.

In this regard, it is appropriate to remind the reader of the words of Vladimir Korolenko, a brilliant Russian writer, who wrote to Lunacharsky, at that time the People's Commissar for Education: 'The very ease with which you managed to carry the masses of our people along with you, shows not our readiness for socialist construction but, on the contrary, the immaturity of our people' (*Novy Mir* 1988 No. 10, p. 207). 'In our country, industrially backwards, with little developed capitalism, it will be easier to organize the economic life in accordance with the communist plan' wrote another equally brilliant Russian philosopher, Nikolai Berdyayev (Berdyayev 1989, p. 87).

They were right but, as is often the case with those who are right and brilliant, they were not heard but were instead sent far away. These first two hundred Russian intellectuals were lucky. Lenin sent the best minds of Russia to the West while Stalin, some years later, chose another direction – the East, Siberia.

There are several reasons to explain why these ideas were accepted in underdeveloped countries. No doubt there was a special attractiveness about the socialist ideas amongst oppressed peoples who truly had nothing to lose except their chains. This, and also the susceptibility of poor masses to collectivist ideas, particularly the ideas of equality and social justice, in countries where individual rights and freedoms were unknown for the majority of the population. But in such countries these ideas acquire, as a rule, the most radical, extremist form, and are implemented in a decisive, uncompromising manner.

In Western societies, where there are more developed and widespread individualistic concepts which place the individual at the centre of society and even of the world order, where the level of societal development has achieved such a degree that practically all of society's members have *something* to lose, in these societies ideas that call for the socialization of all the means of production and the violent overthrow of the existing structures do not find especially fertile soil.

However, in underdeveloped countries, where socialist ideas are more easily accepted and where, to use Lenin's expression, 'it is easy to launch the socialist revolution', only the most utopian ideas and violent means for their implementation can be used. Here the violent introduction of the utopian elements of socialist teaching (nationalization of the means of production, the liquidation of the market, etc.) becomes possible, while at the same time truly valuable ideas (e.g. guaranteeing every person's social and economic well-being, free health care or education) cannot be realized in practice.

Accordingly, in those countries which announced the building of socialism and embraced the practical implementation of the ideas of socialism, considerable limitations and violations of human rights and freedoms always took place; the cults of party and of state leaders developed; and dictatorial regimes emerged.

And this no doubt is not a coincidence. In a society where the essential material preconditions for acceptance of the ideas of social security, free health care, etc. are lacking, where individual rights and freedoms are not developed, where democratic traditions are completely lacking, some aspects of socialist ideas receive one-sided interpretation and application, while other aspects remain only slogans or are simply forgotten. In the name of a class, nation, or people which does not have sufficient political experience, leaders at different levels begin to run public affairs with the support of the bureaucracy. This is why, when the attempt was made in Russia to put into social practice ideas which either generally contradicted the tendencies of social development or which required for their implementation considerably more developed social relations, it was necessary to do it through violent methods.

However, not just the aim – a humane society – but the means of attaining this result has to be humane as well. Otherwise the aim becomes one with the means of its attainment in the sense that the final result will be forged by the character of the means applied.

By this I do not wish to call for obedience to tyrants, the submissiveness of the oppressed, or to deny a people's right to overthrow a government which does not guarantee its rights and freedoms. However, the violence carried out in Russia after October 1917, not only in practice in the form of the executioner's excesses, but also enshrined in instructions and even raised to the level of theory, repeatedly exceeded the measures necessary for overcoming the resistance of the overthrown classes.

As to the representatives of the overthrown classes, the Soviet Chekist (ChK was a predecessor of the KGB), M.I. Latsis, himself a victim of the Stalinist terror in 1928, wrote in 1918:

> We do not conduct a war against separate persons. We destroy the bourgeoisie as a class. Do not search amidst the investigation materials and proofs, for evidence of the fact that the accused acted in either word or deed against the Soviets. The first question which you must pose to him is to what class he belongs to, what is his background, his upbringing, his education or profession. And these questions must determine the fate of the accused. In this is the idea and the essence of the Red Terror. (*Krasny Terror*, 1 November 1918.)

On 2 June 1921, V.A. Antonov-Ovseyenko and M.N. Tukhachevsky, both later shot by Stalin in 1939 and 1937 respectively, while conducting the struggle with Antonov's peasant revolt in the Tambov province, signed order No. 171, which, *inter alia*, declared:

1. Citizens refusing to disclose their names to be shot on the spot without trial.
2. Villages in which weaponry is hidden shall be sentenced by order of the authorities to seizure of hostages, who shall in turn be shot in case of refusal to yield the weaponry.
3. In cases of locating hidden weaponry, persons to be shot on the spot without trial.
4. Families which hide bandits shall be subject to arrest and eviction from the province, and all property to be confiscated. The bread-winner in the family to be shot on the spot without trial. (Feldman 1989 p. 57.)

And finally, let us cite the opinion of yet another victim of the Stalinist terror, A.I. Rykov, in connection with the 'Shakhty Affair'. At the Central Committee Plenum in 1928, he said that the party must subordinate various legal processes to questions of policy, and in general not follow abstract principles of punishing the guilty according to justice; and that as regards the question of arrest, it was necessary to approach this topic not so much from the point of view of the interest of our criminal policy, as from the point of view of our 'over-all policy' (*Pravda*, 3 October 1988).

I have cited only these four well-known revolutionaries and political and military leaders of the Soviet State, in whose personal fate was reflected the fate of the nation. The adherence to violent methods of struggle, to terror in response to the resistance to the Bolsheviks led not only to these people becoming victims of the Stalinist terror, but the whole nation fell victim to the terror as well. Even if violence against violence can sometimes be justified as an unavoidable evil, terror even in response to terror can never be justified, for terror is applied with the aim of striking fear, and its direct victims more often than not are innocent persons, as is well documented in the order issued by Antonov-Ovseyenko and Tukhachevsky, especially in those provisions of the order which speak of shooting hostages or the bread-winner of the family.

After World War II, the Stalinist model of socialism was extended to the countries of Eastern Europe. Of course, those who came to power did not commit crimes comparable to those of Stalinism in every state. However, restrictions and at times gross violations of individual rights and freedoms took place in all these countries. The attempts of some of them to change their Soviet model ended tragically. Yugoslavia was ostracized, and in Poland, Hungary and Czechoslovakia troops were brought in with the aim of putting down attempts to change the existing political order and democratize society.

The sad experience of the former socialist countries, not just in the area of economic development but also in securing human rights and freedoms, inevitably raises the question of the future possibilities for socialism. Socialism as it existed in its administrative-command or barracks form, that 'real socialism' or 'actually existing socialism' which existed in the Soviet Union and in the Eastern European countries, is definitely dead, notwithstanding Castro's obstinacy or the fact that China is still playing around with the terminology. Socialism as a special social, economic and political system, whatever may be meant by that (e.g., different versions of African socialism), which were based on Marx's teaching, have also received a justified blow.

One of the specific features of Marxism–Leninism has always been its exclusiveness. Although the classics of Marxism–Leninism unquestionably relied on the achievements of mankind's previous social thought, as opposed to the works of most Soviet philosophers, there can be no doubt that the so-called founding fathers of Marxism contrasted Marxism sharply with all other tendencies of social thought. Djilas, who is certainly familiar with the phenomenon from different sides, rightly notes that:

> In the pretensions of contemporary Communism of being, if not the unique and absolute, but in any case the highest science, based on dialectical materialism, are hidden the seeds of despotism. The origin of these pretensions can be found in ideas of Marx, though Marx himself did not anticipate them. (Djilas 1965 p. 2)

Such claims are discernable, for example, in the ideas developed by Lenin, that Marxism alone produced answers to all questions of social sciences from A to Z, that Marx's ideas cannot be revised in any way (those who tried to do so were dubbed as revisionists, which was considered by Stalin to be not only a political error but also a crime), that they are all-powerful and comprehensive and so forth.

However, socialist ideas are not limited to those of administrative-command socialism or to Marxism–Leninism and some have a direct bearing on human rights. Even in Russia, as early as 1906, a Russian lawyer, Boris Kistyakovsky, wrote:

> Thus, in the socialist state more than anything the system of subjective rights will be expanded and augmented; the rights of the individual and the citizen will receive in this system complete recognition and decisive formulation. To two categories of public rights, realized in the modern state based on law and order, that is, to the freedom of the individual in the narrow sense and to political rights, there shall be added a third category – socialist rights.

> These rights include the right to work, or the right of every person to the use of land or means of production, and the right of each person to participate in all material and cultural benefits; they will all be united by one general right to a worthy human existence. (Kistyakovsky 1990 p. 156.)

And most importantly, for Kistyakovsky, unlike for Marxists, 'bourgeois' individual rights and freedoms will not be eliminated in a so-called socialist state. They will be supplemented by new rights. With this in mind the Russian scholar says that 'violence can never be justified. Political freedom is such a huge and valuable benefit that it cannot be relinquished for one instant, nor for any temporary gains.' And he asserts that for the sake of realizing the power of the people, one can never, not even temporarily, turn to violence against so-called 'enemies of the people' (ibid., p. 146).

In current terminology all this would mean that civil and political rights should be supplemented by social, economic and cultural rights, that ideas of individual rights and freedoms, i.e. civil and political rights should be augmented by ideas of social justice and the welfare state. And one could forgive Kistyakovsky the use of the term 'socialist state' because what he really described corresponds very much to a welfare state.

Ideas of socialism were born and developed in Western Europe, in countries where various philosophical and religious concepts, based on individualism, were widely accepted. Bhikhu Parekh writes that:

> The view that the individual is conceptually and ontologically prior to society and can in principle be conceptualized and defined independently of society, which we shall call individualism, lies at the heart of liberal thought and shapes its political, legal, moral, economic, methodological, epistemological and other aspects. (Parekh 1993 p. 157.)

Individualism, as an ideology, recognizes the high value of each human being and the interests of the individual. In philosophy, individualism is expressed as the consideration of the individual as the basic and central form of human existence, as the highest expression of the nature of man, and in contrast to many other social, philosophical and religious teachings which attach fundamental importance to supra-individual forces, whether society as a whole or some other human communality (nation, class, etc.). F. Hayek wrote that, 'it is this recognition of the individual as the ultimate judge of his ends, the belief that as far as possible his own views ought to govern his actions, that forms the essence of the individualist position' (Hayek 1944 p. 44).

The absolute dominance of individualism as an ideology can and does have its negative points, especially if its extreme manifestations find expression in the public consciousness and if one speaks only of the individual's rights and freedoms without taking into account the interests of society as a whole and, even more importantly, the interests and rights of other individuals. As David Selbourne puts it:

> The secret of the defects and failures of the modern civic order in its leading democratic form – the form of 'liberal' democracy or democracy which places the freedom of the individual at the centre of its concerns – is not, in essence, to be found in the limits placed upon the exercise of authority over the individual on the part of the state, the government and the law. It is to be found, rather, in the marginal role allocated to the principal of duty in the relationships between citizen and citizen, and citizen and civic order. (Selbourne 1994 p. 26.)

As one should not sacrifice the interests, rights and freedoms of the individual for the sake of the interests, rights and freedoms of any social entity (be it a nation, class or state as a whole), similarly the primacy of individual rights and freedoms over the interests of society should not be made absolute. Both extremes are identically unacceptable and dangerous. A wise compromise must be found between them.

In a society where the individual with his interests, rights and freedoms (both civil and political) is the centre of attention (if not always in practice, then at least in theory and in the public consciousness), the limited nature of individualistic views and practices must be overcome. This involves, as I see it, introducing certain ideas, which may be called socialist as they were initially elaborated in the doctrines of Western social thought, as well as corresponding practical steps, into public life. And this is in fact the practice in most Western countries where liberty of the person, the freedom of speech, the right to a fair hearing, etc. have been supplemented by different social benefits, free health care and other social programs, which have taken the form of social and economic rights. Though I doubt whether it is possible to divide human rights into three generations (civil and political rights, economic and social rights, and so-called third generation rights such as the right to development, to a clean environment, etc.), especially if, as is often the case, their origin is traced respectively to Western, socialist and third world countries. As we have seen, ideas of social rights certainly originated in Western societies, where they have so far also found their fullest (although by no means perfect) realization in practice.

The introduction of socialist ideas into Russia's social life, where not only the economic basis for the acceptance of these ideas was non-existent, but where the ideological preconditions for the acceptance of the truly humanistic ideas of socialist thinkers were utterly lacking (people like Kistyakovsky were certainly in an absolute minority), created the basis for the distortion of socialist ideas; for their dogmatization; and for the recognition of only those positions of Marxist teaching that spoke, for example, of violence as the midwife of history and of the dictatorship of the proletariat as subject to no legal restrictions whatsoever, etc.

The elements of Western socialist theories (e.g., ideas of social justice and social and economic guarantees) which aimed at overcoming the one-sidedness of the individualistic outlook, dominant in the Western world, made little impact where authoritarian and communal ideas and practices flourished and where the individual was of no value at all. Socialist theories which emphasised the interests of the collective, social justice and equality over the individual's rights and freedoms, overlapped in Russia with preexisting local ideas and practices which subordinated the individual to a collective (state, nation, church, community).

Because of the lack of material and spiritual foundations, in practice there came to be realized not, say, the slogan 'the free development of each is the condition for the free development of all', but rather those ideas which were erroneous or utopian.

The very idea of the division of countries into capitalist and socialist ones was erroneous. Many of the so-called capitalist nations have introduced ideas that are essentially socialist, while in many so-called socialist countries these ideas remained only as slogans.

The bitter experience of these nations has discredited the truly humane ideas of socialist teachings, above all those ideas related to the social and economic rights of man. However, the idea of man's social well-being has already found expression in the right to work, to relaxation, to adequate standards of living, to social security, to education, etc. The idea that at a definite stage of a society's development, the society and the state must not only abstain from the violation of inalienable civil and political rights and secure and defend these rights, but also take on, within certain limits, concern for the economic, social and cultural interests of its citizens, is undoubtedly a progressive idea. In many Western countries social and economic rights have become almost as natural as civil and political rights and the International Covenant on Economic, Social and Cultural Rights has approximately the same number of parties as the International Covenant on Civil and Political Rights.

On the other hand, as some authors note, such rights as the right to employment, education and health-care, if claimed as rights in the strict sense of the word, i.e. if they could be legally formalized and enforced by courts, would conflict with the logic of freedom and of the market (Zoo 1993 p. 157; see also Barbalet 1988 pp. 59–79). However, this is a conflict, or rather a contradiction, the resolution of which makes the market more perfect, more civilized.

There does exist, of course, the danger of state paternalism in which it is possible to see, especially where there is an insufficient level of economic and social development, the seeds of totalitarianism. Too much care for the individual on the state's part has the tendency to turn into petty regulation of his or her behaviour. Besides this, strong social programmes do not always beneficially affect the economic activity of both the individual and society as a whole. Therefore, a balance between societal concern for the individual and his own responsibility for himself, a balance between freedom and justice, is essential. 'In theory', writes David Selbourne, 'and especially in the hopes of those still faithful to the Protestant ethic, personal responsibility for the self, and co-responsibility for the well-being of one's fellows, are the moral correlates of the liberty of the individual' (Selbourne 1994 p. 47).

In some of the newly-born countries of Eastern Europe and the former USSR, there is a danger that social and economic rights will not be properly taken care of not only because of the lack of economic resources, but also because of their perceived link with 'real socialism'. The work on different drafts of a new Russian constitution confirms this conclusion. Those who once emphasized social and economic rights, which were at that time considered to have, in the socialist concept of human rights, priority over civil and political rights, now shy away from social and economic rights as from a sin of their youth of which one should feel ashamed. So Yeltsin's draft Constitution, published in May 1993, did not contain any reference to social and economic rights (*Rossiiskie Vesti*, 1993, No. 83 (252)).

One of the authors of the draft, Sergei Alekseyev, a member of the Presidential Council and a well-known professor of law, wrote as recently as 1991 that it was extremely important that human rights under socialism should include not only 'the political and legal protection of the individual' but also 'comprehensive social protection' (Alekseyev 1991 p. 142–3). However, Alekseyev now writes that social and economic rights are not rights at all and that they only express aims, ideas and intentions towards which society is striving, either in reality or often only in declarations (Alekseyev 1993 p. 2).

But the answer is not to shy away from one extreme position only to find oneself in another extreme position. Of course, the economic conditions prevailing at present are rather poor. This in itself puts limits on the full implementation of economic and social rights as these are economically and financially conditioned rights. Nevertheless, it is necessary that Eastern European countries and countries which have emerged in place of the former USSR implement economic and social rights at least to the minimum of their available resources with a view to progressively achieving the full realization of the rights recognized in the International Covenant on Economic, Social and Cultural Rights, as required by Article 2 of that Covenant (6 ILM 360 (1967)).

It is also important not to over-react to another tenet of 'real socialism', that of the inseparable link between the rights and obligations of the individual, which in reality meant the primacy of obligations to the state and to the communist party, over the rights of the individual.

Though it will take a long time in most of the newly-born countries to guarantee declared rights and freedoms, there is at the same time a real danger that, at least during the period of 'wild capitalism', rights and freedoms will be enjoyed mainly by the strongest and by those who are less scrupulous. To minimize this danger (I do not think that it can be totally avoided) these societies should not forget that the abusive use of the real link between rights and duties, which eventually led to the suppression of individual rights by duties to the party and state, does not mean that this link does not exist or that one can ignore it without harming the rights and freedoms of the individual. 'For it is only on the basis of a reciprocity of obligation, in accord with the ethic of the civic bond and the principle of duty, that 'commodious and peaceable living' is possible in the civic order; that civic disaggregation can be arrested without recourse to draconian measures; and that the life, health, and true liberty of the individual can be preserved' (Selbourne 1994 p. 83).

III COMMON HERITAGE AND SPECIFIC PROBLEMS

As a result of the dissolution of the USSR there are now fifteen recognized subjects of international law in the territory of the former Soviet Union with problems and difficulties many of which are common to all or to most of them. Naturally, all of them also have their own specific problems, stemming from historic or religious traditions, their demographic situation, the gravity of inter-ethnic tensions, etc. Therefore, it is possible to speak of the current human rights situation in the former Soviet Union only in rather general terms. The specific problems of the different new states probably outweigh their common heritage (but even here we have an interesting question: why?).

Common problems originate from factors which were shared by all the republics of the erstwhile USSR. The current human rights record of all of them is conditioned, though to a different extent in each case, by their common totalitarian past, by the transition from a centrally planned economy to a market oriented one and by the birth or revival of nation-states after the collapse of the USSR.

All these developments are in a positive direction and are necessary and even inevitable. But at the same time they create enormous difficulties; first, because the past has stamped its birthmarks on the new entities. Notwithstanding democratic slogans and even sincere aspirations, politicians very often prefer to use old and therefore much more familiar methods in furthering their aims. Second, the transitional period has created disorder if not chaos in social relations. In some instances it seems that anarchy is an inevitable path from totalitarianism to democracy. For example, instead of freedom of the press, which presupposes legal guarantees of that freedom and, of course, certain restrictions, those writing and publishing in Moscow, Kiev, Tallinn and other cities of the former USSR frequently enjoy limitless possibilities to interfere in the private life of others and to spread information without any responsibility as to its accuracy. But at the same time, state officials often do not reveal important information, which is of public interest, and take different extralegal (it is difficult always to say 'illegal' because of the absence of proper legal regulation) punitive actions against the mass media.

The immediate effect of all economic reforms in all the republics of the former Soviet Union is usually economic hardship and social strain. Even if, in the domain of civil and political rights, progress is obvious in most newly-born states (except, of course, in regions where armed conflicts are going on), the level of implementation of social and economic rights is even lower than under totalitarianism. And there is hardly any exception. Differences between the various republics are only those of degree.

These are difficulties facing all states born from the ashes of the erstwhile USSR. There are certainly some positive achievements in most republics, especially in the legislative field, though practice very often lags behind. It is impossible to deal, in the scope of this paper, with all republics and with all developments. It would probably, in any event, be a useless endeavour because of the rapid changes in the legislation enacted in all states. In some republics constitutions have not yet been adopted which means that, after their adoption, new rounds of legislative activity will start. Therefore, in my analysis of current developments, I will concentrate upon trends and certainly will draw on the legislation and practices of some states more than of others.

IV THE STRUGGLE OF RUSSIA AND OF ITS SLAVONIC NEIGHBOURS FOR DEMOCRACY

Certain acts of Russian diplomacy and statements by Russian leaders, as well as the position of other states, confirm that Russia is not simply a successor state to the USSR but that it is a continuation of the former Soviet Union.

Among other things which Russia inherited from the USSR was a legal system which Russia has, of course, been trying to reform quickly. Soviet laws were applied only in so far as they did not contradict new realities. In the domain of human rights this meant that Russia already had, by the time of the dissolution of the USSR, certain standards in the form of Soviet legislation passed during the Gorbachev era.

As a continuing state of the Soviet Union Russia also became automatically bound by the Soviet Union's treaty obligations on human rights matters, *inter alia*, by both Covenants on human rights and by the Optional Protocol to the Covenant on Civil and Political Rights, under which individuals can apply to the Human Rights Committee if, after exhaustion of domestic remedies, they feel that their rights under the Covenant have been violated.

At the end of 1991 and during 1992, the Supreme Soviet of Russia adopted new laws which deal with important human rights issues. The Law on mass media[5] prohibits censorship of the mass media and, if the political will of leading political forces were there, would be able to guarantee the freedom of the press. But there were several attempts by the conservative Supreme Soviet, under the chairmanship of Ruslan Khasbulatov, to curb press freedoms (e.g., a proposal to create supervisory bodies for mass media, attempts to take over Izvestia, etc.).

Though there is no direct censorship of the mass media it is hardly possible to be content with the freedom of the press in Russia, especially if one is comparing the current situation in Russia not with the distant Soviet past, but with international standards. J. Wishnevsky is quite right in saying that 'there has been remarkably little progress in the development of free speech in Russia since the fall of communism in August 1991' (*RFE/RL Research Report*, 14 May 1993, Vol. 2, No. 20, p. 86). There are economic and law and order reasons for such a situation, but I agree with Wishnevsky that:

> what may be causing the most harm is the fact that many journalists in the Russian Federation inherited from the Soviet Union the totalitarian concept of the role of the mass media as largely a propaganda tool for this or that political party rather than as a source of information for the public. (ibid.)

Though there are various journals and newspapers in Russia, most of them are clearly partisan. It is very easy to discover the political or ideological orientation of this or that newspaper or journal. Even those which generally support economic reforms and democratization understand democracy as democracy for democrats, i.e., for like-minded people. So after Yeltsin's dissolution of the Parliament in September 1993, State television, which remained firmly pro-Yeltsin, dropped any pretence of objectivity and a newsreader 'began her evening report by reminding viewers that she and her colleagues remain loyal to the Kremlin leader' (*The Times*, 24 September, 1993, p. 15).

In July 1992, the Supreme Soviet of Russia adopted the Law on psychiatric assistance and guarantees of citizens' rights.[6] This Law is especially interesting since abuse of psychiatry for political purposes was one of the most abominable crimes of the Soviet regime against its own people, and it also had wide international repercussions. The new Law is indicative of Russia's resolve to drastically change the situation and, it

---

5 *Vedomosti Siezda Narodnih Deputatov Rossiiskoi Federatsii i Verhovnogo Sovieta Rossiiskoi Federatsii*, 13 February 1992, No. 7.

6 *Vedomosti Siezda Narodnih Deputatov Rossiiskoi Federatsii i Verhovnogo Sovieta Rossiiskoi Federatsii*, 20 August 1992, No. 33.

seems to me, publicly and solemnly to renounce the old practices. Therefore, the Law in its preamble notes that the absence of adequate legal regulation of psychiatric assistance may have been one of the reasons for the use of psychiatry for non-medical purposes with damaging effects on the health, dignity and rights of citizens and also on the international reputation of the state. One of the purposes of the Law, as declared in the Preamble, is to implement in the legislation of Russia those rights and freedoms of individuals recognized by the international community and by the Constitution of the Russian Federation. The Law also provides that, in case of a contradiction between the provisions of international treaties entered into by Russia and domestic legislation, the treaty provisions shall prevail (Article 2). It is also interesting to note that Article 10 establishes that the diagnosis of psychiatric illness shall be made in accordance with generally recognized international standards and that it cannot be based on the non-acceptance by a person of moral, cultural, political or religious values which are accepted by the society.

The Law contains legal guarantees against the abuse of psychiatry. The most important of these is the provision providing that a person can be held in a psychiatric hospital against his or her will only in accordance with the decision of a court (Articles 13, 19, 32–6). A special state body, independent from the national health service, will be created to protect the rights of those in psychiatric hospitals (Article 38) and all hospitals themselves are subordinated to the health service (Article 13(2)), which means that there will not be any more special psychiatric hospitals of the Ministry of the Interior.

The Law on psychiatric assistance is a big step forward, even in comparison with steps undertaken at the end of the 1980s under Gorbachev in this field, and it indicates that the Russian authorities are taking human rights seriously. But the lack of material resources, overcrowding in hospitals and shortage of personnel (who are incredibly underpaid) are some of the main obstacles in the way of implementing this Law.

A positive role in the promotion of human rights in Russia is now played by some former dissidents, who hold key posts in state bodies in charge of human rights. So Sergei Kovaljov, a co-founder together with Andrei Sakharov of the Committee on Human Rights in the Soviet Union in the 1970s, was chairman of the Human Rights Committee of the Supreme Soviet of Russia which was dissolved by Yeltsin. The allegiance of this man, who spent years in Soviet labour camps, to the cause of human rights is no doubt genuine. Currently, Sergei Kovaljov heads the Presidential Commission on Human Rights created in November 1993.

In August 1994 this Commission released a Report on the implementation of human and citizen's rights in the Russian Federation in 1993 (*Rossiiskaya Gazeta*, 25 August, 1994). This is an amazing document which may provoke different reactions.

On the one hand, its contents authoritatively reveal that grave and systematic human rights violations are occurring in Russia. But, on the other hand, the very fact of its publication by the Presidential commission shows that the authorities are serious about human rights and democracy.

The Report states that Russia has undertaken a series of measures to promote human rights in the country and has, *inter alia*, in accordance with the Declaration and Programme of Action adopted in Summer 1993 by the World Conference on Human Rights, elaborated a Federal programme of action on human rights. As positive developments, the Report mentions the adoption of the Constitution in December 1993, which contains all basic human rights and fundamental freedoms, and Russia's active participation in international fora of cooperation on human rights, as well as its rejection of the dogma that human rights are exclusively domestic issues.

But the main thrust of the Report is on the violations of human rights and on recommendations on how to change the situation for the better. The document emphasizes that 'there are serious and often systematic violations of civil and political and, especially, social and economic rights in the country'. It speaks of discrimination based on ethnicity and religion, violation of the rights of refugees and of displaced persons. Especially appalling, the Report states, is the situation in places of detention which is often tantamount to torture or to inhuman treatment or punishment. There are reported cases of torture in places of pre-trial detention to extract confessions from detained or accused persons. The Report characterizes such cases as clear violations of the 1984 UN Convention against Torture and other Cruel, Inhuman or Degrading Treatment or Punishment. The Report found that Moscow authorities have exceeded everybody in the country in the domain of human rights violations.

The 1993 Constitution (Article 27(1)) and the Law on the right of the citizens of the Russian Federation to choose freely their place of residence, of June 1993, are aimed at abolishing the notorious 'propiska' system under which one could not freely choose one's place of residence in the country. But, says the Report, the old system continues to exist in its entirety. Though, on the positive side, the Report mentions the fact that there have been cases when courts, applying the Constitution directly, have maintained this right notwithstanding local decrees, decisions and practices.

Many violations, according to the Report, occurred during the 1993 October emergency situation. Most importantly, such non-derogable (even under an emergency) rights as the right to life and freedom from torture were not respected. The Report also contains concrete information on the violation of social and economic rights and recommends specific measures to change the situation in the whole domain of human rights.

The Report evokes mixed feelings. On the one hand, it confirms that the human rights situation in Russia is worrying. On the other hand, the very fact of its publication raises hopes that Russia has democratic potential to cope with the difficult situation. However, democratic reforms received a new, serious blow when the authorities committed massive human rights violations in Chechnia, calling it an internal affair of Russia.

It is difficult and probably too early to appraise the role of the Constitutional Court of Russia. One of its most noticeable decisions concerned Yeltsin's Decree on the establishment of the Ministry of Security and Internal Affairs of the RSFSR of 14 December 1991. The decision declared the Decree, which purported to merge the KGB and the Ministry of Interior into one super-ministry, unconstitutional, because it did not correspond to the division of powers in the Russian Federation between legislative, executive and judicial branches as established by the Constitution of the RSFSR.[7]

But the Constitutional Court could not become the highest impartial judicial body in Russia. This was felt especially during the acute constitutional crisis and power struggle in the spring of 1993. Chairman of the Court, Valerii Zorkin, made political statements and took sides in the ongoing political battle even before the Court had had an opportunity to consider the matter. This led to a call for the resignation of Zorkin by the Deputy Chairman of the Court, Nikolai Vitruk, who cited the fact that most other members of the Court also disapproved of Zorkin's political activities. Vitruk also voiced the fear that the Court might turn into 'a political instrument in the hands of one or other branch of power' (*RFE/RL Research Report*, 23 July 1993, Vol. 2, No. 26, p. 1) In the autumn of the same year, Zorkin became actively involved once more in the political power struggle.

The absence of a new constitution and the quality of the old one have been, of course, major impediments for the Constitutional Court. But there is also another problem. As we could see in the case of both the Congress of People's Deputies and the Supreme Soviet of Russia, legislative bodies with practically unlimited (or at least unclear) competences, which were elected for a period of five years at a time when the country was in a

---

7 *Vedomosti Siezda Narodnih Deputatov i Verhovnogo Sovieta Rossiiskoi Federatsii*, 6 February 1992, No. 6.

completely different situation and when it was not an independent state at all, became active opponents of democratic reforms. Members of the Constitutional Court were elected for life tenure by the Congress of People's Deputies and some of the members were nominated by hard-line communist organizations.

All this does not necessarily mean that the Constitutional Court cannot, in the future, properly fulfil its functions. Courts and even the Constitutional Court simply reflect the situation in the country. But it does mean that the Constitutional Court, like other links in the judicial system, has to go a long way in order to become a genuinely impartial and authoritative body.

An important event, as has been mentioned above, was the adoption of the new Constitution by referendum on 12 December 1993. The Constitution (*Rossiiskaya Gazeta*, 25 December 1993) contains many interesting developments from the point of view of human rights.

Chapter 2 enshrines a list of human rights which is really comprehensive and corresponds to the requirements of basic international human rights instruments. It includes civil and political as well as social, economic and cultural rights.

Among the guarantees of implementation of declared rights I would like to emphasize Article 17 which states: 'In the Russian Federation rights and freedoms of human beings and citizens are recognized and guaranteed in accordance with generally recognized principles and norms of international law'. Even more important is Article 15(4) stipulating that 'generally recognized principles and norms of international law and international treaties of the Russian Federation are part and parcel of its legal system. If an international treaty of the Russian Federation establishes rules which are different from those provided in laws, the rules of the treaty shall apply'. Article 46(3) contains an important clause: 'Everybody has the right to appeal in accordance with international treaties concluded by the Russian Federation to international bodies for the protection of human rights and freedoms after the exhaustion of all domestic remedies'.

Taking all these Constitutional clauses into account one may conclude that there is a proper constitutional basis for the protection of human rights in Russia. But, as the Report of the Presidential Commission on Human Rights, referred to above, shows, there is a big difference between words and deeds in Russia.

I have no serious doubts that most of the current Russian leaders (naturally, not all) are generally committed to human rights and democracy, though they may often have rather vague ideas of what it means and of how to achieve it in the circumstances. Certainly, there is a trend towards greater care for human rights and fundamental freedoms in Russia. But the difficulties are also immense. All difficulties and factors, which are common for all the newly-born states (the totalitarian past, transition from a centrally planned economy to a market-oriented one and the resurrection of nationalism) apply in full to Russia.

One of the dangers for democratic reforms in Russia, as in many parts of the former USSR and in Eastern Europe, stems from the resurrection of Russian nationalism. Economic hardships, the soaring crime rate, and especially the loss by Russia of its superpower status which for many in Russia is tantamount to a kind of national humiliation, create fertile soil for nationalistic ideas. Therefore, there are certainly some grounds for the gloomy analysis of Walter Laqueur:

> It is easy to think of reasons that seem to favour the growth of some extreme nationalist movement – the feeling of humiliation following the breakup of the Soviet Union; the need to pursue an assertive policy *vis-à-vis* the former republics in defence of Russian interests and the presence of many millions of Russians abroad; the bad economic situation and the need to engage in unpopular reforms; the frequent impotence of the authorities in face of a breakdown of law and order; the fact that democratic institutions are not deeply rooted in Russia; the traditional psychological need for a strong hand; the old Weimar dilemma of how to run a democracy in the absence of a sufficient number of democrats; the deep division on the left. (Laqueur p. 114.)

Though there are extremely vociferous Russian nationalist movements such as the one led by Shirinovsky, or groups are specifically anti-semitic, they are, at least for the present, not in power. The Russian authorities have closed down a number of virulently anti-semitic newspapers and at least three editors of such newspapers (V. Fomichev of Moscow's *Puls Tushino*, A. Andreyev of St. Petersbourg's *Narodnoye Delo*, and A. Batogov of the overtly neo-Nazi *Russkoye Voskressenye*) have been prosecuted for incitement of inter-ethnic and racial hatred.[8] In September 1994 Boris Mironov, the head of the State Press Committee, was dismissed because of his nationalistic views which he had expressed publicly (*International Herald Tribune*, 3-4 September, 1994, p. 2). But the fact that a man who could declare that 'if Russian nationalism is fascism, then I am fascist' was in charge of freedom of the press, and that notwithstanding the closure of some virulent nationalistic newspapers there are still many small newsletters with paranoiac anti-semitic content available on the streets of Moscow and St Petersburg shows that the danger of nationalism in Russia is real.

Nationalistic forces may have influence in matters concerning Russian minorities in other former republics of the erstwhile Soviet Union

---

[8] See *Sovietskaya Rossiya*, 25 February 1993; *Moskovskiye Novosti*, 1993, No. 17, p. 4A; *Nezavisimaya Gazeta*, 26 February 1993.

threatening to use, if necessary, military force to protect their rights, thereby contributing not only to the aggravation of the situation of those minorities, but also instigating armed conflicts with Russia's neighbours. Here the irresponsible behaviour of nationalists in some smaller neighbours of Russia combined with the striving of the Russian imperialists to restore an empire, be it Soviet or Russian, may become dangerous for peace and democracy.

Though nationalists are not in power in Russia, unlike in some other territories of the former USSR, large nations very often do not understand the national feelings of their smaller neighbours or of ethnic groups in their own country and may even get angry when these neighbours or ethnic groups at home want to arrange their own lives according to their own will. But at the same time big nations are, as a rule, less prone to petty nationalism. The Russian citizenship law is probably one example of Russia's broad-mindedness in questions of inter-ethnic relations.

This Law[9] is rather liberal regarding the acquisition of Russian citizenship. The Law establishes that:

all citizens of the former USSR who are permanent residents of the RSFSR on the day of the entry into force of the Law on citizenship will be recognized as citizens of the RSFSR if during a year they do not declare their unwillingness to be citizens of the RSFSR. (Article 13)

The Law also provides that in the Russian Federation nobody can be deprived of his or her citizenship (Article 1) and that Russia encourages the acquisition of its citizenship by stateless persons (Article 7).

On another positive note I would also like to mention Russia's handling of issues arising from the referendum on the independence of Tatarstan. On 21 March 1992, Tatarstan declared itself to be 'a sovereign state and subject of international law building its relations with Russia and other republics and states on the basis of equal treaties'.[10] Though the Constitutional Court of the Russian Federation declared the referendum unconstitutional,[11] the Russian authorities were wise enough not to take any coercive measures against the Tatars. Later the dispute was resolved by the conclusion of a treaty between Russia and Tatarstan. Here Russia's approach is in striking

---

[9] *Vedomosti Siezda Narodnih Deputatov i Verhovnogo Sovieta Rossiiskoi Federatsii*, 6 February 1991, No. 6.

[10] *Report on the Tatarstan Referendum on Sovereignty*, 21 March 1992. Prepared by the Staff of the US Commission on Security and Cooperation in Europe, 14 April 1992, p. 1.

[11] *Vedomosti Siezda Narodnih Deputatov i Verhovnogo Sovieta Rossiiskoi Federatsii*, 26 March 1992, No. 13.

contrast with the USSR's actions in Lithuana, Georgia or Baku. However the massacre in Chechnia showed how easily the balance can be restored.

The respect for human rights is coterminous with respect for law and for the judiciary. But law has never been highly esteemed in Russia. Before the 1917 revolution law was seen by the majority of the population of Russia as a tool against them. In 1909 Kistjakovskii wrote:

> The lack of development of legal consciousness of the Russian intelligentsia and the absence of interest in legal concepts is the result of an old evil – the absence of any rule of law in the day-to-day life of the Russian people ... The total lack of equality before the courts has killed any respect for law. A Russian, by whatever name he goes, will get around or violate the law anywhere he can with impunity; and the government will do the same. (Kistjakovskii 1991 pp. 126–7.)

The Bolsheviks used law and the judiciary as a part of the repressive state apparatus. Legal norms, even in theory, were considered not as measures of freedom or guarantees of rights but as instruments of state policy. Members of the legal profession did not rank high in the eyes of the Communist Party. This tradition goes back to the founding fathers of Marxism–Leninism who derided bourgeois law and lawyers and wrote of the 'withering away' of any law under communism.

It will certainly take time to have such an attitude towards law and the legal profession changed. As Sergei Pashin, head of the Department of judicial reform in the Presidential administration and one of the brightest legal minds in contemporary Russia writes about the rights and freedoms enshrined in the Constitution: 'Declaration of rights without the creation of the judicial or other mechanisms for their implementation is a deception. Though we speak loudly about the state based on law we do not have such mechanisms. We use legal codes of the time of 'undeveloped socialism' and our legislators and practising lawyers are educated on traditions which are not acceptable today' (Pashin 1993 p. 43).

Rather typical was a reaction of President Yeltsin's entourage to ex-president Gorbachev's criticism of reforms of the Government of Russia in June 1992. A spokesman for Yeltsin declared that the ex-President's criticism had gone beyond his competence (I really wonder what this could mean) and that measures would be taken against him. Later it was reported that Mr Gorbachev had been deprived of his limousine. The same story repeated itself in 1993 when the Vice-President of Russia, Rutskoi, was deprived of his limousine and some bodyguards.

Instead of legal action, the deprivation of privileges for bad behaviour and its corrollary, granting certain benefits for good behaviour, were typical methods of the past.

Much has to be done to overcome the psychological reticence of most Russians about going to the courts to protect their rights. The first step should be a reform of the court system and the creation of a really independent judiciary. A step towards this end is the new Law on the Status of Judges of 26 June 1992[12] which, *inter alia*, prohibits any interference in the functioning of the judiciary and provides that judges are to enjoy life tenure. The first trials by jury took place in Russia in December 1993 and January 1994 in Saratov, Moscow region and Ivanovo. In 9 regions of Russia they have become a regular feature of the judicial process (Pashin, op. cit, p. 49).

Economic chaos and transition from the command economy to a market oriented one has created fertile soil for criminal behaviour. The necessity of combating a soaring crime rate entails measures involving increased powers for the forces of law and order. In the circumstances, guarantees for suspects or for detained persons are seen as something secondary or even as detrimental for the effective combat against crime. At the end of the Gorbachev era in the USSR, this false dilemma (though it is necessary to recognise that it is not yet completely overcome in much more developed democracies than Russia): either to effectively combat the soaring crime rate or to introduce effective procedural guarantees such as habeas corpus, trial by jury, the right to have a counsel at the early stages of a criminal procedure, etc. was at the heart of discussions on criminal law and procedural reforms. Rather controversial, from the point of view of human rights, is the Presidential Decree on Urgent Measures to Protect the Population from Gangsterism and Other Forms of Organized Crime, issued by Yeltsin on 14 June 1994 (*Rossiiskaya Gazeta*, 17 June, 1994), which gave law enforcement bodies additional powers to combat violent crime (detention for up to 30 days while the Constitution in Article 22(2) provides for up to 48 hours' detention without judicial control; interference in financial and commercial activities of firms etc.). The Report of the Presidential Commission on Human Rights, referred to above, comments on the Decree of President Yeltsin that the: 'Absence in this Decree of the necessary guarantees of human rights, the necessary measures of judicial control over the activity of the Ministry of Interior and counter-intelligence service ... directly touch upon fundamental human rights and create a real danger of arbitrary arrests, interference in the private life of citizens and the violation of other constitutional rights and freedoms' (*Rossiiskaya Gazeta*, 25 August, 1994). It is interesting to note that Sergei Pashin had written

---

[12] *Vedomosti Siezda Narodnih Deputatov i Verhovnogo Sovieta Rossiiskoi Federatsii*, 30 July 1992, No. 30.

earlier about proposals to increase the maximum term of detention up to a maximum of 30 days: 'Taking into account the conditions in places of provisional detention, where those who are under investigation are detained, it is tantamount to the legitimization of torture in order to extract confessions' (Pashin, op. cit., p. 53).

All this looks rather sinister if one takes into account what the heads of law enforcement bodies think about human rights. The former Procurator-General of Russia was strongly against trial by jury and in his intervention before the Parliament resorted to distortion of the facts in order to show that trial by jury had been deficient in countries where it had been used and was completely alien to Russia (even though there was trial by jury in pre-revolutionary Russia) (Larin 1993 p. 5). Sergei Stepashin, the head of the counter-intelligence service of Russia, who rehired 800 KGB veterans to do 'investigating' work, dismissed worries about their pedigree: 'As regards talk that human rights may be violated to some degree – well, probably yes, but only so that the rights of 99 percent of citizens are defended' (*The Economist*, July 9th–15th, 1994 p. 22). Earlier he had expressed himself even more clearly: 'I am in favour of human rights violations, if this human being is a criminal' (*Rossiiskaya Gazeta*, 24 June, 1994).

Such an approach to the problems of law and order leads not only to innocent people being sentenced but also to criminals remaining unpunished. Nevertheless, in newly born countries, where people demand harsher and quicker measures to deal with violent crimes, politicians and even courts are often eager to please public opinion at the expense of procedural guarantees. And, of course, this is a familiar and therefore easier approach to dealing with crime.

Though citizens of Russia now travel more freely than did Soviet citizens, neither Russia's laws nor practice in matters of foreign travel correspond to international standards. Exit visas for foreign travel, which are still governed by the USSR 1990 Law, have not been needed since 1 January 1993. But if, under the Soviet authorities, foreign passports or exit visas were refused mainly on political grounds, now bureaucrats often ask for bribes. The notorious 'propiska system' (internal resident permits), under which the freedom to choose one's place of residence was violated by Soviet authorities, is still in place, despite the fact that the Committee on Constitutional Supervision of the former USSR found that this system was contrary to the Constitution of the USSR and to the Soviet Union's international obligations.[13]

---

13 *Vedomosti Siezda Narodnih Deputatov SSSR i Verhovnogo Sovieta SSSR*, 21 November 1990, No. 47.

Human rights issues in two other Slavonic republics of the former Soviet Union, Ukraine and Belarus, are much the same as in Russia, though it seems that Russia, leading in the speed of its economic reforms, also has a slight edge, at least at the legislative level, in the field of human rights reforms. The Ukraine is preparing its new Constitution and first drafts have been published and discussed. Belarus passed its Constitution in Summer 1994. Both states have adopted their respective citizenship laws.

The Ukrainian Law on Citizenship provides that all persons who at the moment of the entry into force of the Law are permanent residents of Ukraine, notwithstanding their origin, social or property status, education, language, political opinion, religious views or the nature of their occupation, and who are not citizens of other states and do not object to the acquisition of Ukrainian citizenship, are Ukrainian citizens.[14] The Law on Citizenship in Belarus provides that all permanent residents of the Republic at the moment of the entry into force of the Law on Citizenship are citizens of Belarus (*Zvjazda*, 2 November 1991). The Belorussian Law seems to impose its citizenship on all permanent residents, leaving them no choice.

The Ukrainian Parliament has adopted a Law on Information (October 1992) and a Law on the Printed Mass Media (November 1992) that conform with international standards (*RFE/RL Research Report* 30 July 1993, Vol. 2, No. 27, p. 5). Censorship is banned and the right to receive and disseminate information is guaranteed. There is a variety of printed mass media and even the state-run television, while generally supporting the 'official' line, allows representatives of various political forces to voice their views (ibid.).

It is difficult to predict the speed as well as all the directions of reforms in the field of human rights in Russia, Belarus or the Ukraine. Much depends on the outcome of the struggle between different political forces. Generally speaking, I think, one may conclude that Russia has managed relatively well on its road from totalitarianism via semi-anarchy to democracy, though it is far, of course, from its declared goals. It seems to me that because of its historic traditions, immense economic and social problems, even the vastness of its territory, Russia is predestined, at least during the stage of emerging from a semi-anarchical situation, to choosing a relatively authoritarian political regime. As Eduard Shevardnadze put it: 'Yeltsin is trying to form democratic institutions by using a certain kind of authoritarianism. This is necessary in a transitional period' (*Time*, 25 July, 1994, p. 22). This presupposes a strong executive arm of the government, which, of course, in itself does not predetermine the level of

---

[14] *Vedomosti Verhivnogo Sovieta Ukraini*, 1991, No. 50.

implementation of rights and freedoms of individuals. At the same time, however, strong executive powers, especially in the absence of democratic traditions and an independent judiciary, have a tendency to encroach upon these rights and freedoms.

V SOME REFLECTIONS ON HUMAN RIGHTS IN OTHER FORMER SOVIET REPUBLICS

The Baltic republics (Estonia, Latvia, Lithuania) were at the forefront of processes of democratization in the Soviet Union. At the end of the 1980s it frequently happened that, what was still impossible in Moscow or elsewhere in the USSR, was already possible in the Baltics. For example, the first independent draft of the Soviet law on the mass media, prepared by jurists from Moscow, was published in Estonia and in such a way became known to a larger audience in Moscow and elsewhere in the Soviet Union.

The introduction of elements of a market economy earlier than in other republics of the USSR brought about economic liberalization, which is a necessary basis for human rights and freedoms. In October 1991 Estonia adhered to the most important UN instruments on human rights, including both Covenants and the Optional Protocol to the Covenant on Civil and Political Rights, thereby recognizing the jurisdiction of the Human Rights Committee to consider individual communications (UN Doc. CCPR/C/2/ Rev.3, pp. 3, 96).

In June 1992, Estonia adopted a new Constitution by a referendum.[15] Chapter 2 of the Constitution is devoted to human rights and fundamental freedoms. It corresponds to basic international standards on human rights and enshrines such inalienable rights as the right to life, the prohibition of torture and other forms of inhuman treatment, the right to liberty and security of the person, the right to a fair trial, etc.

The Constitution of Estonia also provides that in cases where Estonian laws or other acts are in conflict with international treaties which are ratified by the Estonian Parliament, the provisions of the international treaty shall prevail (Article 123). It is important and encouraging that the Constitution provides for guarantees of the independence of the courts though much has to be done to ensure a really competent and impartial judiciary.

---

[15] 'Eesti Vabariigi Pohiseadus' ('The Basic Law of the Republic of Estonia'), *Riigi Teataja* (*The State Herald*), 1992, 26, 349.

In April 1993, Estonia and Lithuania were admitted to membership of the Council of Europe which, on the one hand, means that the situation with regard to human rights in these countries is not as tragic as it is sometimes depicted by Russian diplomacy (though this does not mean that there are no serious problems, especially concerning rights of minorities) but, on the other hand, it implies that these Baltic states are now under the scrutiny of European human rights bodies, which certainly will be a very important safeguard for human rights in countries embarking on the road towards democratization.

But citizenship issues, language requirements for the acquisition of citizenship, resident permits for retired military personnel and inter-ethnic problems in general, remain concerns for governments of these states as well as for the world community. In the spring of 1993 Mr van der Stoel, the CSCE High Commissioner for Minorities, made a series of recommendations to the governments of Estonia and Latvia concerning changes in the legislation and practice of these states on minority issues.[16]

The new Estonian Law on elections for local authorities provides that non-citizens who are permanent residents of Estonia can participate in elections. But they cannot be elected (*Riigi Teataja*, 1993, 29, 505). This is, certainly, not the best option, especially for areas where non-citizens are in an absolute majority.

The Estonian Law on aliens, passed by the Parliament on 21 June 1993, not only poisoned relations between Estonia and Russia, but became the object of international scrutiny. The Council of Europe found 'a number of deficiencies in the law and inconsistencies with the norms of European law' (*The Guardian*, 7 July 1993, p. 8). A senior official of the CSCE recommended that Estonia amend the law (ibid.). As a result the President of Estonia did not promulgate the Law and the Parliament had to reconsider the act which it had just passed. After the changes had been made by the Estonian Parliament the European Political Cooperation issued a Declaration in which it commended Estonia for its cooperation with the European institutions and noted that '[t]his political act is a clear indication of the attachment of Estonia to democratic principles and its commitment to political dialogue and compromise and non-confrontation with its communities and its neighbouring countries.'[17]

This Law, which was a logical development of the citizenship legislation, contained very vague language and gave the authorities excessively wide

---

[16] Letters of the CSCE High Commissioner on National Minorities to the Estonian and Latvian Foreign Ministers of 6 April 1993. Reference Nos 206/93/L/Rev. and 238/93/L/Rev.

[17] EPC Press Release, P.66/93, Brussels, 9 July 1993.

discretionary powers. As Anatol Lieven rightly puts it: 'though it is entirely true that Estonian and Latvian policies towards the Russians have so far taken purely legal and non-violent forms, it still forms part of a pattern of exclusivist nationalism which risks tearing apart the entire fabric of Eastern Europe and the former Soviet Union' (Lieven 1993 p. 380). Though, as the EPC notes, the amendments represent 'a substantial improvement of this law',[18] it does not address all the concerns expressed by the experts.

In July 1994, the Presidents of Estonia and Russia signed two important treaties on the withdrawal of Russian troops from Estonia by 31 August 1994 (by the time of writing the withdrawal has been completed) and on social problems of Russian military pensioners in the territory of Estonia.

Article 2 of the second treaty stipulates that military pensioners and their family members shall be issued with resident permits on their personal application. Estonia has the right to refuse a resident permit if an applicant constitutes a threat to Estonian security. A representative of the CSCE will be invited to sit in the Commission which will make recommendations on the issuance of resident permits. Nationalistic forces in Estonia are against the ratification of this treaty as from their point of view this would be a concession to Russia.

Most serious human rights violations take place in areas of armed conflict. Of course, any such conflict in itself is a negation of the right to life. But many other gross and massive violations of elementary human rights and laws of armed conflict are committed in conflicts in the Caucasus, in Moldova, and in Tajikistan. Hostage taking has been widespread and warring sides have boasted of the numbers of hostages taken.[19] In Nagorno-Karabakh both Armenians and Azeris have been engaged, at different times, in 'ethnic cleansing'.

In the Central Asian states of Turkmenistan and Uzbekistan the political opposition is being oppressed and freedom of expression is severely restricted. For instance, Amnesty International reports the arrest in Uzbekistan of two prominent opponents of the Government, B. Shakirov and P. Akhunov.[20] Members of the opposition movement Birlik have been repeatedly harassed.

In Turkmenistan, Amnesty International representatives were detained by militia after less than 24 hours in the country and were forced to leave because of alleged visa irregularities. At the same time opposition leaders

---

[18] EPC Press Release, P.66/93, Brussels, 9 July 1993.

[19] See, for example, Amnesty International *Concerns in Europe*, London, May–October 1992.

[20] *Ibid.*, p. 95.

were placed under house arrest.[21]   In this country it seems that the personality cult of President Nijazov has exceeded the level usually adopted in the former USSR. Newspapers report the Decree of the Supreme Soviet of Turkmenistan on the unlimited production and distribution of portraits of 'Turkmen-pasha' (Leader of all Turkmens). A collective farm, a street, the Academy of Sciences and a steamship have been named after President Nijazov (*Megapolis-Express*, 1992, No. 48, p. 21).

As the head of a group of UN observers in Tajikistan, Livio Bota said: 'The present government of Tajikistan has dealt harshly with its opponents, jailing and, according to some accounts, torturing those opposition leaders it has been able to capture' (*RFE/RL Daily Report*, 19 May 1993, No. 95, p. 3).

VI PROSPECTS OF DEMOCRACY IN POST-TOTALITARIAN SOCIETIES

The experience of all of the former Soviet Republics in the field of human rights shows that the transition from totalitarianism to democracy is not an easy path. It has many pitfalls. Various factors of an economic, political, religious and cultural character and also of a psychological nature, which are not always taken into account in analyses of democratization and of the human rights situation in the Soviet successor states, often play a part in determining outcomes. This means, for example, that differences in social psychology, culture, or historical traditions may lead to different outcomes, though political and economic problems and difficulties may not differ so much. For instance, concepts of pride and honour are different in the Baltics and in the Caucasus. Though the Baltics states are still far from resolving personal or intergroup conflicts in an ideal fashion – through court procedures or political compromises – among some peoples of the Caucasus it would be shameful and a sign of weakness to go to court to resolve conflicts with neighbours or to compromise in politics or in inter-ethnic relations. Compromises are seen as a sign of weakness. The winner has to take all. Power-sharing is usually not an option. Therefore conflicts which in different circumstances could be resolved through protracted negotiations, compromises and power-sharing often end in violent clashes.

In some Central Asian states even under communism, which was supposed to be based on internationalism, republican leaders sought loyalty mainly amongst their tribesmen. The social system existing there may be called a kind of feudal communism. Even now the bases of power for leaders are

---

[21] *Ibid.*, p. 85.

often not political parties in the traditional Western sense but tribes, ethnicities, next of kin.

The events in the former USSR and in Eastern Europe do not in any way mark 'the end of history' and developments towards liberal democracy in some societies cannot be discerned even under a magnifying glass. But even in those societies where democratic reforms have already borne some fruit, difficulties still remain immense. Robert Dahl writes that :

> a country that has had little or no experience with the institutions of public contestation and political competition and lacks a tradition of toleration toward political opposition is most unlikely to turn into a stable polyarchy[22] in the space of a few years. (Dahl 1971 p. 208.)

One of the basic difficulties of the democratization process in countries which have emerged in place of the erstwhile Soviet Union consists in the very nature of this process. Its order is reversed in comparison with processes of democratization in Western countries; it is not gradual but very rapid; its roots do not always, and in some societies do not at all, lie in internal developments of the society, but are external ones.

Dahl speaks of three possible ways in which democratization can arise: 1. when liberalization precedes inclusiveness, i.e. when political contestation starts among a small elite and the population as a whole is included gradually into the political process; 2. when inclusiveness, i.e. inclusion of the population in the political life, precedes liberalization; 3. shortcut which means that a closed hegemony is transformed into a polyarchy by a sudden grant of universal suffrage and right of public contestation (ibid., p. 34). From Dahl's point of view, the first way is the easiest and the most natural, and the last one the most difficult and problematic.

What happened in the former Soviet Union falls somewhere between the second and third ways. There was, of course, universal suffrage in the USSR and the population was to a certain extent included in the political life of the country. But, as public contestation was completely absent, this inclusion was heavily distorted.

But the first two paths outlined by Dahl, it seems, are closed in the contemporary world. The interdependence and transparency of the world and the closeness of different societies mean that the traditional slow ways of democratization, as outcomes of lengthy processes of social struggle and group conflict which themselves created conditions for the consolidation and persistence of democracy (Lewis 1993 p. 300) and having, most

---

[22] R. Dahl reserves the term 'democracy' for a political system one characteristic of which is the quality of being completely responsive to all its citizens. Closest to such an ideal are polyarchies (Dahl 1971 pp. 2, 8).

importantly, completely internal driving forces (England was probably the purest example of this phenomenon) are hardly available any more.

It seems that in the case of the democratization of former socialist states we may have two major variations: the Soviet version, in which political reforms and liberalization precede economic reforms, and the Chinese version in which economic reforms have not yet led to any significant political liberalization. The Eastern European countries fit, at least partly, into the Soviet model, because their democratization started with the sudden collapse of their totalitarian regimes. But, as these regimes were imposed on them by the Soviet Union, and because at least some of these countries had certain more developed grounds for democratization than the former USSR (e.g., economic reforms in Hungary, Solidarnost in Poland, a higher level of economic development in Czechoslovakia) their future seems brighter.

The second variant may be less painful. The political liberalization in the former USSR led to the disruption of economic relations and finally to the dissolution of the country. But I am convinced that in the Soviet case the Chinese version would have been impossible. The Soviet leadership at all levels was ideologically so rigid and numbed that a person who, like the Chinese leaders, would have dared to say that it does not matter whether a cat is black or white, the important thing is whether it catches mice or not, would have been, at best, immediately declared to be an opportunist and politically untrustworthy.

Therefore, political liberalization, which meant, *inter alia*, that Gorbachev gradually had to get rid of the most conservative elements in the party leadership seeking at the same time the support of less conservative ones (and kicking them out during the next round of *perestroika* and *glasnost*), was a necessary precondition for any real economic reforms. At a certain moment Gorbachev needed the support of the population in order to further his reforms, and this meant that the genie was out of the bottle. And in contrast to Aladdin's genie this one would not go back in whatever the wishes of its master.

These difficult and even gloomy prospects facing some of the former Soviet republics, especially in the domain of democratic reforms, inevitably raises the question of whether it is possible at all to export or impose democracy which is certainly a product of Western development and which was gradually, through the method of trial and error, put into practice in these countries. Are not those Russian nationalists who insist that Russia does not belong to Europe, and that therefore the reforms of both Gorbachev and Yeltsin are alien to the Russian spirit, right at the end of the day?

Kishore Mahbubani writes that '[e]arlier theorists of democracy would be surprised by the twentieth-century conceit that democracy can be applied to any society, regardless of its stage of development or its internal social divisions' (Mahbubani 1992). And he suggests that for Third World states 'a period of strong and firm government, one that is committed to radical reform, may be necessary to break the vicious circle of poverty sustained by social structures that contain vested interests opposed to any real change' (Mahbubani 1992).

The recent history of some rapidly developed countries (the 'small tigers' of East Asia and Chile under Pinochet) demonstrate that democracy need not always be a *condition sine qua non* for economic growth.

Governments of all of the newly-born states have to take difficult, rapid and often unpopular decisions in order to cope with their deteriorating economic situation, soaring crime rate, social and often inter-ethnic unrest. This indeed presupposes strong and stable executive powers, and even traditional parliamentary democracies may not do too well under such circumstances.

But at the same time we witness that though democracy is not a precondition for rapid economic growth most dictatorships do not do well even in the economic field. It is not clear whether limitations on democracy, for example in South Korea and Singapore, or massive repressions in Chile under Pinochet contributed in any way to the economic growth of these countries. Moreover, a strong executive power is not at all tantamount to a repressive regime. And the examples of Mobutu, Idi Amin, Bokassa and a host of other dictators shows rather convincingly that a strong government may become not a remedy but a disaster not only for the human rights record of the country, but for its economy as well. Gross human rights violations by authorities in some countries, like Sri Lanka, India or Peru, play into the hands of Tamil and Kashmirian separatists or Shining Path terrorists, helping them to recruit new members.

Moreover, economic growth and social stability are not the only things which matter. In our world it has become really impossible to be indulgent to dictators, even if they do well in the domain of economic growth. The end of the Cold War has made it even more difficult to close ones eyes to gross violations of human rights and to retain normal diplomatic and trade relations with regimes which do not guarantee basic human rights.

At the same time, it seems, it would be unrealistic to request from all countries full implementation of international standards of human rights and, moreover, to always make this a precondition for the development of economic or other relations with all, and especially with newly-born, countries.

The rapid introduction of elements of democracy into societies which have neither economic, social nor cultural prerequisites for accepting democratic institutions and processes may sometimes even be counter-productive. This is especially relevant to countries where economic backwardness is combined with cultural and religious traditions which are not conducive to democratic reforms. It would be unrealistic to expect, for example, that such European countries of the former USSR as the Baltic states, Ukraine, Belarus or Russia, which all themselves face different problems and difficulties, on the one hand, and the Central Asian states, on the other, could move with the same speed in their democratic reforms.

As human rights and democracy are two sides of the same coin, and in a larger sense basic human rights may be considered as a part of democracy, it is difficult to expect that in all the Soviet successor states there will in the near future be full freedom of the press or that all procedural guarantees for detained persons will be observed.

But tendencies and efforts are important even in countries where rapid democratization may be counter-productive. If governments do not guarantee such basic rights as the right to life, liberty, security of the person, or if they torture those who are in opposition to them, then notwithstanding any elections and even the presence of several political parties, there will be neither human rights nor democracy.

Therefore, the world community should monitor the human rights situation in all countries in the light of international standards of human rights but take into account underlying historical, social, economic, cultural and religious factors. What is important is constant progress and not rapid, unprepared reforms which do not take into consideration these underlying realities.

But such an approach to human rights, which calls for taking into account the historic, economic, cultural and religious environment in which human rights are implemented, does not mean that Musa Hitam, a leader of the Malaysian delegation to the Vienna 1993 World Human Rights Conference, was right in saying that '[e]ach country is entitled to its own perception of human rights and forcing developing countries to follow the western perception is unfair and unjust' (Cooke 1993). He added that 'Malaysia views development as very basic to human rights' and that 'civil and political rights should come almost automatically after development has been achieved' (Cooke 1993).

Such an approach is, from my point of view, an abuse of the problems and difficulties stemming from historic traditions and economic underdevelopment. When I call for taking into consideration the social environment in which international standards of human rights are to be implemented, I address the international community of states and special monitoring bodies and I am not preparing excuses for governments of those states which like to hide behind difficulties, often created by themselves, in order to excuse their poor human rights records.

The UN Human Rights Committee, for example, always appreciates the genuine efforts of all states, and especially of Third World countries, which often face real difficulties in the implementation of the International Covenant on Civil and Political Rights, and understands quite well governments which, notwithstanding their efforts, have not yet achieved full implementation of the Covenant. But those governments which usually hide behind the outdated non-interference concept and try to explain away their problems by referring to historical, cultural or religious traditions and economic underdevelopment often simply do not undertake any efforts even to gradually implement international human rights standards.

Sirous Naserri, the Iranian representative to the Geneva headquarters of the UN, for example, at the end of the consideration of the Iranian report on civil and political rights before the UN Human Rights Committee in October 1992, emphasized the need to take into account cultural criteria when interpreting international instruments.[23] But his remark missed the point because the observations and comments of members of the Human Rights Committee did not question the cultural values of the Iranian people or of Islam.[24] Is it really possible to explain discrimination against and even persecution of Baha'is, the death penalty by stoning for adultery, mutilation as a punishment and the fatwa against Salman Rushdie, as cultural requirements which should be taken into account while speaking of human rights in that country?

And do international human rights standards really reflect only Western values and does cultural relativism mean that these rights and freedoms, or at least a part of them, are alien to countries which do not belong to Western civilization?

Certainly, Western countries and consequently Western concepts made the biggest contribution to the elaboration of the major human rights instruments after World War II. But, by the adoption of the International Covenants on Human Rights as early as 1966, not only the Soviet Union and other so-called socialist countries but also most Third World states were able to influence the content of these documents which are now freely ratified or adhered to by considerably more than 100 states, of which the majority are non-western countries. Therefore the World Conference on

---

[23] UN Press Release HR/3215, 30 October 1992 (afternoon), p. 5.
[24] See *ibid.*

Human Rights of 1993 could emphasize that '[a]ll human rights are universal,[25] indivisible and interdependent and interrelated. The international community must treat human rights globally in a fair and equal manner, on the same footing, and with the same emphasis.'[26]

But even more important, in my opinion, is the fact that when one goes further than rather general assertions that the cultural, religious and historic traditions of a given country should be taken into account in assessing its human rights' record, one can hardly say, in concrete terms, how generally accepted international standards conflict with the cultural or religious values of individual societies. It is interesting to note that while the Iranian delegation before the UN Human Rights Committee stressed the necessity of taking into consideration the cultural criteria of any country when assessing its human rights record, the same delegation confirmed that the International Covenant on Civil and Political Rights and the Universal Declaration of Human Rights were compatible with Islam.[27]

Sometimes the arguments of those who deny the very possibility of the existence of universal human rights in the multi-cultural world simply miss the point. I would agree, however, with the Foreign Minister of Singapore Wong Kan Seng who, in his statement at the World Conference on Human Rights in Vienna, said that '[u]niversal recognition of the ideal of human rights can be harmful if universalism is used to deny or mask the reality of diversity'.[28] Later, as an example, he stated that 'Singaporeans, and people in many other parts of the world do not agree, for instance, that pornography is an acceptable manifestation of free expression or that a homosexual relationship is just a matter of lifestyle choice'.[29] Neither the freedom of distribution of pornography nor equality in all respects between homosexuals and heterosexuals are universal human rights norms. Indeed, there are many controversial areas such as euthanasia, abortion, pornography, homosexuality, etc. which touch upon deeply rooted moral and religious sentiments and are considered differently in various societies. Neither is it any excuse that development should be put before civil and political rights. They are not mutually exclusive. Quite the contrary.

---

[25] Not all human rights are, in my view, universal. There are certainly rights which are national or regional. The fundamental, or basic, human rights are universal or, though it may sound like a tautology, we may say that all universal human rights are universal.

[26] *UN Doc.* A/Conf. 157/23, para. 5.

[27] *UN Press Release* HR/3215, 30 October 1992 (afternoon), p. 1.

[28] 'The Real World of Human Rights', Statement by Foreign Minister Wong Kan Seng of Singapore at the World Conference on Human Rights, Vienna, 16 June 1993, p.2.

[29] *Ibid.*, p. 4.

When the Soviet Union's human rights record was criticized it was not because it put social and economic rights first and considered them higher than civil and political rights. The socialist concept of human rights as something different from and even higher than the so-called Western concept was used to conceal the real human rights situation. Human rights were considered not as a practical but as an ideological problem. The lack of civil and political rights was one of the reasons for the stagnation of the economy of the country and consequently for the poor situation regarding social and economic rights as well.

It is true that some fundamentalist religious concepts are really incompatible with international human rights instruments (especially regarding equality between men and women or tolerance towards other religions) but even here, I would dare to assert, we can hardly discover any imposition of specific Western values on culturally different societies. Catholic fundamentalism is not so different from its Islamic counterpart. In Western European countries women were (and in some of these countries still are) discriminated against, while in many European countries heretics were burnt. In Spain the inquisition was abolished only in 1834[30] and in 1925 a school teacher was condemned by a local court in Tennessee, USA, for teaching the theory of the origin of the species.[31] As to the punishment of crimes, Western European countries have moved from such cruel forms of execution as hanging or guillotining to the complete abolition of the death penalty. The main difference between these religious fundamentalisms is that while Catholic fundamentalism was powerful in the Middle Ages, Islamic fundamentalism is a contemporary phenomenon.

This shows that contemporary human rights standards are not immutable values, inherent only in Western countries. These countries themselves, and others as well, came to the acceptance of these values through a long historical process. David Selbourne is right in tracing back 'the historic widening of claims-to-rights in liberal democratic civic orders':

> from claims made by seventeenth-century property owners to the concomitant political rights to which they believed themselves entitled by virtue of their ownership; to claims made by non-property-owners in the nineteenth century to a variety of civic rights which should owe nothing to wealth or position; to claims made by all citizens (and even non-citizens) in the twentieth century to rights of protection from the consequences of misfortune, including the consequences of unemployment, old age, homelessness, and sickness. (Selbourne 1994 p. 57.)

Therefore, I can see no universal international human rights norm which would be culturally unacceptable for any society. It may be the case that

---

[30] *Longman Illustrated Encyclopedia of World History*, London, Ivy Leaf, 1991, p. 463.
[31] *Ibid.*, p. 410.

some time would be needed in some societies to fully implement them, and some quite deeply rooted traditions which are inexcusable from the point of view of these standards could not be immediately eradicated, e.g. India has not yet succeeded in completely eradicating such vestiges of the past as the 'dowry death' (where a wife is killed because of the insufficiency of her dowry), or suttee (where a widow has to commit suicide or is encouraged to kill herself after the death of her husband), but the government is certainly trying to do its best to get rid of these crimes.[32]

There are no inherently Western international human rights standards. It may also be true that for some countries certain rights may seem more important or even that some countries, like Malaysia, may view 'development as a basic human right'. But this does not mean either that if development is guaranteed civil and political rights would automatically follow, or that for securing development the limitation of civil and political rights is necessary. 'While development facilitates the enjoyment of all human rights, the lack of development may not be invoked to justify the abridgement of internationally recognized human rights.'[33]

In my opinion, human rights are conditioned by three categories or levels of factors: anthropological, societal and international. These factors are not immutable in time or space. While societal factors, that is factors pertaining to the characteristics of a given society, have exercised the strongest influence on the content of rights and freedoms of members of a society, international factors are of more recent origin but their influence is rapidly growing. Some rights, like the right to life, freedom from torture and the right to found a family, are of an anthropological nature, though they, as any other rights, can exist only in a society. Robinson Crusoe could have had no rights or obligations before the appearance of Man Friday.

The growing interdependence of the world as a whole and the transparency of most societies mean that international factors, through purposeful efforts as well as through interpenetration of cultures, are influencing human rights concepts as well as practices in different societies. However, this does not and should not lead to global cultural uniformity.

We may probably conclude now, returning to our main topic – human rights in these post-totalitarian societies – that though in many of them democracy or even, using the term proposed by Dahl 'polyarchy', is still quite far away, most newly- or re-born states have sufficient resources for

---

[32] A new offence of 'dowry death' was included in the Indian Penal Code and there is the Commission of Sati (Prevention) Act of 1987 (*Second Periodic Report of India to the UN Human Rights Committee*, 12 July 1989, UN Doc. CCPR/C/137/Add.13, paras. 117, 119.

[33] UN Doc. A/Conf.157/23, 12 July 1993, para. 5.

democratization. Naturally, the efforts of governments and the assistance of other states and of international inter-governmental bodies as well as NGOs, are necessary. Understanding difficulties and problems, and even the recognition of cultural diversity as a universal value, does not mean that one should or could be lenient towards the violation of fundamental human rights in countries which are facing objective difficulties.

4. Human Rights in Russia: Discourse of Emancipation or only a Mirage?

Bill Bowring

I INTRODUCTION

Viktor Zaslavsky, in a recent article expressing optimism for the Russian transition to democracy, declares that:

> Today's Russian youth is thoroughly Westernised. Global Western culture, with its emphasis on democracy, human rights and individual freedoms, is becoming a viable substitution for the traditional political culture in several crucial groups. (Zaslavsky 1993 pp. 49–50)

In an anxious response, Rittersporn asks:

> Why is he discovering the heuristic merits of categories such as 'Western values', 'market' or 'democracy' without trying to see what they denote in the context in which he uses them and without asking himself if they have a clear and unambiguous meaning? (Rittersporn 1993 pp. 59–60).

This chapter is concerned to situate human rights discourse and human rights practice in the context of contemporary Russia; and also to ask what is the content of the 'global Western culture' which contains these praiseworthy virtues – democracy, human rights and individual freedoms, so full of ambiguity in their use in the West. Of course, the dominant discourse of the historical past, what Zaslavsky describes as the 'traditional political culture', regarded human rights in the 'global Western sense' first as a mirage (Pashukanis, 1978 p. 146); and then defined rights in a radically different, and not uninfluential way.

I start, therefore, with the human rights provisions of the latest, 1993 Constitution, born out of the bloodshed of the events of October 1993 (its legitimacy is, at the time of writing (August 1994), increasingly called into question[1]). Of course, contemporary international human rights discourse is very much a product of the post World War II era; although the dominant rhetoric is that of civil and political rights, which were inscribed on the banners of the American and French revolutions. It is of interest, therefore, to trace the development of the concept of rights through the Bolshevik revolution and the horrors of Stalinism. Third, I examine the most recent predecessors of the rights in the new Constitution, as they appeared in the 1978 Brezhnev Constitution, and the evolving mechanisms, for the most part the products of Perestroika, for protection and vindication of human rights, taking into account the role of international human rights instruments and discourse. Fourth, such an itinerary will necessitate consideration of the role of rights in legitimating political power; and, reciprocally, the role of rights in restraining and shaping the exercise of power. Finally, I have my own views as to that framework of human rights which is adequate to present day conditions.

II VARIABLES FOR DETERMINING THE STATE OF HUMAN RIGHTS LAW

There is no aspect, political, economic, or legal, of the present Russian reality which seems susceptible to coherent analysis. It is doubtful whether any predetermined analytical model will assist in conceptualising what has occurred and continues incessantly to transform itself. In his long article on the subject Professor Van den Berg has, nevertheless, sought to diagnose the main problems (Van den Berg, 1992). He suggests a number of seemingly technical problems, which, in addition to the political situation, have had an impact on the state of legislation and therefore on the state of human rights in Russia. These are: 1. The fact that the constitutional system and laws are full of rules from the old system, which were not in agreement with international human rights legislation; 2. Moreover, in the old system, constitutional provisions were said to be directly enforceable, when this was not the case. For example, Article 54 of the 1978 Constitution provided that the secrecy of correspondence was 'protected by law'. Since no laws were enacted, the courts would not apply the provision. 3. Many past laws conferred political, social or economic rights

---

1 See, for example, 'Yeltsin referendum "rigged"' by Tony Barber, *The Independent* 9 April 1994; it is alleged that Yeltsin's supporters in regional administrations and electoral commissions may have exaggerated voter turnouts so that they exceeded the required 50 per cent of the electorate needed to validate the referendum.

only on 'citizens of the republic'; such laws could therefore be discriminatory. 4. Where a democratic tradition is absent, politicians may fail to reflect on what they are doing in human rights terms. 5. In any event, many laws are very poorly drafted, unclear, vague and full of mistakes. 6. The courts have in the past not shown themselves to be independent, and to this day wait for the lawmaker to amend the law. The question posed, therefore, is whether these problems, accurately identified, are being or can be overcome.

More recently, Chistyakova (1993 p. 372) sought to pin down the underlying causes of the Russian problematic. Soviet conceptions of rights in the pre-Gorbachev era reflected three main principles: first, that the state is the sole source of human rights, and the government has the power to define and limit those rights; second, that the needs of individuals must always be secondary to those of the state and the collective; and third, that economic and social rights enjoy a higher degree of protection than civil and political rights.

She concedes that social and economic rights were indeed, to an extent, delivered. The central role of social and economic rights is one of the themes of this chapter. Moreover, Chafetz points out (1992 p. 158) that the implicit Soviet social contract which permitted Communist Party rule guaranteed relative equality, if at the price of economic and social stagnation. The regime, in his view, required a degree of docility from society in order to rule. In return for that docility, society was not asked to work very hard, and was guaranteed increasing standards of living and an extensive social welfare system. In this way the regime enjoyed some considerable legitimacy. It is arguable that through a degree of continuity with the past, a democratic future in which all human rights are adequately protected may be more possible. These points will be kept in mind as we survey the present state and recent history of human rights in Russia.

Furthermore, there is one important consideration which should always be borne in mind, particularly by lawyers of the Anglo-Saxon, common-law tradition. The Russian legal system has, since 1922, been based largely on the German model; the Constitutional Court is a replica of Karlsrühe; and German conceptions prevail. The relationship between the individual and the state is posited in a very much more reciprocal and articulated manner than would be usual in English jurisprudence, where the state is so often cast as an inimical other. This is what a contemporary German textbook writer says about the rule of basic rights in the constitutional order:

> In their function as subjective rights, the basic rights determine and secure the foundations of the individual's legal status. In their function as objective basic components of a democratic and constitutional social order, they insert the individual in

this order, which can itself only become a reality if these rights are given real shape. The status of the individual in terms of constitutional law, as grounded in and guaranteed by the basic rights laid out in the Basic Law, is thus a material legal status, i.e. a status with concretely determined contents, a status which neither the individual nor the state's powers can unrestrictedly adapt at will. This status in constitutional law forms the core of the general status of national citizenship, which, along with the basic rights ... is laid down in law. (Hesse, 1990 p. 113)

But it must also be borne in mind that, as Kudryatvstev (1994 p. 95) points out, the present Constitution has come into being courtesy of the most comprehensive violation (by way of the forcible and in the end bloody dissolution of parliament and the suspension of the Constitutional Court – for an account, see Steele, 1994) of the previous constitutional system. It is not surprising then, that the commentators who have so far reflected on the new Constitution stress the central importance of the separation of powers: see, for example Pivovarov and Salmin (1994 p. 172), who point out dangerous parallels with the French Second Republic, and with the ill-fated Weimar Constitution.

III THE 1993 CONSTITUTION

The Constitution which was approved by the Constitutional Conference in November 1993,[2] and (perhaps) approved in the Referendum of 12 December 1993, is expressly constructed on the basis of human rights. It proclaims:

We, the multinational people of the Russian Federation, united by a common destiny on our land, asserting human rights and freedoms and civil peace and concord ...

and Article 2 spells this out:

The individual and his rights and freedoms are the supreme value. Recognition, observance and protection of human and civil rights and freedoms is the obligation of the state.

This statement amounts to a thoroughgoing repudiation of the former system; it is intended to do so.

Chapter 1 deals with 'Foundations of the constitutional system'. Of great interest, in view of what has been said already about the Soviet social compact, is the fact that Article 7 provides:

(1) The Russian Federation is a social state whose policy is aimed at creating conditions ensuring a worthy life and free development of the individual.
(2) In the Russian Federation people's labour and health are protected, a guaranteed minimum wage is established, state support is insured for the family, mothers, fathers,

---

2　Moscow, *Rossiskaya Gazeta* 10 November 1993, pp. 3–6

children, invalids and elderly citizens, the system of social services is developed, and state pensions, allowances and other guarantees of social protection are established.

Those words might, in today's circumstances, seem to mock the majority of the population, or, at least, to offer a 'bright future' which is perhaps as illusory as that promised under actually existing socialism. Nevertheless, it is significant that this is how the new regime seeks to legitimise the new order; by asserting substantial continuity with the old (on this point, see Aráto, 1994).

Chapter 2 contains the new Constitution's 'Human and Civil Rights and Freedoms'. As we will see, this is a very comprehensive list of rights indeed. Articles 17 and 18 set out the philosophical foundations; and a most important provision as to application:

Article 17
(1) Human and civil rights and freedoms are guaranteed in the Russian Federation in accordance with generally recognised principles and norms of international law and in conformity with the present constitution.
(2) Basic human rights and freedoms are inalienable and belong to each person from birth onwards.
(3) The exercise of human and civil rights and freedoms must not violate the rights and freedoms of others.'
Article 18
(1) Human and civil rights and freedoms have direct application (*yavlaiutsya nyepostredstvenno deistvuishimi*). They determine the meaning, content and application of laws and the activity of the legislative and executive branches and of local self-government and are safeguarded by justice.

This last is a decisive provision. It states without equivocation that not only the Constitution itself, but the whole range of international human rights instruments as well, are to be applied by all the courts, not only as a guide to interpretation, but also as a means of quashing administrative decisions and overturning legislation.

Following Article 19, which contains a comprehensive prohibition of discrimination, there are no less than 35 articles containing specific rights. Of these, 14 contain civil and political rights. Some of these are advanced, and do not appear in the European Convention, for example Article 24, on the prohibition on the collection, storage, utilisation and dissemination of information about a person's private life without his consent, together with the right to see documents and materials directly affecting rights and freedoms, unless otherwise prohibited by law. Furthermore, Article 25 proclaims that dwellings are inviolable; no-one may enter without consent except on the basis of federal law, or on the basis of a judicial decision. Article 26 contains the right to determine and indicate one's own nationality; with the right to use one's native language. It is notable that the State is given, within the Articles themselves, fewer specific grounds for interference with the exercise of these rights than under the European Convention on Human Rights: for example, the guarantee, in Article 29, of the freedom of thought and speech, is limited only by a prohibition on propaganda or agitation exciting social, racial, national or religious hatred and enmity or supremacy. However, Article 29(4) provides that 'Each person has the right freely to seek, receive, pass on, produce and disseminate information by any legal method. The list of information constituting a state secret is determined by federal law.' This is disturbingly ambiguous as to the circumstances in which national security may be claimed; and as to whether the courts may adjudicate as to the state's grounds.

Article 34 provides for the right to make free use of one's abilities and property for entrepreneurial activity, provided this is not directed towards monopolisation or unscrupulous competition. There is a right to private property and inheritance; no one may be deprived of property save by court decision, and compulsory expropriation may only be carried out if full compensation is paid (Article 35). Land may be held in private ownership (Article 36); and Article 37 contains rights of free labour, the right to work in conditions meeting requirements of health and safety, and for not less than the state minimum wage. There is also a constitutional right to resolve individual and collective disputes by methods 'prescribed by federal law', including the right to strike; and a right to leisure. Article 38 places maternity, childhood and the family under the state's protection; concern for children and their upbringing are the equal right and duty of parents. More unusually, able-bodied children who have reached the age of 18 must look after disabled parents. Article 39 guarantees social security in old age, sickness, disability, or for the raising of children.

The most controversial provisions, those against which some of the commentators of the Chicago University-based Eastern European Constitutional Review warn (see in particular Sunstein, 1993), are the provisions for social and economic rights: the right to housing, in Article 40, the right to health care and medical assistance in Article 41, the right to a decent environment in Article 42, and the right to education in Article 43. All of these are to be justiciable; the right to housing is non-derogable. However, the rights protected are somewhat indeterminate. According to Article 40, for example, public bodies are to encourage housing construction and are to create the conditions for the exercise of the right. Housing is to be provided free or at affordable cost to low-income 'and other citizens indicated in the law who require housing' from public stocks. Under Article 41, medical assistance in public health care establishments is to be provided free of charge 'by means of funds from the relevant budget, insurance contributions and other revenue' – enforcement litigation would raise interesting questions of interpretation; moreover the concealment by officials of facts and circumstances creating a threat to people's lives and health carries legal responsibility. The right to a decent environment in Article 42 includes a right to compensation for damages caused by ecological offences. Primary and secondary education are to be free of charge, according to Article 43, as well as free higher education on a competitive basis.

It is, in my view, highly significant that these rights find an equal place in the new Constitution. First, it is arguable that the very notion of social and economic rights as rights finds its origin in the West's response to the Russian Revolution of 1917. Second, the fact that the 1948 Universal Declaration of Human Rights contained both generations of rights, and only under Cold War conditions was it necessary to promulgate separate Covenants in 1966, to complete the 'International Bill of Rights', show that Russia's enthusiastic adoption of international human rights instruments is no one-way-street. Third, Russia's is not the only 'constitution of the transition' to grapple with the justiciability of social and economic rights: in a comprehensively-argued paper, Randal Jeffrey (1993) demonstrates, with wide international reference, just why the new South African Constitution can and must contain justiciable second generation rights.

Although Article 55 provides that the rights and freedoms must not be interpreted as negating or diminishing other universally recognised human and civil rights, and laws abolishing or diminishing human and civil rights must not be promulgated in the Russian Federation, the third paragraph states:

> Human and civil rights and freedoms can be curtailed by federal law only to the extent to which it may be necessary for the purpose of protecting the foundations of the constitutional system, morality and the health, rights and legitimate interests of other individuals, or of ensuring the country's defence and the state's security.

This would appear to give the State an unacceptable degree of licence to interfere with basic rights. It will be interesting to see how the courts deal with this potential problem.

Nevertheless, Article 45 provides that state protection of human and civil rights and freedoms is guaranteed; and Article 46 that each person is guaranteed judicial protection of his rights and freedoms, that the decisions and action or inaction of public bodies can be appealed in court, and that Russian citizens may appeal to international treaty bodies. There are also rights to receive qualified legal assistance (Article 48), the presumption of innocence (Article 49), the *ne bis in idem* principle (Article 50), the right not to testify against self or family (Article 51), and a right to compensation from the state for damage caused by the unlawful action or inaction of public bodies.

Finally, the derogation provision in Article 56 is, on the face of it, exceptionally restrictive on the freedom of action of the state, and is progressive in comparison to other instruments. Unlike the ECHR, it insists that individual restrictions of rights and freedoms in a state of emergency can only be introduced with an indication of their extent and duration; and only in order 'to ensure the safety of citizens and the protection of the constitutional system in accordance with federal constitutional law'. The rights to life (Article 20), against torture (Article 21), to inviolability of private and family life and personal honour (Article 23(1)), against collection of information without consent (Article 24), to freedom of conscience and religion (Article 28), to entrepreneurial activity (Article 34(1)), to housing (Article 40(1)), and the series of due process rights contained in Articles 46 to 54, are all non-derogable.

There are a number of obligations: as well as the duty to look after disabled parents, already mentioned, there are duties to ensure that children receive basic general education (Article 43(4)) to display concern for preserving the historical and cultural heritage (Article 44(4)), to pay legitimate and non-retroactive taxes (Article 57), to protect nature and the environment (Article 58), and to protect the fatherland and perform military service (Article 59).

Chapter 7 of the Constitution provides for judicial enforcement of these rights. Article 125 contemplates a Constitutional Court consisting of 19 judges (the present 13, with the election, by the Federation Council, of a further 6 judges). By Article 125(1) the Court may be moved by the President, either chamber of parliament, one fifth of the members of either chamber, the Russian government, the Russian Supreme Court and Superior Court of Arbitration, and the legislative and executive bodies of the components of the Russian Federation, in order to decide the constitutionality of, first, federal laws and 'normative acts' of the President, parliament, or the government; second, the constitutions of republics and charters of components of the Russian Federation, and laws and normative acts issued by them; third, treaties between components of the Russian Federation; and fourth, international treaties of the Russian Federation not yet in force.

Most significantly, for our present purpose, as well as having power to resolve disputes over areas of jurisdiction between components of the Russian Federation, the Court, pursuant to Article 25(4):

> on the basis of complaints regarding the violation of citizens' constitutional rights and freedoms and at the request of judges, examines the constitutionality of the law that has

been applied or is applicable in the specific case, in accordance with the procedure laid down by federal law.

The new Constitution, therefore, on paper, appears to provide a complete and water-tight system for vindicating rights.

The experienced commentator Vladimir Kudryavtsev adopts, however, a somewhat more pessimistic view (1994 p. 97):

> Let us look now at the picture of the lower level – at the legal status of the rank-and-file citizen. On paper it does not look at all bad. The new Constitution anew enlarges the list of rights and freedoms of the citizen. During the referendum campaign there were many declarations and appeals to this effect.
>
> However, we must turn to the practical side of things. The legal situation of the citizen is not lived out on paper, but in everyday life – at work, on the street, on holiday, in existence. And there reality seems to be not very comfortable.
>
> First, the citizen will continue to collide with the unclarity and instability of laws [particularly banking and insurance laws] ...
>
> Second, the practice of vindication through law, as before, is extremely bureaucratised. Red tape in the courts and administrative establishments, despite all sorts of strong instructions and elucidations, reduces each case into a tedious, long-drawn-out, and, at the end of the day, expensive procedure. It is possible to cut through this red tape, practically speaking, only in two ways: by bribery, or by connections 'on high' ...
>
> The result of the inefficiency of legislative and legal vindication mechanisms is the legal defencelessness of the citizen and his lack of faith in the force of the law.

Kudryavtsev calls for a range of reforms, including a really powerful human rights ombudsman, and much greater rights for consumers, amongst others.

IV BOLSHEVIK RIGHTS

To trace the changing Russian attitude to rights, we must look back to the October Revolution. Russia's first Constitution came into force on 19 July 1918. Lenin said: 'If we are now able to submit a Soviet Constitution to this Congress, it is only because Soviets have been set up and tested in all parts of the country; only six months after the October revolution, ... (we are) able to write down what already exists in practice' (Lenin, 1964 p. 515). On Lenin's suggestion, a 'Declaration of the Rights of the Working and Exploited People' was added to the preamble. These rights did not include any of the civil and political rights one would expect in a modern constitution; rather, they were the rights of victors in the class struggle.

Following the devastation of the Civil War and in conditions of the New Economic Policy, when stability was once more of the essence, a Criminal Code was enacted in May 1922, a Civil Code shortly afterwards (both based closely on German models), and then Agrarian and Labour Codes. In 1923, the foundation of the USSR was accompanied by the creation of a

Supreme Court, subject to the higher authority of the Central Executive Committee, and acting as its agent (Carr 1970 p. 97), as well as a Procurator of the USSR, to act as an organ of control of the lawfulness of administrative action, as well as prosecuting authority. Nevertheless, the Constitution was not to be enforceable by any court.

Yevgeny Pashukanis published his 'Law and Marxism: A General Theory' in 1924, and it went through two further editions until 1927. His views on the rule of law were forthright. The constitutional state, the Rechtsstaat, was, he said, a mirage, but one which suited the bourgeoisie very well, since it replaced withered religious ideology and concealed the fact of the bourgeoisie's hegemony from the eyes of the masses. The beauty of the ideology of the Rechtsstaat was that, while it did not fully reflect objective reality, it was still based on this reality:

> Power as the 'collective will', as the 'rule of law', is realised in bourgeois society to the extent that this society represents a market. From this standpoint, even police regulations can figure as the embodiment of the Kantian idea of freedom limited by the freedom of others. (Pashukanis, 1978 p. 146)

At that time, in the 1920s, Pashukanis set the tone. Others did not attain the same sophistication. A scholar named V. Diablo, for example, argued in 1926:

> What accounts for the contrast between bourgeois and socialist legality? This contrast is entirely a product of the contrast between the foundations of the 'law-governed bourgeois state' and the dictatorship of the proletariat.

In his view, the theory of the law-governed state supposes that the state is unfree, since the individual's freedom is limited not by the state, but by nature or reason; while the individual rights of citizens do not constrain Soviet power, but 'are rather granted only for the development of the country's productive forces'. In other words, only the Soviet state could enter into a transparent freedom of action, both actual and theoretical, in which the concept of the rule of law would have no place.

Following the adoption of the first Constitution of the USSR, on 31 January 1924, a new constitution was prepared for the Russian Socialist Federation of Soviet Republics, in which the Declaration of Rights of the Toiling and Exploited People was omitted; also, the words of the 1918 Constitution guaranteeing the dictatorship of the proletariat, *inter alia* for establishing state power, were replaced with words 'establishing socialism'.

a) Stalin's Constitution, and the Birth of the United Nations

In September 1934 the USSR joined the League of Nations, and was elected a permanent member of the Council. A new Constitution was unanimously approved on 5 December 1936. According to the notorious Vyshinsky, prosecutor of the Moscow Trials, the 1936 Constitution reflected the following changes:

> The complete triumph of the socialist system in all branches of the national economy, the fundamental realisation of socialism, the liquidation of the exploiter classes, the annihilation of man's exploitation by man ... all these factors evoked the necessity of changing the Constitution of the USSR so that the new Constitution should reflect all the changes ... since 1924. (Vyshinsky 1948 p. 120)

With regard to the rights enshrined in it, it was, sadly for them, taken seriously by those closest to power. Nikolai Bukharin, one of the members of the drafting Commission, who boasted later that he had written the document from the first word to the last (Kochan & Abraham, 1990 p. 377), thought that the new Constitution was a document 'which would make it impossible for the people any longer to be pushed aside'. It was indeed, for its time, a model document, giving paper guarantees of freedom from arbitrary arrest (Article 127), inviolability of the home and secrecy of correspondence (Article 128), and freedom of speech, of the press, of meetings and of demonstrations (Article 125). That Bukharin thought it would be implemented shows that he imagined that a genuine relaxation was taking place (Conquest, 1971 p. 134). But, as is now well known, this was but a lull in the Great Purge of 1934 to 1938; as a result of Stalin's activities, Conquest estimates, some 10 to 15 million people died. The rights inscribed in the Constitution were unenforceable; there were no remedies. The regime saw no need to be shy about the significance of this. Vyshinsky permitted no illusions as to the nature of rights:

> Proletarian declarations of rights frankly manifest their class essence, reflecting nothing of the desire of bourgeois declarations to shade off and mask the class character of the rights they proclaim. (Vyshinsky 1948 p. 554)

By a supreme irony of history, Vyshinsky was, in March 1953, at Stalin's death, appointed the USSR's permanent delegate to the United Nations; he had been made Foreign Minister in March 1949 (Vaksberg, 1990 p. 279), having attended the Third Session of the UN General Assembly at the end of 1948. That was the session which adopted, on 10 December 1948, the Universal Declaration of Human Rights. 48 states voted in favour of the Declaration, while 8, including the USSR, abstained.

In the introduction to a collection of Russian translations of major human rights instruments, Lev Shestakov, now Head of International Law at Moscow State University, asked why the USSR abstained. He gives three reasons (Shestakov 1990 pp. 6–7); these were also Vyshinsky's reasons. First, in the opinion of the Soviet delegation, the draft Declaration had limited itself only to fixing formal rights, and did not contain measures for the material and legislative guaranteeing of those rights. Second, the draft failed to contain the right of peoples to self-determination, on which the USSR had insisted, as a principled question. Third, Articles 19 and 20 (freedom of expression and freedom of association) had been drafted in such a way as to permit fascist propaganda; the USSR wished to include in Article 19 the words 'the inalienable right of every human being is ... the fight against fascism in the fields of ideology, politics, state and social life.' It is notorious that the USSR ratified practically every human rights instrument thereafter.

V RIGHTS UNDER THE BREZHNEV CONSTITUTION

What rights, if any, were guaranteed in the Constitution which has only recently been swept away? Did human rights find any protection at all? Chapter 7 of the 1977 USSR Constitution (there is a translation in Feldbrugge 1993 pp. 321–78) was entitled 'The Basic Rights, Freedoms and Obligations of Citizens of the USSR'. Article 39 stated that 'Citizens of the USSR enjoy the full range of socio-economic, political and personal rights and freedoms proclaimed and guaranteed by the Constitution ... In exercising their rights and freedoms, citizens may not injure the interests of society and the state or the rights of other citizens.' According to Feldbrugge, 'Fundamental rights are granted by the state and the citizen participates in them by being involved in the socialist system of production. The most basic right was therefore the right to work (Article 40) ...' (Feldbrugge, 1993 p. 217). This was followed by the right to leisure (Article 41), the right to health care (Article 42), the right to social security (Article 43), the right to housing (Article 44), the right to education (Article 45), the right to use the achievements of culture (Article 46).

These socio-economic rights were followed by political rights. First, there was the right to participate in the administration of state and public affairs (Article 48), ensured by the possibility of participation in elections to the Soviets etc. Next came the right to submit proposals for improvement, and to have these answered (Article 49). Article 50 guaranteed freedom of speech, of the press, of assembly, of meetings, street marches and demonstrations; but 'in accordance with the interests of the people and in order to strengthen and develop the socialist system', so that the exercise of these freedoms was ensured by making public buildings etc. available to 'the working people and their organisations'. Article 51 provided for the right to unite in social organisations, but only in 'accordance with the goals of communist construction'.

Personal rights came last. Article 52 guaranteed freedom of conscience. Articles 54 and 55 guaranteed inviolability of the person and the home, save on the basis of a court order or the sanction of the procurator. Such orders were readily given, and there was no redress for unlawful or oppressive searches or seizures. Private life and the secrecy of correspondence and telephone conversations was, by Article 56, to be protected by law. There was no such law, in practice. There was no freedom of movement; foreign travel was possible only with special permission; and internal movement was restricted by the systems of the *propiska* (residence permit) and internal passports.

Finally, a series of duties included Article 60: 'Conscientious labour in one's chosen field of socially useful activity and observance of labour discipline is the duty and a matter of honour for every Soviet citizen who is able to work. Avoiding socially useful work is incompatible with the principles of a socialist society.'

An Example: The Right to Housing

What was the reality of these fundamental social and economic rights? Van den Berg (1989) has provided us with a highly detailed study of the right to housing (Article 44). This right was:

> ensured by the development and protection of the state and social housing fund; by assistance to co-operative and individual housing construction; by a fair distribution, under social supervision, of living space, made available in accordance with the realisation of the programme for the construction of well-built housing; and by moderate payments for rent and municipal services.

The *Principles of Housing Legislation of the USSR*, enacted on 24 June 1981, provided that living accommodation should be allocated 'as a rule in the form of a separate apartment for each family'. The view of a number of Soviet authors reviewed by Van den Berg was that the right to housing was, although it was effectively unenforceable in the courts, a 'subjective civil right', and 'one of the elements of the legal status of a USSR citizen'. But neither the 1977 nor the 1936 Constitutions contained a right to freedom of choice of residence; indeed, on 27 December 1932 a Uniform Passport System was introduced, and to this day local authorities, now, notoriously, the city of Moscow, assert and enforce the right to restrict the freedom of choice of residence, through the *propiska* (residence permit) system laid down in a Decree of the USSR Council of Ministers of 20 August 1974, despite the fact that the system has now been declared unconstitutional – see below (of course, as Van den Berg points out, the Netherlands has a system of residence permits the *woningvergunningen*, which were in 1986 considered not to infringe the European Convention on Human Rights (*Gillow v The Netherlands*). As late as 30 June 1987 a *Law on Judicial Review of Administrative Acts*[3] was enacted for the USSR providing for the right to challenge in court cases of unlawful actions of officials (but not 'collegial bodies'), infringing upon a citizen's rights; but it is not known how many cases were heard.

There was clearly, therefore, a conflict between the right to housing and the freedom of choice of residence; this is because although the right is proclaimed by the state, it has to be realised by local authorities, who are first of all responsible for their own residents: 'the system of residence certificates is an effective tool in the hands of local politicians, who are concerned with the welfare of the local population...' (Van den Berg, 1989 p. 383).

VI THE RIGHTS AND REMEDIES OF PERESTROIKA

Is there any experience, therefore, of vindicating the many rights which are to be found in the new Constitution? To a limited extent, there is. Chapter 2 is closely based on the *Declaration of Rights and Freedoms of the Person and the Citizen* adopted by the Russian Federation on 22 November 1991 (following the USSR's *Declaration of the Rights and Freedoms of Man* adopted on 5 September 1991 and incorporated, as Chapter 5, into the Constitution of the Russian Federation dating originally from 1978 – see the translation in Feldbrugge 1993 p. 383–444). It is notable that Article 32 provided that 'Generally recognised international norms concerning the rights of the person prevail over laws of the Russian Federation and directly create rights and duties for citizens of the Russian Federation.' We shall see how that provision was implemented by the Russian Constitutional Court. The adoption of the Declarations, in Feldbrugge's words 'signified the return of the Soviet Union to the general fold of mankind' (1993 p. 226).

At an early stage, transition to a 'law-governed state' was seen, by Gorbachev (1988) and others, to be inextricably connected to the creation of a constitutional court (see, in the English-language literature, Yakovlev 1988, Kudryavtsev 1988, Vaksberg, 1990 and Kazimirchuk 1991). In the words of Sergei Pashin, who drafted the Law of 6 May 1991 '*On the Constitutional Court of the RSFSR*':

A Constitutional Court is an organ which is unknown to the state structure of Russia during the whole course of its existence. Rudiments of a constitution were bestowed

---

3   *Vedomosti SSSR* 1987 No. 26 Art. 388.

upon the subjects of the Russian Empire on 17 October 1905, but autocratic rule was preserved right up until the February Revolution of 1917. The October coup which followed shortly afterwards extinguished the constitutional basis of legality and recognition of human rights. V I Lenin stressed (Complete Collected Works, Vol. 31, p. 342): '... The whole legal and factual constitution of the Soviet republic is built upon the fact that the party directs, prescribes and builds everything on one principle.' The USSR Constitution of 1924 imposed on the Supreme Court the duty of giving, at the request of the Central Executive Committee of the USSR, judgments 'on the legality of enactments of the Union republics from the point of view of the Constitution', but this jurisdiction was not developed and was repealed in 1929. (Pashin 1992a p. 4)

The first step was the creation of the Committee for Constitutional Supervision, the CCS (a full account of the CCS and of the early days of the Russian Constitutional Court may be found in Hausmaniger, 1990 and 1992). Although such a body was first proposed by academics in 1977, there was no legislation until December 1988 'with the goal of guaranteeing the strictest correspondence of laws and Government decrees with the Constitution of the USSR'.[4] It started work in April 1990, and was dissolved, together with the other supreme organs of the Union, and the USSR itself, in December 1991. The *Law on Constitutional Supervision in the USSR*,[5] adopted on 23 December 1989, disappointed many commentators. The powers of the CCS were severely circumscribed, and subordinated to the legislature. The CCS could not quash unconstitutional executive decisions. It could only give a declaratory judgment. There was no power to suspend the implementation of a Law of the Congress of Peoples Deputies, or the Constitutions of subordinate Union Republics. The CCS could only refer the question back to the Congress, which could reject the CCS' judgment by a two thirds vote. Only where laws violated 'human rights and freedoms codified in the USSR constitution and international covenants signed by the USSR' could the CCS declare them void, with effect from the date of judgment (Article 21).

The CCS was also subject to procedural limitations. It could consider the constitutionality of a Republican law only on the initiative of the Congress of Peoples Deputies and the Supreme Soviet of the USSR, the highest organs of power of the Union Republics, the Presidium of the Supreme Soviet; and, later, the Speaker of the Supreme Soviet and the President of the USSR. Butler, writing in 1990, feared that the restrictions placed upon the CCS seemed: 'likely to encourage a mechanistic and literalist attitude to constitutional matters and to diminish the opportunities for the rule of law through constitutional maturity' (Butler, 1990 p. 84; see also Arkady Vaksberg, 1990 p. 188).

---

4 Materials of the XIX All-Union Conference of the CPSU, Moscow, 1988, p. 146
5 *Vedomosti SSSR* 1989 No. 29, Art. 572.

Nevertheless, it should be noted that the CCS worked within a context of much greater respect for international human rights norms. On 10 February 1989 the Presidium of the Supreme Soviet passed a Decree recognising the compulsory jurisdiction of the International Court of Justice with respect to six human rights treaties, including the 1948 *Genocide Convention*, and the 1984 *Convention Against Torture.*[6] Schweisfurth (1990 p. 111) commented that 'this move marked a positive shift in the previously negative attitude of the Soviet Union towards the principle judicial organ of the United Nations'. He saw, rightly I think, these developments as exemplifying a farewell to the traditional strict positivistic approach to human rights.

During the period of its work the CCS heard 29 cases. Some of these were of considerable significance, demonstrating the seriousness with which the CCS took human rights considerations. Here are a few examples. First, in the *Unpublished Laws Case* of 29 November 1990 the CCS ruled that all unpublished USSR regulations affecting the rights, freedoms and duties of citizens (there were many such 'secret' laws) violated international human rights norms and would lose their force unless published within three months.[7] Second, in the *Right to Defence Counsel Case*, the CCS (petitioned by the Union of Advocates), decided that the USSR law of 10 April 1990 on reforms to the criminal law, which restricted the right to defence counsel, violated both the Constitution and international conventions. Third, in the *Ratification of the Optional Protocol Case* (4 April 1991), in a move which put the USSR ahead of the UK and the US, the CCS requested the Supreme Soviet of the USSR to secure ratification by the USSR of the Optional Protocol to the *International Convention on Civil and Political Rights* (ICCPR).[8] The Soviet Union had ratified the ICCPR but not the Protocol. There was a commendably prompt response. On 5 July 1991 the Supreme Soviet adopted two Resolutions acceding to the Optional Protocol and recognising the jurisdiction of the Committee for Human Rights under Art. 41 of the ICCPR.[9] Fourth, in the *Dismissal on Attainment of Pensionable Age Case*,[10] the CCS considered the USSR Presidium Edict amending labour law by adding as a ground for termination

---

6   Reported in (1989) 4 Interights Bulletin 3; the other treaties were the 1949 *Convention for the Suppression of Traffic of Persons;* the 1952 *Convention on Political Rights of Women;* the 1965 *Convention on the Elimination of Racial Discrimination*; the 1979 *Convention on the Elimination of Discrimination Against Women.*

7   *Vedomosti Syezda Narodnikh Deputatov SSSR i Verkhovnogo Sovyeta SSSR,* 1990 No. 50 item 1080.

8   *VSND SSSR* ibid, 1991, No. 17, Art. 502; see also 'Sovetskaya Yustitsia', 23 December 1991, p. 17.

9   *Vedemosti SSSR*, No. 29, items 842, 843 (1991).

10 *Vedemosti SSSR*, No. 17, item 501 (1991).

by the employer 'attainment by the worker of pensionable age with entitlement to old age pension'. The CCS declared:

> The rights and freedoms granted to citizens in carrying out any form of activity in the field of work and occupation not forbidden by law form a most important part of human rights, and indicate the level of social protection attained in a society. In a law-governed state every human must be guaranteed equality of opportunity in the possession and use of these rights ... The principle of equality before the law is enshrined in the Constitution, in statutes, and in international legal acts on human rights and freedoms ... and its main guarantee is the prohibition of discrimination.

For Bernard Rudden, the tone of that passage 'recalls the righteousness of many a Soviet sermon' (1994 p. 75). He is critical of failure of the CCS to give the respective dates of the enactments referred to by it, or to discuss the *lex specialis* or *lex posterior* type of argument, or to reveal the international legal acts with which the ground for dismissal is said to clash. But he appears to miss the path-breaking nature of the Committee's adjudications.

Finally, and to illustrate further where I believe Rudden to have missed the point, in the *Residence Permit Case* (11 October 1991), the CCS decided that the system of '*propiski*', permissions to reside in a particular place, plainly contradicted the rights freely to move about and choose one's place of residence, enshrined in international treaties and in instruments such as the 1948 UDHR, but not even mentioned in the then Soviet Constitution[11].

Savitsky (1993) believes that the role of the CCS 'was a secondary one and amounted to the publication of a number of purely symbolic 'conclusions' that were binding on no-one'. With all due respect for Savitsky's eminence, I disagree. Furthermore, in the view of Van den Berg (1992 p. 206), the work of the CCS 'in the field of human rights on the whole was positive'; it was not an illogical institution; he considered that 'In fact it had much more power than most constitutional courts throughout the world ...'

VII THE ROLE OF THE CONSTITUTIONAL COURT IN PROTECTING HUMAN RIGHTS

The period of gestation of the Russian Constitutional Court coincided with the failed August 1991 putsch; the Court started work immediately following the dissolution of the USSR, and consequent disappearance of the

---

[11] *Vedemosti SSSR*, No. 46, item 1307 (1991) *Conclusion of the USSR Constitutional Committee Concerning the Residence Permit Procedures Applied to Individuals.*

CCS. The *Law of the RSFSR on the Constitutional Court of the RSFSR*,[12] drafted by Sergei Pashin, was signed by President Yeltsin on 12 July 1991. Pashin (1992) commented that the Law represented 'an important guarantee of the right of the citizen to judicial protection'. He wrote that the provisions of the new Law were based on Chapter 4, Article 93 of the German Constitution, which provides that the Federal Constitutional Court considers cases 'by way of petition on constitutionality, which may be laid by any person considering that one of his basic rights has been infringed by the state power'. Furthermore, the Chief of the Secretariat of the Court, Yuri Kudriavtsev told the commentator Brzezinski (1993a p. 673) that 'the basic structure of the Court is a reflection of the democratic traditions of Western Europe, and our hope is to bring Russia's legal and constitutional structure even closer to these Western traditions'. Its jurisprudence was shaped by Article 32 of the Russian Constitution, as amended in April 1992, and referred to above, which stated that universally accepted human rights norms have precedence over the laws of the Russian Federation and have direct effect.

How great a role did these norms, and the new human rights provisions of the Constitution, play in the work of the Court? The subsequent jurisprudence of the Court, in particular the *Age Discrimination Case* (4 February 1992),[13] where the Court set aside the dismissal of two workers for having reached pensionable age, and ordered an amendment to the Labour Code, demonstrated a determination to secure a rule of law grounded not only on strict observance of the now much-amended 1978 Constitution, but also on implementation of a wide range of international human rights instruments. In that case, the Court applied not only the Russian *Declaration of Rights and Freedoms* (not by then incorporated into the Constitution), but the 1966 *International Covenant on Economic, Social and Cultural Rights*, and a range of International Labour Organisation instruments.

Bernard Rudden is critical of the 'ebullience' of the jurisprudence of the Constitutional Court (Rudden, 1994 p. 63). He claims that the Court had no jurisdiction to hear a challenge by private individuals to the constitutionality of a statute, but only on the standard judicial application of law (Article 66(1) of the Law); but on the contrary, individual petition was the only way in which such 'standard application' could be challenged (see Pashin 1992a p. 17). Nevertheless, Rudden considers the Court's ruling tone a 'sideways challenge'. He is also critical of the Court's failure to

---

[12] Full text at '*Sovetskaya Yustitsia*', 21 November 1991, pp. 37–53.
[13] *Vedemosti Verkhnovogo Sovyeta RSFSR* No. 13 Art. 669.

consider contrary policy arguments, its partial reading of Article 2(2) of the 1966 ICESCR, and misreading of ILO Convention No. 111 and Recommendations 1980 No. 162 and 1982 No. 166. He is worried about the tendency to constitutionalise the civil law (1994 p. 82). But this criticism seems to me to miss the point, which is, that a court was for the first time seeking to enforce international human rights standards.

Another case referred to critically by Rudden is the ruling of 23 June 1992[14] on *Time Limits for Challenging Unfair Dismissal*, where a number of workers filed petitions complaining of the unconstitutionality of amended legislation providing for two year time limits for challenge. The Court ruled in their favour, finding that the amendments infringed five norms of international law and 14 articles of the Constitution.

The most controversial case heard by the Court was the *Case of the Communist Party*. It also devoured an inordinate amount of the Court's time: proceedings began on 6 July 1992 and the decision was handed down on 30 November 1992. Yuri Feofanov considers (Feofanov, 1993 p. 623) that in refusing to declare the criminal nature of the Party the Court failed the hopes of the democratic party. 'But by that fact it affirmed that the establishment of a legal order in Russia was becoming a reality.'

The Court was a victim of the same events which ushered in the new Constitution. On 9 September 1993 Judge Zorkin was ordered to vacate his state dacha by 13 September. On 21 September 1993, Yeltsin issued his Decree No. 1400 *On Progressive Constitutional Reform in the Russian Federation*, suspending the work of Parliament, providing that the 1978 Constitution should remain in force so far as it did not contradict the present Decree, and ordering the holding of elections for the State Duma of the Federal Assembly on 11–12 December 1993. He also 'recommended' that the Constitutional Court should not sit until after the forthcoming elections. The Court sat all night, and, in a decision which has called forth from certain judges allegations that Judge Zorkin falsified the result, condemned the Decree, and paved the way for impeachment by Parliament. Parliament responded immediately with a Resolution providing that the President's powers should be exercised by the Vice-President, Rutskoi. In a persuasive article,[15] Jonathan Steele argues that Yeltsin's problem was how to close the Parliament, albeit illegally, and to convince key players in the Russian political game to approve of what he had done. The solution was to spring a deadly trap for Rutskoi and his followers, on 3 and 4 October 1993, in which many innocent civilians were killed (for a further

---

[14] *Vedemosti Verkhovnogo Sovyeta RSFSR* No. 30 Art. 1809 (1992).
[15] '*The Guardian Weekend*' 13 November 1993.

account, see Semler, 1994; also Steele's own extended analysis in Steele, 1994). On 6 October 1993, Judge Zorkin was forced to resign as chairman of the Constitutional Court; the same day, in a television address, Yeltsin told the nation that he considered the Constitutional Court to a large extent to blame for the events. Shortly afterwards, he suspended the activity of the Court, pending new elections, although, in a speech on 2 November to the Council of Ministers, he referred to a 'de facto absence of constitutional control'.

I have already pointed out that a Constitutional Court is a centrepiece of the new constitutional order, essential for the vindication of human rights. It is of the greatest importance, in my view, that continuity has been maintained, and that the President has respected the principle that the judges have been elected for life. By August 1994 the new *Law of the Constitutional Court* had passed its third reading in the State Duma; there should be no barriers to signature by the President, and election of the remaining six judges.

It may therefore be said that October 1993 marked the end of an era. Van den Berg, attempting an evaluation in 1992, identified a number of remnants of the past. First, he pointed out the conflict between the Soviet model of merger of legislature and executive, and the doctrine of the separation of powers. Second, there was the problem of constitutional review of Presidential edicts. Third, the independence of the courts had been threatened not only by the necessity to decide cases like that of the CPSU, and the constitutionality of the referendum on the sovereignty of Tatarstan, but also by the formidable political role played by Judge Zorkin.

Have these problems been in any way resolved? It is noteworthy that the new Constitution, in Article 3, preserves the notion of peoples' power, expressed through 'the referendum and free elections' (note the order of these terms). But the State Duma has shown itself capable of providing an effective opposition, and of working constructively with the President. Presidential Decrees are more controversial. While the Constitutional Court, in one of their first decisions, quashed Yeltsin's decree merging the interior ministry and KGB,[16] and Yeltsin accepted the decision, Article 90 of the new Constitution empowers the President to issue decrees and directives, implementation of which is mandatory throughout Russia, save that they must not contravene the Russian Constitution and federal laws. Finally, the Court's survival, playing a key role in protecting a very wide range of human rights, is one of the more reliable guarantors of a state based on those rights.

---

[16] *Vedomosti Verkhovnogo Sovyeta RSFSR* No. 6 Art. 247 (1992).

VIII HUMAN RIGHTS AND PROBLEMS OF LEGITIMACY

This is the point at which I consider whether it is now possible to attempt a more adequate analysis of the role of rights in the new Russia. Habermas, who has published several short articles on similar themes in recent months, interprets human rights as the government of laws and not men – that is, human rights are homologous with the classic definition of the rule of law (see Habermas 1994, 1994a). By human rights he means the 'negative', civil and political rights. Human rights, thus defined, and popular sovereignty, in the sense that the members of a democratic community govern themselves collectively, are, he argues, the modern pillars of legal legitimacy and political power. He contrasts liberal or 'Lockean' political traditions which conceive human rights as the embodiment of moral autonomy, prior to popular sovereignty, with 'republican' (more recently, communitarian) traditions which conceive popular sovereignty as the expression of ethical self-realisation of a people, with priority over human rights. He suggests that in order to transcend this dichotomy, private and public autonomy should be given original and equal weight, so that:

> the substance of human rights resides in the formal conditions for the legal institutionalisation of those discursive processes of opinion – and will – formation through which the sovereignty of the people can be exercised.

It may be that such an integrative approach, albeit that it is limited by its exclusive focus on discursive processes (as if the content of the life-world is exhaustively described in terms of discourse), and, consequently, on civil and political rights (those rights which guarantee the discursive realm), can nevertheless provide a basis both for beginning to explain the specificity of the former Russian focus on economic and social rights, in the context of what was in essence a 'republican' social project, and to suggest the legitimation processes at work in the new order. What is at stake is whether 'formal conditions' can or should include the social and economic rights, as part-guarantees of legal effectiveness.

Habermas' analysis can therefore, I suggest, be enriched in the following way. The Soviet hostility to human rights, or at least of the first generation civil and political rights, owed much to Marx's critique in *On the Jewish Question*. For Marx, none of the so-called rights of man (as set out in the French Declaration) go beyond egoistic man, as an individual withdrawn into himself, into the confines of his private interests and private caprice. Marx wanted, on the contrary, to conceive human beings as species-beings, constituting and constituted by society. Now the development of human rights discourse since World War II can be read as an enrichment and extension of rights which, in part at least, respond to the Marxian and socialist critique. As Ted Benton (1993 p. 118) points out, the 1948 UDHR:

> affirmed more than the traditional liberal agenda inherited from the early modern period. Not only were civil liberties and the traditional 'rights of man' reaffirmed, but universal rights to full democratic participation in the political sphere were consolidated, and a range of new rights to economic and social security were added, not merely as conditions for the 'positive' exercise of legal and political rights, but as morally valid claims in their own right.

This represents a shift to a more 'positive', concrete specification of rights, so that the impressive range of human rights instruments worked out since 1948, and now incorporated into the new Russian Constitution as, quite obviously, its legitimating agent, do acknowledge bodily well-being, social belonging and cultural identity as indispensable to the interests of individuals (for Habermas' thoughts on the legitimation process, and for fruitful applications of his analysis to the Russian predicament, see Habermas 1990 and 1992a, and Williams and Reuten 1993).

IX CONCLUSION

Constitutional provision, and even the existence of an active and fearless Court are in themselves inadequate guarantors of human rights. Fortunately, there are a number of significant human rights actors both in and outside government in today's Russia. The Commissioner (Ombudsman) for Human Rights appointed by the State Duma pursuant to Article 103(1)(e) of the new Constitution is Sergei Kovalyov, who is a respected campaigner for human rights – he chaired the Human Rights Commission of the former Supreme Soviet, and acted as a staunch critic both of the President, and of Khasbulatov and Rutskoi. On 21 July 1994 the State Duma approved a draft law giving him 'unlimited powers' – access to state and commercial secrets, the ability to order checks on any state organisations or establishments, and power to take them to court if necessary.

He has not been silent. On 30 July 1994 he identified, with considerable publicity, the areas in which human rights had been violated most seriously during the past year: first, the rights of refugees and forced migrants (of whom there are now huge numbers, many from the Caucasus and central Asia); second, human rights in prisons, which still retain the Soviet model;

third, freedom of movement and the choice of a place of residence,[17] and fourth, human rights during military service, where there are many suicides, and at work. He described President Yeltsin's recent decree on fighting organised crime as a serious violation of human rights.

Furthermore, his Commission has published a Report on the 'October Events' between 3 and 18 October 1993, detailing 'mass infringements of the rights and freedoms of individuals in the city of Moscow', including unwarranted use of firearms, causing deaths and injuries, the holding of 6,000 detainees in solitary confinement, beatings, and more.[18]

In addition, there are now several human rights Non-Governmental Organisations in Russia. Kovalyov is a board member of the Moscow Research Centre for Human Rights, which is an umbrella organisation, part-funded by the EU, providing a roof for a number of activist groups – Jewish rights, mothers of servicemen, freedom of expression, and so on. His fellow board members include Yelena Bonner, Andrei Sakharov's widow (who is establishing a Sakharov Foundation in his memory), and Judge Ernest Ametistov of the Constitutional Court. The Centre is headed by Alexei Smirnov, a dissident who spent a long period in prison under the former regime. Other organisations include Helsinki Watch (Alexander Petrov), which produces excellent research reports; Oleg Orlov's 'Memorial' human rights centre; and Yuri Shmidt's Russian Bar Association for Human Rights. Amnesty International has assisted in the setting up of an Amnesty group. The only unsavoury side of this healthy proliferation is the hot competition for grant-aid from the west.

But, in my view, it remains the case that the refashioned Constitutional Court will be of paramount importance in vindicating human rights. It is conceivable that the Court, through its interpretation and enrichment of the rights provisions in the new Constitution, will make a real contribution to answering the vexed question whether economic and social rights may or should be justiciable, and effective.

---

[17] See the *Helsinki Watch Report* 'Russian Residence and Travel Restrictions' (August 1992).

[18] Extracts were published in '*Nezavisimaya Gazeta*' (*Independent Newspaper*) on 23 July 1994.

5. The Politics of Human Rights in Post-Communist Poland

Jacek Kurczewski

Human rights were the main mechanism that transferred the former opponents of Communist rule in Poland into leading positions within the first post-Communist administration. As it is often assumed that the post-Communist countries entered the era of human rights out of nothing. I will allow myself a few lines to put the case in its historical context. The old Polish political culture (cf. Ogonowski 1993 pp. 20–35), being based upon the late medieval charters of fundamental rights and freedoms, was enjoyed above all by approaching 10 percent of the population who constituted the gentry. It was finally demolished under the internationally accepted alibi of the partitioning powers that Polish 'golden freedom' equals anarchy and ungovernability and was supplanted with tough absolutist measures. Towards the end of the nineteenth century Polish political interests were represented in the parliamentary life of Prussia and Austria, while the idea of Polish independence was considered unrealistic. In the Russian zone, politics was dominated by the absolutist concept of sacred Tsarist rule, while liberalism was a weak faction amongst the intellectuals and parliamentary life only started as late as the first decade of the twentieth century (Walicki 1987). Polish nationalists in this area were fighting not only against alien rule but also against an absolutist regime and in this they cooperated with Russian revolutionaries. After 1917 cooperation changed into open conflict, culminating in the Polish–Bolshevik war of 1919/1920 that ended with the recognition of the independent Polish state by Bolshevik Russia. We have gone so far back in history in order to trace the beginning of the opposition between the national and the socialist set of values (Kurczewska 1989). Polish socialists were patriotic and became an important political force during the Second Republic in 1918–1939. There was, indeed, also a different faction that supported the national values and opposed themselves to the socialists, but the difference was more in relation to another set of values as the opposition between the nationalists and the socialists in Poland was mainly related to the opposition of the former to the liberal concepts supported by the Polish Socialist Party. All the main political parties in Poland were opposed to the revolutionary message of Communism. In the face of an attempt to revolutionise the masses against democracy and independence, Polish Socialists promoted in 1918 the State that since the beginning granted suffrage to women and limited the length of the working day, an interest in socioeconomic rights that was institutionalised in its first Constitution of March 1921. The years that followed were filled with growing controversies and conflicts over social and economic expectations, the scope of representative democracy that was allowed and the collective rights of various minorities inhabiting the recovered Polish state. Pilsudski's coup d'état of 1926 ushered in moderate policies but it nevertheless undermined the democracy and led to the 1935 Constitution which attempted to secure the dominance of the executive branch and went some way in the direction of establishing a unitary state.

The 1935 Polish State did not yet have at its disposal a totalitarian ideology and movement, despite attempts by some of the followers of Pilsudski. It was closer to a Bureaucratic-Authoritarian State of the Latin American type than to the Party-State of the Fascist not to speak of the Communist type. It was busy with developing industrialisation, a goal that was taken over by the totalitarian system in the second half of the Century and achieved, but at the price of the displacement of the economic market and of the mechanisms of political democracy. Elsewhere I have sketched the process of the resurrection of rights in a social landscape that doctrinally seemed alien in relation to the concept (Kurczewski 1993). In the 1970s, the Helsinki agreements provided the anti-Communist opposition with the third basket of human rights as the normative point of reference surpassing the arbitrary power of the Party-State. 'Solidarity' itself was both in substance and in form the effect of the human rights movement. Freedom of association in those days needed to be reinforced by the specific ILO Convention on freedom of trade unions that didn't need the approval of the State in order to function as internationally recognised subjects. This was the legal foundation of the new democratic order recreated first, within the mass movement of 'Solidarity' in 1980–1981, and then, after the 1989 Round Table agreements, within the political realm of the state that soon changed into the Third Republic. As was predicted, this has opened up the new political process in which rights and freedoms have not lost their importance but instead have become the focus of the political process in which the emerging Polish democracy is shaped. The following is just one of several occasions on which this process has presented itself with almost purposeful clarity.

I THE CONSTITUTIONAL TRIANGLE

On 21 January 1993, the Polish Seym met to discuss the drafts of two Constitutional laws: the Charter of Rights and Freedoms proposed by the President of the Republic and the Social and Economic Charter proposed by the post-communist Alliance of the Democratic Left (SLD).[1] President Walesa in his introduction stressed that the constitutional laws passed until this point in the transformation process had dealt only with the relations between the various branches of government and hadn't touched upon relations between the government and citizens, and that the Charter of Rights and Freedoms is meant to fill exactly this gap in the new constitutional law by 'setting up the frontiers that no government may trespass'. The President took a clear and direct position in the debate on the constitutional safeguards applicable to social and economic rights when he said:

> The proposed Constitutional law omits controversial issues. It legislates only those rights that are considered as inalienable and inviolable in the civilised world. The Charter is not a programmatory or ideological declaration. It secures only what the state can fulfil, that is civic rights and freedoms, political rights and also basic social rights. The Republic has no means to satisfy all the needs of various social groups. The Charter of Rights and Freedoms cannot entail promises without support, it cannot be a set of good wishes. Its great merit is that it guarantees the necessary minimum of social rights and doesn't remove the already acquired rights.

Post-Communist MP Danuta Waniek, when introducing on behalf of the SLD the draft of the Socio-Economic Charter, indirectly disputed the President's view by saying that 'in the last years in Poland a majority of [social and economic] rights have been limited or even abolished either in the parliamentary way or through the method of *le fait accompli*'. Describing the SLD's draft as parallel to the President's draft Charter of Rights and Freedoms, Ms. Waniek observed that they crosscut each other only partially and expressed the hope that in future both may be harmonized. Ms. Waniek, in a lengthy introduction, reviewed in detail the draft Social and Economic Charter of which she observed generally that 'it goes beyond the traditional forumla of a catalogue of civic rights as the law incorporates the decisions concerning the systemic mechanisms safeguarding the widely understood implementation of these rights, starting with pointing to their economic foundations through outlining the mechanism for releasing the social conflicts and ending with judicial ways

---

1   The following description and citations are based upon the Transcripts of the 35th Session of the Seym of the Polish Republic on the 21st, 22nd and 23rd January and on 3rd and 4th February 1993, Warsaw 1993 (translation mine – JK).

of achieving one's due, one's rights'. As basic values 'labour, property and social partnership' were mentioned.

In this way a debate was opened that involved representatives of all political groups in the then Polish parliament. MP Wlodzimierz Cimoszewicz (SLD) started by expressing approval for the Presidential draft and support for the doctrine of human rights but criticised the Charter of Rights and Freedoms for its 'marginal treatment and far-reaching narrowing of the scope of social, economic and cultural rights', formulating them, in some instances, more narrowly than the Constitution of 1921. According to the Left, public authorities are co-responsible for the living conditions of citizens. Cimoszewicz also stressed that in times of crisis the right to unemployment benefit is more important for many than the right to exercise a vote in elections. Acknowledging in advance possible criticism of the SLO Charter because of its programmatic character, Mr. Cimoszewicz said vaguely that the authors 'see the possibility of searching for more specific formulations'. Many MPs from parties of the Centre and the Right criticised the SLD draft as unrealistic even if touching on the real issues. Donald Tusk (KLD: Liberal-Democratic Congress), for instance, while supporting without reservation the Presidential draft remarked that the 'over-detailed provisions of the Social and Economic Charter mainly grow out of, as one may suppose, the tradition of the over-protective state that in return for a protection of unreliable worth stripped its citizens of their freedom. Today', he continued, 'instead of promises the Charter of Rights and Freedoms offers citizens what may be really safeguarded, that is freedom and the right to the individual pursuit of happiness. Approval of the Social and Economic Charter may in effect lead only to prolonged tension between the activated expectations of the people, on the one hand, and the opportunities that the public administration has, on the other. This would ruin the effects of the Charter of Rights and Freedoms, that is the real identification of citizens with the state, and inevitably feelings of hostile estrangement from the democratically established and functioning power would emerge.' This was the reason why liberals as well as Democratic Union, 'Solidarity', People's Agreement (pro-Solidarity agrarians) and the Realpolitik Union were for the Presidential draft and against the Social and Economic Charter. Agrarians from PSL, nationalists from the Confederacy of Independent Poland, MPs representing the German minority and the new Left Labour Union supported both drafts, criticising various aspects of each. But there was also a third option presented to the House and which was perhaps most vividly expressed by MP Marian Pilka from the fundamentalist Christian-National Union

(ZChN) who pointed out that the Charter of Rights and Freedoms is based upon:

a false philosophy of man, a philosophy according to which the imagination puts forth abstract and, in reality, non-existing individuals opposed to all collectivities in which they are living, that is family, nation, state, as if the social environment of man were a threat to him and not the natural outcome of his social nature. ... The temptation to 'liberate' the individual from the dominance of family, society, culture, custom, nation and state, also from the repressive aspects of these institutions has many times demonstrated itself in history and has bore such fruits, among others, as the events of the French or Bolshevik revolutions. ... The authors of the Presidential draft forget that man is spoiled by original sin, that his development is possible only within society, that the State must care for the healthy functioning of society exactly for the sake of the good of man who is born and brought up in the family, in local and professional environments; that the identity of man is shaped by religion and national culture ... The individual apart from rights also has duties, not only towards himself but also towards collectivities in which he lives. Finally, it should be remembered that due to the spoiling of human nature by Original Sin there must be law and a penal system keeping in check asocial individuals. ... The basic right of a citizen is the right to have a state that is able to safeguard both its own security as well as the security of its citizens. A strong state safeguards also the development of the nation, family, order and public morality. The idea outlined in the Charter aims at the total disorganisation of the state disabling its possibilities of efficient functioning ... and ... is an expression of the fanatical and militant liberalism aiming at the imposition of this extreme ideology in public life.

This view was supplemented by more specific arguments in some other interventions. MP Józef Hermanowicz (Christian Democracy) stressed the need for a developed constitutional description of the rights of the family including the right to marry or to stay single, the protection of maternity, of giving birth to offspring, of the raising of children, of economic security (employment), of social security in case of various social handicaps, of housing conditions adequate to the needs of family life and of the inviolability of the home: 'Such an understanding of the rights of the individual, conceived above all as as a social being and not as an individual, presumes constitutional guarantees by the state of specially weak families, that is of families with many children, of single parent families, of families handicapped by invalidity or by some pathology and of migrant families'. Similar views were expressed by the Centre Alliance and by the Polish Convention.

It is remarkable that in this debate the basic triangle was formulated so clearly. Triadic elements reappear even in the internal structure of each of the three conflicting views. The Presidential draft lists as three basic values *Human Dignity, Freedom* and *Equality Before The Law*. In the draft Social and Economic Charter, *Labour, Property* and *Social Partnership* are listed. Finally, the fundamentalist, anti-liberal critique itself refers to yet another triad of *Family*, *Nation* and *State* as organic collectivities in which the social proclivity of human nature may be fulfilled.

Figure 5.1 Triangle of Constitutional Values

human dignity
freedom
equality before the law

labour	family
property	nation
social partnership	state

Individual votes on the fate of both drafts were unfortunately unrecorded. The voting was on whether to refer the draft to the House's Extraordinary Commission, that would work on it, or to reject it already at this stage. The Presidential draft Charter of Rights and Freedoms was sent further on with 72 MPs voting against it, 251 voting for and 34 MPs abstaining. The Post-Communist draft Social and Economic Charter was rejected by 190 MPs, with 139 MPs in favour and 27 MPs abstaining. Behind these figures, there were fundamentalist Right parties voting against both drafts, various 'Left' (including strongly anti-communist populist Right) parties voting for both drafts and the liberal Centre supporting President Lech Walesa's draft Charter of Rights and Freedoms only. To the latter information one may add that the Center was in the main composed of the Democratic Union party whose identity was formed in the electoral struggle of ex-Prime Minister Tadeusz Mazowiecki against Lech Walesa for the Polish presidency in 1991. This means that one would not predict the voting pattern on the basis of the explicit frontline political allegiances and conflicts. The voting on that day reflected something more fundamental in Polish democratic politics, making the everyday political identities just mere epiphenomena at the surface level.

In other terms there are two ways to describe the pattern of voting. On the one hand, Labour, Property and Social Partnership won the allegiance of 139 deputies, Family, Nation and State of 72 deputies and Human Dignity, Freedom and Equality Before the Law of 251 deputies altogether, but on the other hand, the victory of the liberal-individualistic draft was possible due to the support of the 'Left' and the failure of the socialist-collectivistic draft to the lack of support on the part of the ideologically and politically coherent Centre totalling $251 - 139 = 112$ deputies. This voting, in my judgement, reflects in the purest way the structure of the first democratically elected Polish Parliament. One should note that the widely understood Left was already strongest due to the fact that those who used to call themselves Right were internally divided into two mutually exclusive ideological camps of the collectivist Right and of the individualist liberal Centre.

II UNEXPECTED REASONS FOR THE INCOMPLETE DE-COMMUNISATION

To understand the events described above we need to look into the wider context of the political life of post-1989 Poland. Three major areas of debate, conflict and controversies have been, in my opinion, the basic *foci* around which the political process has concentrated in these years: de-communisation, re-christianisation and economic liberalisation. None of these processes has been concluded. In fact, what we can observe is a triad of antithetical conflicts which, however, due to their mutual interconnection, must be interpreted not as three separate issues but as a triangular structure which was already in evidence in constitutional debates of the type aforementioned.

As to de-communisation it must be recalled that, though for a while the voice of the Communists was unheard, it was obvious that socially this group included not just a small group of the former ruling elite but also the vast sector of those who were linked directly with the past political system. The Party bureaucracy was most evidently in this position but one should remember also the hundreds of thousands of other Party members plus their families whose entire careers had been spent on the side of the Party. Even in the domain of the trade unions, Solidarnosc never became the sole actor and, after the peak of its popularity in 1981, Communist trade unionism was restructured by the martial law authorities and emerged from those days with quite a stable clientele as, contrary to what the anti-communist opposition had expected, masses of workers surrendered to the mixture of blackmail and persuasion and joined the officially approved trade unions once 'Solidarity' was abolished. In fact, it seemed for a long time that the average employee found himself in a quite satisfactory position as the addressee of offers directed to him by two competing unions and by their professional militants and leaders. Communists politicians of the former ruling Party and their followers have not disappeared from Polish politics at all. The Party officially supported the deal struck with the democratic opposition which permitted it, together with its allies, to retain 65 per cent of the seats in the Seym, the lower house of the Polish Parliament, during an interim period scheduled to last until general elections planned for 1993. Thus, the Party's disappearance was peaceful as it was protected by the transitory semi-democratic arrangements it helped to generate. Under this safety net, new parties emerged out of the former ones of which the Social Democratic Party (SLD) won the hearts of most of the still politically active members of the former Polish United Workers' Party. In the elections brought forward to 1991, this Party was confronted not by the unified anti-Communist front but by several mutually competing parties that developed out of the previously almost unstructured opposition and, due to this, the SLD won the second place in the Lower House and thereby legitimised itself as an important actor in Polish democratic politics with all the normal rights and duties. In contrast to 1989, the 1991 elections were not a plebiscite for or against Communism but represented a full-fledged electoral battle in which dozens of the freshly created political units took part. This was repeated in 1993 when post-Communists won 20 percent of the active electorate, a result that, with the help of new electoral laws aiming at the consolidation of Parliament, was enough to give it first place in the new Seym and to secure it 171 out of 460 seats, that is 37.1 percent. This short electoral history shows that though the elimination of Communist rule is the necessary prerequisite of democracy, once this is achieved the other focal points of the clash of interests, beliefs and sentiments immediately come to the forefront of post-Communist politics.

Let us recall here how widespread Party membership formerly was in society. Normally, it was about ten percent of the adult population, thus if one adds whole households the recent election results would not surprise us numerically. The fact is, however, that there are many more persons who had at one or another moment in their history been members of the Party, especially amongst those who have held career positions at work, whether it was in a university, in a state agency or in a state-owned company. Among opposition politicians of the middle generations many were once themselves members of the Party. The shock following the disclosures of the crimes of Stalinism, in 1956, resulted in resignations from the Party by many previously zealous activists. Ranks were soon filled again by the new generation recruited during the stagnant economic conditions that prevailed under Gomulka, and then under Gierek's developing socialist welfare state. In contrast to other socialist states, the history of Communist Poland was that of recurrent political crises in which the ruling Party was struggling against rebellious sectors of the population. Each of these political crises, whether in 1956, 1957, 1966, 1968, 1970, 1976, 1980 or in 1981, was marked by the departure from the Party of some intellectuals and members of the intelligentsia. Finally, it looked as though a line would be drawn at

13 December 1981, and that only those who were ousted from the Party after the introduction of martial law or who left themselves would be acceptable in the eyes of the democratic opposition; but soon politicians who had favoured the liberalisation of the martial law regime, like one of the former secretaries of the Central Committee of the Party, were allowed to enter the ranks of the anti-Communist democratic parties.

All this shows the complexity of the process of de-communisation in a country like Poland where the process of transformation was endogenous, and the disorganising effects of de-communisation when introduced as a political program by some political forces. First, given the fact that the Communists ruled Poland for forty-five years (not to mention the Soviet occupation of the Eastern territories in 1939–1941) and that since 1956 there were successive waves of defectors, it would be extremely difficult to put up a clear dividing line between Communists and non-Communists. It was a common joke among non-Party members that the new membership should be carefully checked before being allowed into their ranks. Some of the ex-Communists, after leaving the Party, were at least as instrumental in ending Party rule as the representatives of the anti-Communist opposition who survived Stalinism. It is no surprise then that the opposition in 1989 and afterwards was not uniform on the issue of de-communisation that became one of the decisive factors used in the formation of the public identities of new political actors. Unable to eliminate Communists from public life, more radical politicians of the political Right, who entered parliament after the first free elections in 1991, were able only to pass the 'lustration' resolution addressed to past collaborators with the political police, that is against those who mostly have not themselves been in the Party. With records damaged, information dubious and results which put in doubt the reputation of some of the leaders of the anti-Communist opposition, the outcome of this resolution was a further division in the ranks of the non-Communist political class and the fall of the government who supported the measure (Kurczewski 1993a).

Second, as it was from the very beginning assumed that the transition would be made in accordance with due process of law, legal continuity being left intact, and thus only transgressions of the law *as it was prior to 1989* giving rise to possible criminal sanctions (plus recognition of the amnesties that marked the transition period and the lapse of time for certain crimes), it was practically impossible to deal with cases and persons who committed deeds contrary to the *now prevailing* legal and political standards. Let it suffice to say, that it is impossible to judge Party officials who authorised various political measures as these were neither constitutional organs of State power nor the sources of law. Parliamentary investigation of the circumstances surrounding the introduction of martial law continues in the present Parliament, led now by Prof. J.J. Wiatr who advised the Party in 1981 and presciently predicted Martial Law in his publication in the Fall of that year. It has meant also that judges have been left in office without the clearance measures that were applied to the reorganised public prosecutor and state security services.

It is obvious and should perhaps be said in the first place, that sharp de-communisation would have been possible in 1989 when the anti-communist opposition was at its peak and when the remembrance of the past oppression and misery was at its height. But in order for that to have happened something totally contrary to what occurred in reality should have happened as well. The timing of the liberalisation was decided by the Communists who retained the initiative. The whole process took the shape of a negotiated evolution with formal compromise being reached at Round Table talks, with the Catholic Church as the moral supervisor. There was no V-Day on which masses destroyed the Bastille. Instead, quite ominously, the headquarters of the Polish Communists were handed over to the University and rented to the Warsaw Stock Exchange, while the First Secretary became the first President. This evolutionary and negotiated process prevented a black-or-white solution. In Poland there was enough political force behind the reformist wing of the Communist Party to control the whole process with the permanent blackmail of possible Soviet military intervention.

Last, but by no means least, one may doubt whether there was much public support for de-communisation if it meant the personal cleansing of the administration and of the political world of former Communists. In my 1988 nation-wide representative survey conducted by OBOP 20 percent (!) approved the Communist ban on the functioning of 'Solidarity' while 62 percent were openly against it; in a 1990 survey only 26 percent supported the idea of banning the activities of political parties continuing the Communist tradition and 55 percent were against it.[2] Certainly, the mood of the nation was for peaceful democratisation and not for sharp de-communisation. Moreover, in the attitudes of Polish public opinion we discover the same approval for political rights and freedoms extended equally to both anticommunist 'Solidarity' and to Communist organisations. One may say that this is the benefit Polish communists obtained from their

2 Here, and throughout the paper I refer to my three surveys of political and moral opinions of Polish society made for me by the OBOP polling centre on a nation-wide representative Sample of $n = 926$ in 1988, $n = 898$ in 1990, and $n = 1319$, as well as to the 1993 survey made by the Department of the Sociology of Custom and Law, IASS, University of Warsaw, also through OBOP ($n = 1111$).

politics of complex maneuvering between, on the one hand, the official demands of doctrine and, on the other, the resistance of the population; one may say as well, though, that both maneuvering and resistance resulted from the existing ethos of individual rights and freedoms. So, whatever the arguments on the viability of de-communisation, how may one imagine the implementation of this ethos in the practice of the new democracy without contravening its basic tenets?

III LIBERAL CATHOLICISM VERSUS INSTITUTIONALISED FUNDAMENTALISM

The same remoteness from public opinion was the reason for the failure of radical policies in two other disputed areas of post-Communist politics: welfare state versus the market economy and Christian (i.e. in Poland Catholic) values versus the lay state separated from the Church and religion.

To discuss religion in the context of Polish post-1989 politics one needs to remember that the Catholic Church was the only institution that emerged from the communist period both morally and organisationally strengthened. The hierarchy supported 'Solidarity' in general, whatever its concern at the influence of the lay and democratic wing of the democratic opposition could have been, and the Church defended all martial law prisoners and victims impartially, independently of their religious beliefs or even the lack of them. In 1989, the 'Solidarity' structures, which had been illegal until then, were basically too weak to act on their own in the countryside – in contrast to the industrial centres – so when the elections came the Church, who supported the opposition throughout the 1980s, was often the only institution to be asked to help select the candidates to the new political class from those who, in defiance of the old system, used to gather around the Church to organise independent social aid, charity and cultural work. Some of them were politically active people subscribing to various shades of non-Communist opinion. Some were simply lay Church activists, likewise priests and bishops some of whom were involved in political or trade-union activities, whilst others kept close to the Church and to religion. New political parties needed to rely on the Church at the local level in developing their influence over the electorate through the authority of the priests, the only official figures who were publicly acknowledged as independent from the communist 'Party-State', and through the parish-related network. This quickly led to competition over whom preferences should be given to, and as to who is more Catholic. In this way some men of the Church became more directly involved in politics and some parties developed a brand of radical political Catholicism, demanding an end to the division of State and religion which they characterised as a legacy of the officially atheist and anti-religious Communist rule. Once such a political orientation develops it is always difficult for the Church and clergy to reject an offer to have institutionalised influence over the State, though in fact it might not have been the Church but this or another political party who aspired to the position of being the guardian of the spiritual propriety of the State.

How the Church and politics intermingle was demonstrated in the abortion issue which has plagued Polish politics since 1957 when, during the post-Stalinist liberalisation, the law allowing for free abortion, including abortion on the grounds of the economic circumstances of a woman, was passed. Since then the freedom of abortion was subject to permanent criticism by the Catholic Church until, in 1992, a parliamentary majority finally passed the law that limits abortion to cases where the life of a pregnant woman is threatened, or where a continuation of the pregnancy poses her severe health hazards. The law in fact was a compromise that satisfied neither the Church nor the anti-abortion politicians. Here it is important to notice that the issue served to mobilise on both sides political actors on a matter that for most parties had not been part of their platform (cf. Fuszara 1993 pp. 221–52). Thus, for instance, the centre Democratic Union has included both MP Hanna Suchocka, who signed the anti-abortion draft law, and MP Barbara Labuda who organised the nationwide movement to reject this very draft law. The political class as a whole was subject to the pressure of Church and of Church-related lay organisations fighting against abortion. For each political party it was necessary to find a way out of the dilemma of appeasing both the Church and the electorate who, as will be shown, by no means accepted the ethical doctrines of the Catholic Church. Most parties resolved this matter simply by not taking a party stand on the issue and by relaxing its parliamentary discipline which, on the other hand, left individual MPs without a much needed excuse to resist the demands of the Church. But at least one of the significant parties at the time, the National Christian Union (ZChN), took advantage of the situation, being a party in favour of the ban on abortion. It therefore gained strength from all those individual votes that together formed a majority in favour of the new restrictive legislation.

The debate on abortion that developed already in the final Communist parliaments and that continues until today with the 1993 elected Seym removing some of the restrictions (an initiative that certainly promises to lead to a counterattack by the Catholic fundamentalists in the future) has been, along with debates on lustration and on de-communisation, one of the liveliest controversies in the public life of the New Republic. Both sides engaged in sometimes abusive arguments, demonstrations and petitions involving tens of thousands of people, debates in the mass media were supplemented by arguments expressed from the pulpit. The unquestionable authority of Pope John Paul the Second was introduced to counter the otherwise undoubted silent resistance of the majority of Polish public opinion which was in general favourable to freedom of abortion. The debate helped Polish feminists to organise but also assisted the formulation of the whole doctrine of limits that natural law places on legislation. Human rights and freedoms were introduced in the debate as a weapon used by both sides, one referring to women's freedom to choose whether to give birth to a child or not, the other to the human right to life from the very moment of conception.[3]

Yet another debated issue was the teaching of religion in public schools which was reintroduced after 1989. The debate, which continues, is complex and is fragmented in terms of the various legal and administrative aspects of the issue. The problems were how to give effect to freedom of conscience, whether the marks for religion should be recorded on the pupil's school certificate, whether the teaching of religion by the clergy should be financed from the state's budget, and similar questions. The debate around these issues centred on the question of whether the relevant solutions were constitutional and, above all, how these solutions related to the basic human right of freedom of conscience.

On a smaller scale, this conflict was repeated over the 1992 law on television and broadcasting that helped to create a public media, in coexistence with the licensed private media, out of the previously State-run television and radio. To this long awaited law, however, militant Catholics under the guidance of the ZChN Party, inserted a clause vaguely stating the need for both public and private media to respect Christian values under sanction of losing their license. One needs to remark that the law established a national board for the media to implement these and other controls which the law provides.

After all these legislative victories it would not have been surprising if the National Christian Union, and other parties which make Catholicism their political platform, had won the 1993 elections. However, this was not the case, and if the Church was not compromised by all of this it was only because the Church had been wise enough not to get involved in the

---

3 More generally, on family legislation and on Catholic politics in contemporary Poland, see Kurczewski 1994 pp. 25–52.

electoral campaign on behalf of its zealous self-proclaimed partisans. After all, the Church already felt that the victory in the abortion controversy had been achieved against the will of a majority of the public at large which was also, and most likely because of this fact, overwhelmingly against the direct involvement of the Church in public matters.

Here again the results of the nation-wide representative surveys I have conducted through OBOP may substantiate the claim and allow us to understand the normative currents in Polish culture and society, which were running somewhat contrary to what was the, at least temporarily, prevailing direction within the political class or at least its new branch. First, results of the survey evidence the growing secularisation of sexual ethics exactly at the moment when the Church and its representatives were given the fullest chance to influence national legislation. Divorce by mutual consent of a couple with children was held to be sinful in 1988 by 76 percent, but a majority, 49 percent as against 39 percent, was willing to grant the couple the right to divorce in such a situation. In 1990, the percentage of those finding such a divorce sinful, from the religious point of view, went down to 60 percent, and in 1992 it went down further to 50 percent, while the number of those who accepted the right to divorce under these circumstances first fell insignificantly to 47 percent and in 1992 went up to 50 percent. Sexual cohabitation outside marriage was considered sinful by 81 percent in 1988, by 69 percent in 1990 and by 61 percent in 1992, while approval of the right of couples to cohabit outside marriage, after gaining 44 and 40 percent in 1988 and 1990 respectively, went up to 55 percent in 1992. Teaching about contraception in schools was already regarded as proper by a majority, 70 percent, in 1988, but the approval, despite – or because of – the Church's partly successful attempts to limit sexual education, went up in 1990 to 76 percent and in 1992 to 79 percent, while the share of those considering such education sinful went down from 35 to 22 to 10 percent in those years. In 1990, 13 percent of the nation-wide sample were of the opinion that abortion should be totally banned while 23 percent accorded women full freedom of choice, the others opting for more or less restricted sets of circumstances in which abortion was permissible, such as where the material conditions of life were unsatisfactory or where the life of the pregnant woman was endangered. In 1992, just before the restrictive legislation on abortion was adopted, a total ban was supported by 9 percent, while unlimited freedom of choice was favoured by 22 percent of Polish public opinion. When asked in a more general way about the public influence of the Catholic Church in Poland, only 9 percent in 1990 and 8 percent in 1992 supported the view that, as a majority of Poles are Catholics, Catholicism should be established as the State religion and that the Church should have guaranteed influence upon decisions regarding public matters. A majority – 61 percent in 1990 and 68 percent in 1992 – supported the statement that 'the state should be fully separated from religious matters, that it should remain the private affair of the citizens'. It is interesting to note that the proportion of those who define themselves as affilitated with the Church and of those who believe in some basic religious tenets, such as God, the Last Judgement or sin, has remained practically unchanged during the four years covered by our surveys. As we have pointed out in another publication (Kurczewski 1990 pp. 269–99), the process of the liberalisation of the *anima* leads to the privatisation of the body and the widening of freedoms in the polity and in the economy inevitably leads to the specific process of developing a more Protestant style of ethics of the individual conscience within the general structures of Catholicism. Polish society is not escaping from the Church, it wants to remain close to it and at the same time to decide freely on its own what is appropriate and what is not.

IV THE TRAP OF INHERITED ENTITLEMENTS

The two already mentioned controversies – on de-communisation and on re-christianisation – have attracted most attention. In a sense they were the substitute controversies, as critics of the public life of the Third Republic used to complain. Those who say that tend, however, to underestimate the role of values and of symbols in social life. Myself, I would rather observe that the amount of energy displayed over these controversies may be explained by reference to the apparent availability of a solution. The more real problems, as the critics would say, are at the surface more difficult to solve for structural reasons. With this we depart from the areas of political ethics and of religious faith and enter the dark realm of economics.

The noncommunist governments that ruled Poland from 1989 to 1993 faced the formidable task of restructuring the national economy under two handicaps: first, the huge external debt, amounting to 65 percent of GNP, left by the Communist elite of the 1970s; second, the general recession in the world economy that prevented the mass economic assistance needed when Communism surrendered. Communists relinquished their power not only because they were unable to fulfill the new aspirations for material well-being of the societies they ruled but also because the constitutionally recognised economic and social rights to free health services, education, employment, as well as the accumulated burden of social benefits due to the aging of the society, were put at risk by the economic crisis that started in

Poland in the mid-1970s after the failure of the accelerated modernisation program started by Gierek, Bozyk et al., and could not remain anaesthetised forever under the martial law introduced on December 13th, 1981.

The new governments, united in their contempt for the Communist past, were of various economic and political orientations. The fact remains that whatever their preferences may have been, they were obliged to impose budget cuts touching all areas of life and leaving nobody unaffected. The austere policies of Professor Leszek Balcerowicz, Finance Minister in the first two post-1989 governments of Tadeusz Mazowiecki (UD-Democratic Union) and of Jan Krzysztof Bielecki (KLD – Liberal Democratic Congress), resulted in greater credibility with the international-financing institutions, a credibility that each Polish government since then, left, right, or centre, has striven to safeguard. Each of these governments, independent of its political composition, needs, nonetheless, to fight not only with the opposition but against the resistance of its own constituency and with its own parliamentary base in order to pursue the appropriate policy of economic austerity.

Almost non-existent for decades, registered unemployment rose continuously from 10.7 percent of the labour force in 1991, to 13.6 percent in 1992 and to 15.4 percent in 1993. In some regions it extended to one-fourth of the labour force. Unemployment results from lay-offs in the enterprises undergoing fundamental economic transformation as well as from the closing down of entire enterprises not fitting the new open market economy. To this should be added the hidden unemployment which was estimated at 13.1 percent of those employed in 1991. An expert writing on the subject in the Autumn of 1993 concluded grimly that in the near future Poland may have to deal with two consequences of transformation at once; on the one hand, the perpetuation of hidden unemployment that makes the majority of companies uncompetitive and liable to bankruptcy if not subsidised from the state budget and, on the other hand, a further increase in open unemployment as the process of economic restructuring becomes more accelerated leading inevitably to mass lay-offs. The inherent conflict is thus exacerbated by the strong position of trade unions who defend the employees and the still weak position of managers (Czerwinska 1993 pp. 47–61). All this means that, though Poland became the first post-Communist country to record an actual increase in its GNP after some years of contraction (–11.6 percent in 1990 as compared with 1989, –7.6 in 1991, +1.5 in 1992 and +4.0 in 1993),[4] the move forward will be accompanied by

---

4 Information on the Socio-Economic Situation of the Country, Year 1993, Warsaw: Main Statistical Office, 1994, p. 108 (in Polish).

the accumulation of social tensions resulting from the increase in unemployment leading to a further weaking of the over-centralised and bureaucratised social security system which has not been reformed as yet and which collects less and less money with time, despite the fact that 48 percent of the earnings of each employee is put into it. This situation results from the fact that the number of those paying into the pension savings scheme went down by 12.4 percent in the years 1989–1993, while the number of those receiving pensions has risen by 21.4 percent. It was estimated that if savings are to balance pensions, contributions should increase to 64 percent of salaries by the year 2005.[5]

'Resolving the public pension crisis can prove to be one of the most formidable challenges in eastern Europe and the countries of [the] former Soviet Union', an expert from the World Bank wrote recently (Fox 1994 p. 3). Since 1989, Polish governments have been busy drawing up reforms and Parliament has taken some measures to give effect to them, though the results so far are far from satisfactory. Already on February 9 1990, a law was passed that abolished the special privileges of the top national and regional officials of political parties and of the central cooperative unions (sic). Nostalgia for the Communist past usually does not take into account these less widely, or not at all publicised, pieces of law that created the complex system of class inequality, so it is good to learn some details. Basically, the privilege in question entitled those who held one of the top positions for at least 5 years to retire on a full pension five years earlier than the normal retirement age (after 20 years' employment for women and 25 years' for men) plus an increase of the pension-to-salary coefficient by 1.5 percent for each year of employment in the top position. Soon, on 24 May 1990, this was followed by the abolition of similar privileges formerly enjoyed by top-level public officials. Next, after these decisions of great symbolic, though economically slight, value Parliament reworked the government's and post-Communist party's draft pension regulations that, among other things, introduced the three-monthly indexation of pensions according to the forecasted increase in average earnings. On October 17, 1991, a new law was passed that introduced the increase in 5 percent of effective average wages in the previous three months as the reference, instead of the forecasts. This was soon amended by the Law of February 15, 1992 that mandated the recalculation of pensions only if the respective increase in average wages was not less than 10 percent. The legislature also debated other proposals by the Government such as the postponement of

---

5   Report on the State of the State, Przeglad rzadowy, Office of Council of Ministers, 10, 1993, pp. 64–5 (in Polish).

the recalculation of pensions, lowering the base for purposes of recalculation from 100 percent to 91 percent of average earnings, abolition of special schemes for those working in hard conditions, etc. It should be added that during these years the relation between pensions and earnings first rose from 53.3 percent in 1989 to 75.7 percent in 1991, then declined to 71.7 percent in 1992.

But the changes that had already been made to pensions law had become the matter of fundamental controversy:[6]

> The most important was the Law of October 17, 1991, that eliminated (partially) the accumulated unmerited discrimination against some groups of elderly pensioners and farmers. Many provisions in that law have touched the basic principles shaping the system of social insurance – social security and the inviolability of justly acquired rights. The Law abolished the privileges of some groups that enjoyed them justly and of some that did not. By abusing justly acquired rights the law has opened up the political 'unlimited bargain' on the vindication of lost rights. In the insurance systems, justly acquired and basically inviolable rights are those that were acquired according to the principle of insurance, that is, acquired through the payment of contributions.

14 critics observed that the law in question suffered from lack of discrimination between 'rights acquired through payment of contributions and rights acquired through the support principle' as well as from the lack of 'principles of combination and the mutual exclusion of rights acquired through the payment of contributions (insurance principle) and through the principle of social solidarity (support principle).'[7]

Surveys I have conducted during the transition period in which there have been changes of political regimes point to the tendency to uphold expectations of the State as these were shaped under the influence of Socialist ideology. In 1988, 91 percent of the sample thought that it should be a duty of the State to secure to everybody stable jobs according to their skills, 93 percent believed the State should secure to everyone the minimum income or pension that would allow them to live, and 66 percent believed the State should secure welfare entitlements for everyone. In the years that followed support for the last expectation dwindled to 33 percent in 1990 and to 34 percent in 1992, while the State's duty to provide everybody with a job matching his skills retained the support of 79 percent in 1990 and of 80 percent in 1992, and the duty to ensure minimum earnings was approved by 94 percent in 1990 and by 96 percent in 1992. Thus, a guaranteed minimum wage or pension, which is an almost universal expectation, and the provision of welfare benefits to individuals by the State, which is the expectation of a (significant) minority, seem to be acceptable within the

---

6 Hrynkiewicz and Krynicka 1993 p. 276.
7 Ibid.

scheme of the rational market economy which is emerging. However, symptomatic of the troubles reformers are encountering is the fact that three quarters of Polish public opinion expects the State not only to ensure full employment but also employment according to one's qualifications and experience.

V THREE ETHICAL ORIENTATIONS

Three major areas of political debate reveal more fundamental divisions. As advanced pluralism is the most characteristic feature of political life, the competition between groups trying to distinguish themselves from one another on the positions they adopt on each of these issues may be of decisive importance. The election process, on the one hand, is a competition between candidates and party lists for the votes of citizens but, on the other, it is also a competition between political actors for symbolic identities that mediate between them and the voter. In this competition the pool of normative references is permanently under scrutiny. In my analysis of the process of resurrecting rights in Poland under Communist rule (Kurczewski 1993), I referred to the underlying normative structure taking it as basically uniform; now, the internal inconsistencies are starting to reveal themselves.

First, there is still the powerful ethos of freedom which finds its most radical expression in the rejection of any limitations on individual freedom, even if those limitations originate from the democratically established authorities themselves. Though the libertarian and anarchistic extreme is sometimes manifested, in its moderate version this tendency has been apparent, for instance, in the activities of the Polish Helsinki Committee, a private association established independently of the Communist authorities which continues to monitor legislation and the implementation of human rights standards in Poland today. In fact, it was this Committee which was responsible for preparing the draft of the Charter of Human Rights and Freedoms which was submitted by President Walesa to Parliament in 1992. This approach is linked with the strictly individualistic and anti-collectivistic concept of rights that are to be enjoyed through the direct petitioning of independent courts and of supra-national tribunals in the case of violations, putting the state and all other collectivities in a subservient position. It is not surprising that proponents of this view have been, for instance, strongly against de-communisation or lustration, understood as class discrimination or retroactive justice, against the ban on abortion as discriminating against women and against a right to employment as fictitious and thus as destructive of the real value of the concept of justiciable rights.

As such, the liberal orientation is a reaction to the experience of totalitarian socialism in which individual rights and freedoms were systematically violated in exchange for socio-economic standards conceived of as developmental goals and not as judicially enforceable rights. So the fundamentalist approach is also a reaction to the past while it puts stress on the traditional values of Polish and Christian culture and on the necessity of their rigorous application. From this perspective, the legacy of communism means, above all, the psychological erosion of society, which is deprived of full contact with the Church and which is exposed instead to the officially institutionalised system of double talk, closed communication circuits, unabashed propaganda and suchlike. This standpoint of the Roman Catholic Church, which is shared by parties of the Right and by 'Solidarity', is embodied in the triad of 'Person – Family – Nation' as expressing an absolute and organic set of moral subjects. Not surprisingly, it was from this wing that the proposal came to enact the constitutional Charter of Family Rights that would recognise the family as a collective subject of some rights against the state and, possibly, against its individual members as well.

Finally, the third orientation manifests itself in the tendency to exact various social and economic rights from the State. Because these rights were legislated with largesse and applied with discretion by the previous regime, this orientation is often taken as conservative. In fact, the matter is more complicated as this very orientation was employed for decades to resist the breach of promises by the Communist Party-State. Pointing out that social protest in the then People's Republic had always involved stress on human dignity and civic liberties should not, however, make us blind to the equally obvious and ever-present socio-economic dimension. So the resurgence of this orientation today should be taken as the interweaving of circumstances, in which the impetus for the fulfillment of the socio-economic promises of the previous era coincides with the dissatisfaction aroused by the diminishing institutional safeguards for the individual against the risks inherent in the market economy. The intertwining of these expectations and exigencies is nicely illustrated by the further history of the draft Charter of Social and Economic Rights, introduced by the SLD, that would have made post-Communist Poland possibly the only country with almost all of these rights enforceable through the courts. The draft Charter was not reintroduced in Parliament when the Democratic Left Alliance (successor to the Communist Party) won a share in government and could easily have legislated it. Paradoxically, it was the strongly pro-market government of Hanna Suchocka which drafted legislation, negotiated with the trade unions and with the business community, that would install in a projected Pact on Enterprise the principle of tri-partite cooperation and which 'Solidarity' is willing today to raise to the level of constitutional institutions at the expense of representative democracy.

Leon Petrazycki used to distinguish between three essential types of juridical relations: (1) One's right to *accipere* to which corresponds another's obligation of *dare*, as when, for instance, a beneficiary has the right to receive the amount of a debt, the debtor is obliged to pay this; this has been called a positive claim; (2) the right to *non pati* and its correlative obligation of *non-facere*, as, for instance, the right to immunity from certain types of actions by others, called the protective right; (3) the right to *facere* and the correlative obligation to *pati*, for instance, the duty of an offender to surrender to authorised punishment by the State.

If one follows this typology then the three delineated ethical orientations might be linked with some of these types of rights and duties. The individualistic-liberal orientation might be defined as the orientation towards the protective rights of the individual; the individualistic-socialist orientation as putting an accent on the positive claims of the individual against the state, and the collectivistic orientations as those that lay emphasis on the broad authority of the state *vis-à-vis* its citizens. The previously discerned fundamentalist orientation appears, against this background, as different inasmuch as it is the collective subject in whom the defined rights and duties are vested – not the state but supposedly natural communities like the nation and the family.

VI MECHANISMS, INSTRUMENTS, AND PROSPECTS

Democracy started after 1989 as a result of decades of pressure for the implementation of human rights which had been recognised by the Soviet Bloc in international agreements and in internal constitutions. Polish constitutional law, in contrast to most other post-Communist countries, is an expression of the gradualist and compromise-oriented approach so typical of Polish history after World War Two. It is composed of provisions of the 1952 Communist Constitution that abounds with social and economic rights and of post-1989 legislation that reintroduced the division of powers and established a complex institutional arrangement in which a strong Presidency is forced to coexist with a strong Parliament. In this system, the Constitutional Court remains limited in its jurisdiction due to the vestiges of the Westminster-like concept of the sovereignty of Parliament that was effectively implemented in the period 1989–1992, before the last constitutional amendments were made. What it means practically is that when a piece of legislation is defined as unconstitutional by the Court, for instance because it is in conflict with some of the basic rights, the Parliament may still, by a qualified two-thirds majority vote, decide to overrule the judgment of the Court. As this entails a stronger majority than in ordinary voting, the government in such a case needs to win wider support than was the case with voting on the legislation that is under scrutiny. The procedure, itself defined by constitutional law, is thus perfectly legal and constitutional. Undoubtedly, though, the Rule of Law would be realised more fully if, as all political actors promise, the Constitutional Court were granted powers of full and definitive review of legislation.

One may wonder, and in fact many do, if under these circumstances human rights in Poland are sufficiently well protected? In fact, nobody should ever be satisfied with the scope and degree to which these rights are implemented. I wish, however, to point to two institutional arrangements that help in their implementation. First, there is a set of internal institutions in which not only the Constitutional Court along with other courts may be listed but, more specifically, the Ombudsman or the Spokesperson on Civic Rights, as the office is called. In the late 1970s, when I addressed the Communist authorities with a memorandum calling for the introduction of this institution, I was informed that there is no need for an Ombudsman in Poland as, according to Lenin's concept, the Prokuratura (Supreme Prosecutor's Office, functionally independent from the Ministry of Justice) should also intervene on behalf of the citizens whose rights have been abused by other State organs, not to mention by private persons and organisations. Towards the end of his direct rule, General Jaruzelski, as part of a series of reforms, created the office which was filled by Professor Ewa Letowska. This office, with an uncharacteristically wide range of functions, and operating under new political conditions, became the principal instrument for the implementation of various rights. Similarly, the present Polish ombudsman, Professor Tadeusz Zielinski, apart from exerting pressure on the administration, has the right to institute proceedings before the Constitutional Court, serving as a substitute for class action. This single-person office, similar in this respect to the Presidency, has given its successive incumbents the opportunity to develop a highly visible and widely popular line on civic rights policy that has strengthened the office itself and has preserved the human rights element as one of the basic ingredients of Polish political culture, debate and discourse after 1989.

Another instrument, much less visible at present but inevitably gaining in importance with the passage of time, is the European Convention on Human Rights and Freedoms. For the Communist societies the existence of the CSCE process and the Helsinki agreements that established the recognised standards of human rights against which the performance of the Communists was judged were of major importance. Similarly, for the post-Communist democracies the existence of supra-national structures to which they aspire or to which they belong, which may monitor them, are of extreme value. This role was, in the years immediately following 1989, performed by the Council of Europe which provided information and assistance to the young democracies, and monitored their progress, to ensure that they complied with internationally recognised human rights standards. Entrance into the system of the European Convention serves, however, as the next stage. Since 1992, Poland is a party to the Convention and the first cases against the Polish government are finding their way to the Human Rights Commission and to the European Court of Human Rights in Strasbourg. This in fact seems to be the most effective mechanism available at present as it puts the State under permanent scrutiny. In other words, the Rule of Law under construction in post-Communist Poland is the rule of internationally recognised human rights. After self-limitation imposed upon themselves by the enlightened absolutist rulers who put forward the ideal of the *Rechtsstaat*; after the national system of the Rule of Law based upon the constitutional division of powers, the time came for the supra-national Rule of Rights (Kurczewski 1989, 1993b, 1994a).

But all this may function only within a specific context. First, it is difficult to imagine an interest in human rights if poverty, disorganisation and discontent would exceed a certain level. Visibility of crime, new types of crime, the influx of criminals from abroad and the availability of weapons make crime control problems the most vulnerable point in the barrier that divides human rights-friendly societies from those that put other considerations above human rights. The Polish police find a strong following among the public when applying for sterner measures against organised crime and crime in general, and in this climate very often ideas are put about that, if put into practice, could endanger the proper respect and protection of human rights. Until now, however, the problem has not achieved the scale that would lead to the real endangerment of the rights in question.

This is related to the second factor, that is the functioning of democracy. However critical society is in assessing the performance of democracy nobody can doubt that in Poland governments and parliaments are changed by the will of the people expressed in free elections. The same can be said of local government which was also introduced after 1989 in a deliberate attempt to engage society in democracy and to decentralise the power of the State. Freedom of expression is above all secured by the free and uncensored private press that represents all shades of political opinion and that aggressively investigates the functioning of various branches of power. Finally, one thing that Polish democracy abounds in is plurality, which makes it unlikely that the actions of parties in power would remain uncontrolled and uncriticised by society. Each of these elements, and we have only listed some, when viewed in conjunction represent democracy in action, increasing the likelihood that human rights will be fostered and that the abuse of human rights will be hampered.

A third, related factor is the desire of the Polish nation and of its political class to resume its place within a unified Europe as soon as possible. This hope has been frustrated by complex diplomatic games that have postponed the entrance of Poland into NATO, the Western European Union, not to speak of the European Union itself. But due to history and present-day realities entrance into a unified Europe is seen in Poland, as well as in other Central European countries, as the only way to secure cultural identity and real social development. Seen from that perspective, the question of human rights in Poland, or anywhere else in the region, is at the same time a question about human rights in Europe as a whole.

Finally, we have cited evidence, and one could cite much more, that human rights and freedoms remain well ingrained in the Polish ethos. Polish politicians themselves were very often victims of the systematic abuse of human rights. This in itself would not suffice. However, it is surely of decisive importance that human rights have not been under threat since democracy was reconstituted. Rather, the main controversies have dealt with the question of which rights are to be given priority under the conditions of a changing moral, political and economic order.

6. The Constitutional Court of the Czech Republic and a Legal–Philosophical Perspective on the Sovereignty of the Law

Jirí Pribán

I INTRODUCTION

This essay seeks to describe the Constitutional Court of the Czech Republic, its position within the system of constitutional bodies, and its first practical steps in the field of protection of the principles of the rule of law, legality and constitutionality, which includes the protection of human rights as defined in the Bill of Fundamental Rights and Freedoms. I shall concentrate on the first judgment of the Court concerning the illegitimacy of the Communist regime which, against a deep legal–philosophical background, analyzes precisely those general principles of a legal state (*Rechtsstaat*) which make the protection of human rights possible. The critique of the Court is centred around the principles of the sovereignty of the law and formal rational law which are reduced by the judges of the Court to techniques or practices of political power.[1] I shall seek to prove that the autonomy of modern systems of positive law requires a formal rational concept of law and principles of legality and sovereignty of the law not only as legal techniques, but as fundamental principles of any modern

---

1 The judgment of the Court speaks literally about the sovereignty of the law, not about the rule of law principle. Although both concepts are closely related to one another, they must be distinguished because the sovereignty of the law concept, unlike the rule of law concept, indicates a more formal and legalistic attitude towards law. The sovereignty of the law principle also corresponds to the language and concepts of continental philosophy of law, especially to Kelsen's pure theory of law (Kelsen 1991) which is implicitly criticized in the judgment of the Court.

law and as necessary conditions for the reconstruction of a democratic legal state defending the rights and liberties of its citizens.

II DISCONTINUITIES IN THE DEVELOPMENT OF THE CONSTITUTIONAL SYSTEM OF CZECH SOCIETY

The last sixty years in the constitutional history of Czech society has been a confused period full of sudden changes. These changes reflected the profound differences between the numerous political regimes that have governed Czech society during this period, as well as policy shifts by individual regimes.

Between the two World Wars Czechoslovakia was a liberal democratic state governed in accordance with the Constitution of 1920. Although its population consisted of several nationalities (Czechs, Slovaks, Germans, Hungarians, Poles, and Ukrainians) and despite the fact that the state had not been established (for many political reasons) as a federal state, the constitutional protection of the rights of minorities was relatively highly developed during this period (Seton-Watson 1943, pp. 313–46).

The German occupation of Bohemia and Moravia, in 1939, brought an end to liberal, democratic Czechoslovakia and resulted in the 'protectorate regime' which formally preserved, to a limited extent, but in fact destroyed, independent Czech political institutions (Seton-Watson 1943, p. 350ff.). The German occupation of Czech territory also resulted in the establishment of a nominally independent Slovakia and in the annexation of the eastern province of Ruthenia by Hungary. After the Second World War and the re-establishment of an independent and united Czechoslovakia, a three year struggle for political power ensued. This struggle was won by the Communist Party, which immediately confirmed its political victory with constitutional changes and the adoption of a new Constitution. This Constitution, although similar in structure to the liberal Czechoslovak Constitution of 1920, breached the principle of the division of powers and contained obvious instruments of a totalitarian political system, such as *the principle of the leading role of the working class* and the integration of all political parties into the National Front which was headed by the Communists.

After approximately eight years of severe repression, with the imprisonment and execution of opponents of the regime, the Communists began slowly to replace brutal political violence with much more sophisticated and ideologically-based, but less repressive, forms of ruling the country. These political changes were partially reflected in the second communist Constitution adopted in 1960.

The last major constitutional change during the period of Communist power occurred in the extraordinary year of 1968. This was not only a 'quixotic attempt' to introduce a model of socialism with a human face, but also involved the most important and striking manifestation of Slovak national interests represented by the elite of Slovak Communists who ruled Czechoslovakia and dominated the Communist Party at that time. This elite introduced one of the most important post-war constitutional changes and Czechoslovakia became a federal state, nevertheless retaining the one-party political system. This constitutional system survived until the very end of the communist regime in November 1989.

Fundamental constitutional changes accompanied the loss of political power by the Communists after the 1989 'Velvet Revolution' (a new government, dominated by non-Communists, was formed on 10 December, while Vaclav Havel was elected President on 29 December). During the first months of 1990 some important constitutional laws were enacted, such as laws introducing a traditional division of powers and abolishing the one-party political system of the Communist Party dictatorship. The Federal Assembly also passed the Bill of Fundamental Rights and Freedoms (n.23/1991Sb.), and the Constitutional Act concerning the Constitutional Court (n.91/1991Sb.). The process of constitutional change, however, was soon overtaken by a crisis between Czech and Slovak political interests and between politicians from both republics of the federation. This crisis was mainly caused by different ideas about the reconstruction of the administrative system and the division of powers between federal bodies and those of the constituent republics of the Czechoslovak state. The transformation of the centralised federal bodies and the adoption of new constitutional laws intended to change the country into a decentralised federation, proceeded too slowly to prevent a growing political, economic, and cultural gap from emerging between Czech and Slovak societies. During 1992, the last year before the split, the political crisis and the alienation of Czech and Slovak political representatives developed so rapidly that there was no chance of implementing or even articulating ideas of constitutional and administrative reform. There was finally no escape from the dissolution of the Czech and Slovak Federal Republic which happened on 31 December 1992.

The newly born Czech state adopted a new Constitution which is quite different from the previous federal one. The Czech Constitution was adopted by the Czech National Council, which had been the Parliament of the Czech Republic within the old federal system, on 28 December 1992.

The new Constitution gives a more powerful role to the President, establishes a bicameral Parliament consisting of the Assembly of Deputies and Senate, and strengthens the position of the Government and Prime Minister. The new Constitution also established a new Constitutional Court. This Court differs substantially from the previous federal one which had been working for only a couple of months before the dissolution of the federation. The Bill of Rights and Fundamental Freedoms, which had formed part of the federal constitutional system, was incorporated into the newly established constitutional system of the Czech Republic. It defines and protects individual, political and social human rights, including the rights of ethnic and national minorities. The Constitutional Court plays a unique role in the mechanism of human rights protection because it is the supreme and, in specific cases, even exclusive judicial body in that field. Therefore, we will turn our attention to the first public experience with this body which is so fundamental to the whole system of human rights protection in the Czech Republic.

III THE CONSTITUTIONAL COURT OF THE CZECH REPUBLIC

1. The Procedure for the Establishment of the Constitutional Court and its Legitimacy

The Constitutional Court of The Czech Republic is, according to the text of the Constitution, the judicial body responsible for the protection of constitutionality (article 83 of the Constitution). The Constitution also defines the functions of the other top judicial bodies – the Supreme Court and the Supreme Administrative Court. The Supreme Court is the highest judicial authority with general jurisdiction, except in cases reserved to the Supreme Administrative Court or to the Constitutional Court (article 92 of the Constitution). This means that the judicial power of the Constitutional Court, set out in article 87 of the Constitution, has a residual nature.

Judges of the Constitutional Court are appointed by the President of the Republic with the approval of the Senate, the upper chamber of the Czech Parliament. The 15 judges of the Court are appointed for a period of 10 years. They must have – a character beyond reproach, a university legal qualification, a minimum age of 40 years and have worked in the legal profession for a minimum of 10 years (article 84(3) of the Constitution). As noted above, the right to appoint constitutional judges is vested in the President of the Republic who can thus influence, albeit indirectly, the general development of constitutional law. In this context it is worth noting that the President of the Republic does not have the right to return constitutional bills to Parliament once they have been adopted, although he is empowered to return so-called 'ordinary' bills that are not subject to the specific and more rigid parliamentary procedure governing constitutional bills (articles 84(2) and 62 of the Constitution). However, a presidential veto will be merely suspensive in effect, provided that the Chamber of Deputies reaffirms the bill by a majority of more than one half of all deputies (Article 50(2) of the Constitution).

We can thus see that the immediate source of the legitimacy of the position of constitutional judges is the presidential will followed, secondly, by the approval of the Senate. The original source can, however, be traced back to the Parliament, because both chambers together elect the President of the Republic. This constitutional mechanism is further evidence that the Czech constitutional system has features typical of parliamentary regimes.

2. The Jurisdiction of the Constitutional Court

The most important power of the Constitutional Court is undoubtedly the right to declare void acts of the Parliament or individual statutory provisions, if they contradict a constitutional provision or international treaties on human rights and freedoms which have been ratified and promulgated by the Czech Republic (Article 87(1)(a) of the Constitution). A constitutional provision consists of the Constitution, the Bill of Fundamental Rights and Freedoms, and a complex of other constitutional acts which are enacted using the same procedure as the Constitution and which are usually adopted so as to specify in detail certain principles enshrined in the Constitution. The Constitutional Court can, moreover, declare void other legal regulations (or parts thereof) if they breach the constitution or international treaties concerning human rights and fundamental freedoms (article 87(1)(b) of the Constitution).

In addition to the primary function of the Constitutional Court of the Czech Republic, which is to protect legality and constitutionality, there are other substantial functions of the Court – jurisdiction over complaints against unconstitutional interventions of 'the organs of public power' that violate constitutionally guaranteed fundamental rights and freedoms, and jurisdiction over complaints of 'organs of territorial self-administration' concerning an unlawful intervention by the state (article 87(1)(c) of the Constitution). These powers signify the strong protection of individual and collective human rights by the Court and important limits on the system of centralized public power. The administrative system of the Czech

Republic, it should be observed, is extraordinarily dominated by a centralism which is not rooted only in the last four decades of the Communist regime. Its origins lie deeper – in the period of the enlightened absolutism of Empress Maria Theresia and her son Joseph the Second (see e.g., Okey, 1986, pp. 48–53). Thus Czech society has had a long experience of a centralized administration. Although this has often been criticized, Czechs have also became partially accustomed to a centralised administration, thus making it more difficult to reconstruct the system of administration in the Czech Republic. This still remains one of the important political tasks for the present Government. The unwillingness on the part of politicians to solve this problem has become an important feature of contemporary Czech political debates. The Constitutional Court, with its wide jurisdiction, can both positively influence and place limits on the decisions of the Government and of all administrative organs in relation to the autonomy of local governmental bodies.

The Constitutional Court has important functions not only with respect to the legal order of the country, but also with respect to its political system. The Court can review decisions concerning the dissolution of political parties and certain other decisions concerning the activities of political parties. Here, the Court may apply not only the principle of constitutionality but also that of legality, thus broadening its power and its jurisdiction (article 87(1)(j) of the Constitution). Accordingly, the Court is the institution which has the last word in determining the legality of subjects of the Czech political system. Thus, the Court's jurisdiction meets here the real political life of Czech society and directly places the constitutional judges within a political context. We shall see later that this political aspect of the activities of the judges can intrude into all spheres of the Court's jurisdiction and can become a definite temptation to an institution whose competences were originally defined mostly from a legalistic perspective.

3. The Establishment of the First Constitutional Court of the Czech Republic and Social Expectations of its Functions

The judges of the Constitutional Court were appointed by President Havel after prolonged political discussions in the summer of 1993. They were not approved by the Senate, which has not yet been established, but by the

Assembly of Deputies which, for the time being, discharges the powers of the Senate.[2]

It took approximately six months before the Court began work. The greatest public expectations of the Court were probably concentrated on the protection of human rights and on the correction of legislation. The Czech Parliament, like legislative bodies of other Central and Eastern European countries in the period of transformation, suffers from legislative hyperactivity. This hyperactivity has resulted in some bad laws and legal regulations being adopted. Laws often serve only as an instrument for the enforcement of a transient political will and can be out of date even at the moment of their adoption. There have also been certain laws which are inconsistent with the rest of the legal system. Although Parliamentary deputies were aware of this inconsistency when adopting these laws, they did nothing to prevent this legally very dangerous situation from arising.[3] For all these reasons citizens expected that, together with the protection of human rights and individual freedoms, the Constitutional Court would become a constitutional body that would be able to target and correct mistakes arising from parliamentary legislation.

Furthermore, there was felt to be an urgent need for an institution standing above political parties, similar to the President of the Republic, since modern Czech political culture is characterised by the enormous role and influence of its political parties. Society would thus value a constitutional body with the capacity to introduce neutral technical expertise into the political system.

---

2 Chapter VIII of the Constitution of the Czech Republic transformed the Czech National Council, the Parliament of the Czech Republic under the old federal system, into the Assembly of Deputies, the lower chamber of the Parliament of the new independent Czech state. Chapter VIII of the Constitution also states that the Assembly of Deputies shall discharge the powers of the Senate until the latter is established. Political disputes and doubts about the importance and sense of establishing the Senate are, however, one of the most serious and symptomatic problems of contemporary Czech politics. There is no political consensus about the desirability of establishing the Senate and, for the time being, it seems that the election of Senators will not take place this year or even in the first half of 1995. The Senate thus remains a 'dead letter' as far as the Constitution is concerned.

3 One typical example is a recent change to the Criminal Code of the Czech Republic. Due to pressure of time, the Parliament adopted changes in the Criminal Code containing obvious mistakes, refused to correct them during a parliamentary debate, and recommended instead to President Havel that he should use his right to return bills adopted by Parliament and thus initiate a new parliamentary process which would correct those mistakes. This particular example is illustrative of a more general tendency in the Czech legal system and of the irresponsibility of Czech legislators.

Have constitutional judges fulfilled these expectations? The controversy accompanying their first judgment on the Act of the Lawlessness of the Communist Regime and of Resistance Against It (n.198/1993Sb.) suggests that they have not. This judgment shows that even the Court is in danger of colonizing purely legal problems with pragmatic political language. This is a general and possibly quite natural tendency which may apply not only in autocratic and totalitarian, but also in liberal democratic systems.

IV THE SOVEREIGNTY OF THE LAW AND A LEGAL– PHILOSOPHICAL CRITIQUE OF JUDGMENT N.14/1994SB OF THE CONSTITUTIONAL COURT OF THE CZECH REPUBLIC[4]

1. The Act on the Lawlessness of the Communist Regime and on the Resistance Against It (n.198/1993Sb)

Czech society's expectations of the Court were strengthened by the fact that the first judgment of the Court concerned the constitutionality and legality of the Act on the Lawlessness of the Communist Regime and on the Resistance Against It (n.198/1993Sb.), which was adopted by the Parliament in the summer of 1993.

The Act itself caused a huge public debate. The main political purpose behind the adoption of this law was an attempt to make a clear dividing line between the present political regime and those of the past and to condemn totalitarian political practices. Criticism of the Act came, however, not only from those politicians representing the former regime, its ideology and political programme. Many lawyers and liberal politicians also expressed their objections to this Act which, in their opinion, consists of many vague formulations and legally meaningless provisions. Most sections of the Act use the language and expressions found in the preamble where, in accordance with Czech political practice, the political intentions of the legislators are contained.[5] More than three quarters of the text of the Act is

---

4 Most of the quotations from the judgment are taken from the translation made by Mark Gillis, an assistant to one of the judges of the Court. However, I reject his translation of 'the sovereignty of the law principle' as 'the sovereignty of statute law principle'. The latter is a narower and thus misleading concept which does not reflect the nature and tradition of the Czech legal system and of Czech legal culture.

5 It is a feature of the Czech legal system and of legal texts that preambles of important laws indicate the intentions of the legislators and put the law in a broader social, political and cultural perspective. Therefore, the language of the preambles of statutes

devoted to a description and analysis of the Communist regime and its criminal nature. Parliament has thus made certain judgements on history, its meaning, and on historical truth. Moreover, Parliament expressed a capacity to know the thinking and motives of citizens when it proclaimed, in one part of the Act, that 'the Communist regime ... forced citizens by persecutions or the threat of persecutions to demonstrate publicly their consent even with what they considered to be a lie or a crime' (see section 1, paragraph 1/a of the Act n.198/1993Sb). Parliament has thus made the dangerous assumption that some political or constitutional body can say what people 'truly' thought about some parts of their personal history. Public life thereby colonizes private spheres of thinking which is thus given a 'proper content'. Although there is no doubt about the criminality of the Communist regime and the atrocities committed by its representatives, and although most of the judgements in the Act are, in my view, correct, it remains a serious question whether any Parliament has a general right to articulate moral and historical judgements, and especially to give them a legal form.

However, in Act No. 198 of 1993, the Czech Parliament not only analyzes the criminal nature of the Communist regime, but also introduces the whole Act with a sentence of clearly normative, though vague, content. This proclaims: 'the Parliament will respect this Act in its future activity' (see the preamble of the Act). Moreover, there arose doubts as to whether those sections containing and speaking about the joint responsibility of the Communist Party and its defenders for crimes committed by the regime (sections 1/2, 2 and section 5 of the Act) did not introduce a criminal liability outside the criminal law. Because of these many confusions and doubts raised by the Act not only legal experts, but also the general public, was impatiently waiting for the judgment of the Constitutional Court.[6]

2. The Sovereignty of the Law Principle from the Perspective of the Judgment

The judgment of the Court was, however, a big disappointment for many and brought confusion instead of clarifying the problem, the nature of which presumes arguments based on a wide legal–philosophical knowledge. Although the judgment also deals with some purely positivistic aspects of

---

differs, naturally, from that employed in the operative provisions of the statutes themselves.

6 41 members of Parliament initiated a proceeding before the Constitutional Court on 15 September 1993 and asked the Court to declare void Act n.198/1993Sb on the Lawlessness of the Communist Regime and on the Resistance Against It.

the law, we shall confine our remarks in this essay to the first part of the judgment, which analyzes general problems of legitimacy, the relation between law and morals, and the relation between values and positive law.

The judgment rejects a purely legalistic approach and, unexpectedly, makes a critique of a formal rational concept of law and legality a central point of its reasoning. This is strange, especially for a Constitutional Court, as such judicial bodies usually assume the principle of the autonomy of legal rules and the irreducibility of law to concrete political life as a basic principle of all reasoning and decisions (see e.g., Walter 1994). The Constitutional Court of the Czech Republic has thus evidently entered a field where law and politics coincide and has crossed over from the legal world into the world of everyday politics and momentary political disputes which characterizes contemporary Czech society. And what are those parts of the judgment like which shift the activity of the Court to a purely political discourse? Firstly, the fourth paragraph of section A of the judgment states that:

> the joint responsibility of members of the Communist Party ... should be understood as an effort to instigate reflection on the part of those who were, or from then on continue to be, members of an organization, the leadership and political activities of which over and over again departed markedly, not only from the basic values of humanity and of a democratic law-based state, but also from its own program and laws.

The Court speaks just about a moral responsibility in this connection and does not interpret this part of the Act as expressing imperative legal rules. It is not so much a question of whether particular statements about responsibility can have criminal legal consequences, but more a question of fact that Parliament can adopt laws or other legal regulations the text of which, instead of having legal aspects and consequences, judge the moral dimension of the actions of individuals and of other legal subjects. Constitutional bodies thus switch from enforcing the rule of law and claim instead to behave like bodies of a moral, or at least moralizing, state. Liberal institutions can thus easily turn into political institutions which use particular moral arguments and feelings of compassion as a main source of justification for the use of power and for political violence. The dangers of such a foundation for any political or constitutional institution have been analyzed in detail, for example by Hannah Arendt (Arendt 1964, 1970). In addition, the judgment states that criminal liability is excluded because the relevant parts of the 1993 Act have, 'a moral-political and not a juridical nature' (see section A, paragraph 8 of the judgment).

The Constitutional Court tolerates, besides the moralizing content of the law, its purely pragmatic political goals when the Court states that:[7]

> the introductory declaration of Parliament ... cannot be considered a legal norm which would bind Parliament. It concerns an expression of political will of a programmatic character, a will established at a certain time and with a certain line-up of forces in Parliament, a fact which may not be interpreted inconsistently with the right of Parliament, in the area and within the bounds of its competence, to adjust the matter differently at another time, nor inconsistently with the principle of the free exchange of views on the floor of the Parliament

Law and laws are thus reduced to a mere expression of political will and lose the characteristic of generally valid rules which are directed essentially to all subjects of civil society. This interpretation is paradoxically and dangerously similar to the famous Marxist thesis that law is just the pure will of the ruling class. Law, as it is understood by the Constitutional Court, loses its enduring quality and its autonomy. Such an understanding creates an opening for the use and misuse of law by various political elites which momentarily hold political power. Law turns into an instrument of this power. Although we should have no doubts about the influence of political systems on law and about the open character of any legal system, the judgment of the Court casts doubt on the autonomy of law itself and the content of law becomes subservient to a momentary distribution of political power and to a particular political system (on the autonomy of legal rules see e.g. MacCormick 1978). Instead of protecting the autonomy of legal rules, the Court diminishes the meaning of the Act of Parliament by reducing most of its contents to the mere expression of political will.

3. Problems of Legality and Legitimacy in the Judgment of the Court

The biggest problems, however, arise from a third level of the Court's legal–philosophical reasoning, which focuses on the legitimacy of political power and its relation to formal rational law and legality. The Court stated that, 'Czech law is not founded on the sovereignty of the law' (section A, paragraph 21 of the judgment). The Court contrasted this legal principle, although it is contained in the Bill of Fundamental Rights and Freedoms, with democratic values and principles, and rejected a formal rational concept of the legal state. It considered the principle of 'the sovereignty of the people who are the bearers of supra-governmental power, constitutive power' (section A, paragraph 21) to be a founding principle of the democratic legal state. A political regime is, according to the judges of the Constitutional Court, 'legitimate if, on the whole, it is accepted by the

---

7   Section A, paragraph 10 of the judgment.

majority of citizens' (section A, paragraph 18). An effort to oppose the legal state based on democratic values to a legalistic and value-free concept of the legal state ends up in a reduced understanding of democracy as merely the will of the majority. While the Court identified the evil of the Communist regime first of all in the coincidence of formal constitutionality and crimes against humanity, it omitted to say that the majority-will principle, though undoubtedly one of the constitutive democratic principles, has helped to 'justify' and commission, under certain conditions, much the same types of crimes. These conditions are, in particular, the absence of formal legal checks upon government and of rights for minorities which, in the absence of the sovereignty of the law, can easily be victimized by certain interests and by the will of a majority within society.

The judges of the Constitutional Court have sought, in this judgment, to fill the constitutional and legal framework of the new Czech republic with positive democratic values; but they have not taken sufficient account of the fact that it was precisely the principles of the majority will and of the sovereignty of the people which were, in their deformed meaning, used by the totalitarian Communist regime for its own purposes (Arendt 1951). In stating that the new Czech Constitution is based on democratic values and 'does not bind positive law only with formal legality' (section A, paragraph 16), the Court has, in fact, reduced those values to the above- mentioned principles of the majority will and the sovereignty of the people. The Court even criticises formal legality so widely that it attributes it, in quite a simplistic way, to the Communist regime. The legal state itself can, however, hardly scorn the sovereignty and formal rationality of law, although it remains clear that the contents of laws can correspond to particular group interests, bringing advantages for some groups and discriminating against others (see e.g., Norrie 1993).

The formal rationality of laws and bureaucratic administration are necessary characteristics of every modern liberal state. This does not mean that such features cannot be misused, but it is decisive that we cannot imagine a modern democratic legal state without this kind of administration as its constitutive element (Weber 1921). The judges of the Czech Constitutional Court attempted to subordinate formal legality to higher principles and ideas of democracy without taking into account the autonomous nature of modern legal systems. Finally, they end up in a famous paradox of every modern legal system (see e.g., Luhmann 1983, Teubner 1991) when they explain that 'legislators are bound by certain basic values which the Constitution has declared to be inviolable' (section A, paragraph 21). Is not the Constitution – one of many positive laws of the Czech Republic, in spite of its supreme position in the legal system –

just one form and fulfilment of the principles of formal legality and the sovereignty of the law? The Constitution would then, as a text of positive law, define and protect values and principles which should have been superior to the validity and obligatory force of the Constitution itself. Should we not rather understand the whole problem of the influence and relationship between democratic values (and all extralegal phenomena) and the positive legal system as a mutually conditioned cyclical movement, in which there are no superior and inferior components? At the moment of codifying these principles and values in the Constitution they would become a part of the system of positive law, albeit they are not reducible to norms of positive law and to the principle of the sovereignty of the law. On the other hand, the sovereignty of the law would naturally become one of the most important values and principles of a modern democratic legal state which transcends particular positive laws and any formalistic perspective. Such a tendency of modern legal systems leads us to the conclusion that we have to reject those legal–philosophical perspectives which Ronald Dworkin sums up as the 'plain fact' view of the grounds of law (Dworkin 1986). Thus, the true nature of modern law was ignored by the judges of the Constitutional Court of the Czech Republic. A question remains, did the Court ignore this fact for purely legal–philosophical reasons or was the Court simply reflecting the momentary political interests and will which they mentioned several times in the judgment?

V CONCLUSION

The intent of this chapter was not, naturally, to excuse or diminish the criminal nature of the Communist regimes which ruled under the supervision of the Soviet Union in the Central and Eastern European countries for the last four decades. There is no doubt about the crimes and atrocities committed against the peoples of these countries. A central theme of the chapter was, however, to ask if Parliament or any other constitutional body, for instance the Constitutional Court, can reserve the right to describe, evaluate and morally judge the Communist regime by means of law. If we accept a positive answer to this question, we can make citizens' ideas about law, its nature, content and language weaker and vague. The constitutional position of the Constitutional Court and its primary legal functions make it absurd that this body, protecting legality and constitutionality, should accept purely political arguments and justifications for laws enacted by Parliament. It is not possible, for that reason, to understand the judgment of the Court in any other way than as a failure at the very beginning of its existence. Although this is hardly exceptional in a liberal society, we have to point out the potentially dangerous consequences.

The judgment of the Constitutional Court of the Czech Republic also indicates that the principle of formal legality is neither a historical feature of weak democracies, like the Weimar Republic or pre-war Czechoslovakia, nor a demonstration of the imperfect nature of contemporary legal systems. Although imperfect, like any other human creation, formal rational legality remains one of the founding principles of the contemporary democratic legal state which cannot be omitted.

7. The Protection of Human Rights in Poland and Hungary

Gábor Halmai

In 1989, the year of the East and Central European transitions, Francis Fukuyama predicted, with more than a hint of wistfulness, the end of history and the triumph of western liberal ideas, and the consequent demise of all viable alternatives (see Fukuyama 1989 pp. 3–18 and 1992). Well now, I live in a part of the world where, in the opinion of many, history is just starting or *re*starting. In the wake of the rapid collapse of Soviet-type regimes in Central and Eastern Europe the following question is sharply raised: where and how should we proceed? Is there really only one way out?

It is undeniably true that liberal democracy – which has had in the course of this century to meet the challenge of both fascism and communism – has even in this region no viable alternative in the long run. These days, however, there are still ferocious political fights going on throughout the world and advocates of liberalism are almost everywhere in the minority. What is more – in order to comfort Fukuyama – in Central and Eastern Europe essentially divergent models are emerging.

Even in countries accepting the basic principles of liberalism there are several options that may be taken, as is also exemplified by the divergent practices of western democracies. What are the foundational principles and what are the alternatives open to the countries of the region? Guaranteeing human rights and power-sharing. These are the two fundamental pillars of constitutionality and their institutionalization is today the central task in the process of transforming the political system. But how?

As regards our topic, that of human rights and their protection, one of the possible solutions is the German model, i.e. regulation partly by the constitution, partly through separate Acts of Parliament. The 1949 Bonn Basic Law can serve as our model here. It has already proved effective in the democratic transformation of both Portugal and Spain (see Llorente 1988). This is one of the ways to abolish dictatorial regimes.

It is important, on the other hand, for us to investigate Anglo-Saxon legal systems as well, since a truly liberal solution is represented by the well-known maxim contained in the 1st Amendment to the American Constitution:

> Congress shall make no law respecting an establishment of religion, or prohibiting the free exercise thereof; or abridging the freedom of speech, or of the press; or the right of the people peaceably to assemble, and to petition the government for a redress of grievances.

This means that human rights are recognised even without a specific basis in statutory law. In accordance with this thinking, which was influential in the newly-established United States and which itself was based on the theories of John Locke, the original text of the US Constitution, of 17 September 1787, contained no catalogue of fundamental rights. This omission was due, in large measure, to the belief that rights do not derive from their enactment in law and that a constitutional enunciation of rights could be positively harmful as it might allow future governments to limit the exercise of freedoms which had not been expressly recognised in the constitution itself.[1] The belief that fundamental rights are the natural birth right of man, which are independent of government, is illustrated by the 1st Amendment to the American Constitution, cited above, and by the 14th Amendment which provides, 'nor shall any State deprive any person of life, liberty, or property, without due process of law, nor deny to any person within its jurisdiction the equal protection of the laws'.

Naturally, I am perfectly aware that there is a long way to go before we reach the German '*Rechtsstaat*' or the Anglo-Saxon 'rule of law', and that numerous conditions for arriving at this goal are missing in Hungary and in the other post-Communist states of Central and Eastern Europe. But I want to call attention to the fact that, yes, the objective is attainable. An example of this is the development of Japan, which, after the Second World War – even if not totally of its own accord – did successfully transform itself from a constitutional state of the German type to a state governed by the rule of law (See Takada 1985).

This would imply, naturally, that the role of the courts, particularly in terms of their jurisdiction, should be changed at the base, which is not unimaginable with a long term constitutional model. In such a system, which would be very similar to the American system of constitutional protection, the courts would base their judgments on the constitution rather than on statute and other laws (of course the personnel needed for this system could not be organized from one day to the next).

---

1 For a fuller discussion of this point see Halmai 1994 pp. 36–37.

As Alexis de Tocqueville said about the power of judges in the United States: 'The right of American courts to proclaim that a law is against the constitution, is one of the strongest obstacles ever put in the way of the tyranny of political groups' (See de Tocqueville 1874 p. 109). Such judgments about laws are only possible in individual cases which have been brought before the courts. The Anglo-Saxon solution represents a distinctive form of restricting state power by protecting the Basic Rights laid down in the Constitution and by giving a much larger role to adjudication than any of the continental legal systems found in Europe, which generally prefer legislation. But we know, from Isaiah Berlin, that it is not the form of restricting state power, but the effectiveness of the restriction in question that really matters (See Berlin 1969).

The former socialist countries do not seem, however, to be as yet in a position where they could choose the option of doing without a statutory foundation for basic human rights. Today, unfortunately, a system which only guarantees rights by listing them in a constitution, without elaborating the scope of those rights in statutes, would not yet offer real guarantees. The historical ballast of past decades makes it necessary,[2] for a shorter or for a longer period, to limit state power by means of detailed legal regulations in order to protect human rights. The German model can thus provide a precedent for us, then, not because it is perfect and offers absolute salvation, but simply because Germany has had a similar history of authoritarianism and illiberalism.

Liberal constitutional traditions which can be found in the history of certain countries in Central and Eastern Europe can also help to shorten this process of transition. This is particularly true of the Czech Republic and, to a somewhat lesser extent, of Poland and Hungary.[3]

Amongst the different countries of the region there are several potential variations for the constitutional regulation of human rights. However, the big paradox, in terms of constitutional developments in Central and Eastern Europe, is that in some countries, where abolishing the *nomenklatura* has met with significant obstacles or where a particularly serious economic crisis requires some sort of reform centralization for a transitional period, there are already new constitutions in place (Russia, Bulgaria, Romania); on the other hand, in countries which have realized a more rapid pace of economic and political transformation – such as Poland and Hungary –

---

2 For a more detailed consideration of the 'historical ballast' with which the states of Central and Eastern Europe must contend see e.g. the chapters by Vernon Bogdanor and by Istvan Pogany in this volume.

3 See e.g. the chapter in this volume by Jacek Kurczewski and his book, Kurczewski (1993) *The Resurrection of Rights in Poland.*

there has been (as yet) no constitution-making National Assembly. Instead, as political power relations have gradually shifted, the respective constitutions have been modified accordingly.[4]

Parallel with the undoubted advantages of the Hungarian approach, however, there are also disadvantages that have already begun to appear. There is, for example, a considerable demand today for stability of the legal system. For this, of course, a basic law is needed that is respected for its supreme or higher law character. To encourage such respect will be the duty of institutions empowered to protect constitutionality, primarily the Constitutional Court. This is the way that the much desired, sometimes even anticipated, rule of law can emerge. There is only one secret to all of this – like grass in England it needs careful tending, for about three hundred years!

The new coalition government (comprising the Socialist Party and the Free Democrats) which was formed in Hungary, following elections held in May, 1994, has resolved that a new, post-Communist constitution should be adopted within a year. However, it has become apparent that the minority partner in the coalition, the Free Democrats, have been pressing for the rapid adoption of a new constitution, while the Socialist Party has been dragging its feet.[5]

I THE POLISH BILL OF RIGHTS[6]

Poland is the only country of the former Soviet bloc in which, following the 'revolution' of 1989, no new constitutional catalogue of human rights and freedoms and instruments for their protection has been adopted. Thus, individual rights are still governed by Chapter Eight of the 1952 constitution. This 'Soviet' constitution enumerated most of the rights recognised in the democracies of Western Europe, although certain significant rights and freedoms are absent, notably the right to privacy, the right to information, property rights, the right to self-government, the right to citizenship, and freedom of movement. Moreover, these rights are frequently expressed in a manner which is self-limiting, while the 1952 constitution failed to safeguard these rights from encroachments by statute

---

4   On this lack of a new constitution in Poland see Ackerman 1992 Ch. 4. For a critical review of Ackerman's book by Richard Posner see Posner 1992 p. 35.

5   For details see e.g. *Heti Világgazdaság*, 10 September 1994, pp. 7–8.

6   The following analysis is based, largely, on the commentary of a senior Polish lawyer who was involved in the drafting of the Bill of Rights. See Osiatynski 1992 p. 29.

or governmental decree. In any event, they remained largely hortatory as they were legally unenforceable.

Thus, while the resistance to the Communist regime throughout the '70s and '80s was inspired, to a significant extent, by a commitment to human rights and, perhaps, by an underlying Polish predisposition towards freedom,[7] the establishment of a democratic political order in Poland has not, as yet, resulted in significant improvements *at the domestic level* to the constitutional protection of human rights. Nevertheless, the transformation process in Poland, as in the other post-Communist states, has been characterised by significant developments in the protection of human rights at the *regional* and *international* levels. Most importantly, Poland ratified the European Convention on Human Rights and Freedoms on 19 January 1993 and accepted the right of individual petition to the European Commission on Human Rights on 1 May 1993.[8]

At the domestic level, however, the two major reforms of the constitutional order in Poland which have been carried out since the transition to democracy, the amendments to the 1952 Constitution of 29 December 1989 and the 'Little Constitution' of October 17, 1992 ('Constitutional Act on the relations between legislative and executive branches of the Republic of Poland and on local self-government'), do not deal with the recognition of rights and freedoms except to a very limited extent. However, some constitutional provisions concerning the relationship between individuals and public authorities, have been changed, notably article 1 of the 1952 Constitution. This provision, in its amended form, states that Poland 'is a democratic state governed by the rule of law and implementing the principles of social justice'. It has been relied upon by the courts in litigation concerning the scope of the largely unchanged provisions of the constitution governing rights and freedoms. In December 1989, an unequivocal constitutional guarantee concerning the protection of property was also introduced: 'The Republic of Poland shall protect ownership and the right of succession and shall guarantee comprehensive protection of personal property. Expropriation may be allowed exclusively for public purposes and against just compensation' (Article 7).[9] However, it may be noted that the protection of private property, while undoubtedly an acknowledged human right,[10] is also an integral part of the process of

---

7 On the significance of this see e.g. the chapter in this volume by Jacek Kurczewski.

8 Information supplied by the Directorate of Human Rights of the Council of Europe, 18 July 1994.

9 On the Round Table Agreement and on the constitutional amendments in 1989 see Garlicki 1990.

10 It is included in the Universal Declaration of Human Rights, for example.

marketization and is of fundamental importance in attracting foreign investment, a matter of particular importance to heavily indebted, capital and technology-deficient states such as Poland and Hungary.

In November 1992, Polish President Lech Walesa submitted the draft Bill of Rights to the Parliament. The text had been largely prepared by members of the Polish Helsinki Committee for Human Rights, although in the final stages legal experts on the staff of the President were involved in the drafting process.[11] An earlier draft had been published in a number of Polish newspapers, and had been the subject of extensive discussion and analysis. In January 1993, the draft Bill of Rights and Freedoms received a first reading in Parliament, after which the matter was transferred to a specially constituted extraordinary commission, the members of which are the 46 deputies from the Lower House who sit in the Constitutional Commission of the National Assembly. In order to secure adoption, the draft, in common with other constitutional amendments, must receive a two-thirds majority in each of the Houses of the Polish Parliament.

The first chapter of the Bill contains three general principles. These are human dignity, which is the source of the specific rights, freedom and equality before law. It should be noted that the chapter also confines the scope of the Bill to relations between individuals and public authorities, thus preventing the horizontal application of the Bill, i.e. to relations between natural persons or between natural and legal persons. Nevertheless, one should not lose sight of the 'revolutionary' character of Chapter One, Article 1.2 which provides that the rights and freedoms enshrined in the Bill are *directly binding* on public authorities. As Osiatynski notes, 'this formulation is revolutionary in Poland, where constitutions have traditionally been perceived as a set of programmatic goals rather than binding laws' (Osiatynski 1992 p. 30). Similarly, another Polish constitutional expert, Andrzej Rapaczynski, has observed that in Poland, as in may other European states, constitutions have traditionally been viewed as (Rapaczynski 1993 p. 93, pp. 104–5):

> primarily symbolic, uniting the people behind certain principles by which the state was morally and politically obliged to be guided, but which did not function as legal norms in the American sense. In particular, though the courts would consider constitutional provisions when interpreting various aspects of the law, traditionally they were not supposed to enforce the Constitution by striking down conflicting normative pronouncements of the political organs of the state. Constitutions set the institutional framework of the state and defined the identity and the aspirations of the people in their sovereign capacity.

---

11 For details see e.g. Osiatynski, op. cit., p. 30.

It is against this background that the importance of Article 1.2 of the draft Bill of Rights should be judged!

Chapter II of the Bill comprises 22 basic civil and political rights. Some of these, such as the right to information, including the right of everyone to have access to any files on them which are held in state offices, or the right to privacy, were not previously recognised in Poland. The right to privacy, as formulated in the draft Bill, also states that 'no one can be made to declare his convictions, ideas, denomination or nationality'. Other projected rights, not previously recognised under Polish law, include freedom of movement, property rights, and the right to engage in free enterprise, as well as the prohibition of the extradition of Polish citizens.[12] It may be noted that the rights set out in this chapter were formulated in accordance with the European Convention on Human Rights and with the International Covenant on Civil and Political Rights. Reliance on such international standards in the drafting of domestic laws concerning human rights has been a common feature of the transformation process in Central and Eastern Europe.

As mentioned previously, the 1952 Polish Constitution contained a broad array of social and economic rights, albeit without enforcement measures. Nevertheless, people in Poland, as in the other former socialist states, came to rely upon such measures of social and economic support by the state, even if they were not in fact justiciable.[13] The omission of social and economic rights from the draft Bill, particularly during a difficult and painful period of economic transition, was not deemed to be politically realistic. However, the economic constraints within which the Polish government was operating also had to be recognised.

Accordingly, the Bill of Rights represents something of a compromise in that it creates two categories of social and economic rights, one of which is enforceable and one of which is not. The former category, contained in Chapter III of the Bill, comprises certain very basic rights and entitlements regarding the right to education (at the elementary level), freedom of employment (in the sense of freedom to choose rather than an actual entitlement to a job), the right to safe working conditions, to medical care (of a very basic kind) and to social security. While the range and content of the rights found in Chapter III is limited, they are nevertheless intended to be justiciable.

The second (non-enforcable) category of social and economic rights are contained in Chapter V which, significantly, is entitled 'Economic, social

---

12 For further details see see e.g. Osiatynski, op. cit., p. 31.
13 For an interesting discussion of this point see e.g. the chapter in this volume by Jacek Kurczewski.

and cultural tasks of public authorities'. The 'rights' found in this chapter include, 'the betterment of working conditions, full employment, aid to families, health care beyond the basic level, education beyond the elementary level, the protection of the cultural heritage, the protection of consumers and of the environment' (Osiatynski 1992 p. 31). Nevertheless, while these 'rights' are not legally enforceable they are intended to be of political and constitutional importance. Nor could these principles simply be ignored by Polish governments. Thus, the Bill provides that: 'The obligations of public authorities described in this chapter cannot be claimed in court. Public authorities shall fulfill them according to economic possibilities. The Council of Ministers and the executive organs of self-government shall submit, along with their yearly reports ... the report on the implementation of tasks described in this chapter and an assessment of the effectiveness of actions undertaken.' (Quoted in Osiatynski 1992 p. 31.)

Provisions regarding the enforcement of the (enforceable) rights and freedoms contained in the Bill are found in Chapter IV. These include recourse to the ordinary courts for the enforcement of specific rights, as well as the right to ask a court for a restraining order before judgment has been given. However, persons may also petition Poland's Constitutional Tribunal for a determination of the constitutionality of a statute or of any other legislative act, or refer the matter to the ombudsman for citizens' rights. As a further expression of the internationalization of the constitutional process, particularly of the recognition and protection of human rights, the Bill states that its norms should be interpreted in conformity with the Universal Declaration of Human Rights and with international treaties ratifed by Poland (Osiatynski 1992 p. 31). However, the reference to the Universal Declaration is perhaps surprising, as this text was not drafted with a view to creating legal (as opposed to moral or political) obligations and is, in international legal terms, a non-binding resolution of the UN General Assembly.[14]

Thus, the Bill 'introduce[s] a dualism in the protection of rights' by permitting recourse to either the Constitutional Tribunal or to the ordinary courts in the case of rights violations (Osiatynski 1992 p. 32). However, it should be borne in mind that these are two entirely different kinds of procedures, as a reference to the Tribunal will be concerned solely with a determination of the constitutionality of a law or other legal measure rather than with a consideration of the merits of an individual case. Where a court may be confronted with a problem about the application of a law whose

---

14 Of course, the argument can be made that the resolution, while originally merely recommendatory, has now acquired the status of customary international law. Its treatment in the draft Polish Bill of Rights would reinforce such a conclusion.

constitutionality has been challenged, it is assumed that the Court will refer the matter to the Constitutional Tribunal for a ruling before giving judgment (Osiatynski 1992 p. 32).

According to the current Polish constitution, the decisions of the Tribunal with respect to the constitutionality of statutes are not final. A statute struck down by the Tribunal returns to the Sejm, which can override the Tribunal's decision by a two-thirds majority. The draft Bill of Rights, if accepted, would thus introduce a distinction between two kinds of constitutional rulings. With respect to rights and freedoms, the Tribunal would have the final say, but with respect to other constitutional matters its decisions would retain only suspensive force. Nevertheless, the Bill would introduce in Poland the supremacy of the constitution over the parliament, at least with regard to fundamental rights and freedoms.

However, parliamentary consideration of the draft Bill of Rights must must now be coordinated with work on a new Constitution, as this process has started again following the passage of a law in April 1992 on the procedure for drafting and adopting a new constitution. Since that time, seven draft constitutions, proposed by different parties and organisations, have been submitted to the Constitutional Committee of the National Assembly. Amongst these is a draft from the President which is intended to operate in conjunction with the draft Bill of Rights. Another of the drafts is a 'public initiative' supported by more than one million citizens whose names have been collected by the trade union 'Solidarity'. (An amendment to the above-mentioned constitutional law on the procedure for preparing and adopting the constitution extended the right to submit draft constitutions to groups of 500,000 citizens and above.) This means that the Presidential draft is now no longer the only proposal dealing with the issue of the constitutional protection of human rights.

II HUNGARIAN FUNDAMENTAL RIGHTS AND THEIR PROTECTION

Amid the frequently stormy political events of 1988–89 in Central and Eastern Europe, Hungary took a decisive and (in contrast to Romania or the former East Germany) entirely peaceful step towards the goal of becoming a constitutional state, a state governed by the rule of law.[15]

According to article 16 of the celebrated French Declaration of the Rights of Man and of the Citizen: 'A society where rights are not guaranteed

---

15 On this process see e.g. Halmai 1990–1991 p. 552–555; Paczolay 1993 Ch. 2.

institutionally ... has no constitution'. In this sense Hungary ceased to be a state possessing a constitution when the 1949 Constitution of the People's Republic, modelled on the 1936 Stalinist Constitution, was adopted by the Hungarian Parliament.[16] This Constitution declared part of the basic citizens' (not human!) rights to be a privilege in the newly-established 'party state', without any possibility of legal enforcement. In a period when, in the Western half of Europe, the rule of law was established in a substantive sense both at the national and at the regional levels, in Hungary even the formal rule of law guaranteeing basic legal procedures was almost entirely undeveloped. Nevertheless, this generalization should not disguise the fact that, in 1972, during the 'socialist' era, the Constitution was amended significantly to give fuller expression to basic rights (albeit of a generally unenforceable nature), while in 1984 a Constitutional Council was created with limited advisory powers.[17]

However, in broad terms, this 'lack of a constitution' continued until the comprehensive amendments to the 1949 Constitution which took effect on the 23rd of October 1989 and which reinstated the Republic in place of the 'People's Republic' of Hungary. These amendments themselves followed, and were the product of, extensive 'Round Table' talks in which the Party participated together with delegates from the major opposition groupings and parties and delegates from certain (supposedly) neutral social bodies and institutions.

The idea of replacing the socialist Constitution was first raised following important personnel changes which took place in May 1988 at the top of the ruling Communist party, i.e. before the transformational process involving oppositional elements had begun. It was thus an initiative of the ruling Communist Party itself which possessed, in contrast to the Communist Parties of the then Czechoslovakia or East Germany, an increasingly influential reformist wing. On 25 August 1988, the Ministerial Council decided that a thorough review of the Constitution should be undertaken and that a Secretariat for the Preparation and Codification of the Constitution should be created (see e.g. Holló 1993 p. 75, *et seq.*). The Secretariat began work on 2 January 1989, while separate working groups were set up to examine specific issues such as fundamental rights. In terms of this latter question, a dilemma arose as to whether the German model was preferable, i.e. a regulatory system of a positive character ('you are allowed to do only what the law specifically allows') or whether the Anglo-

---

16 Of course, the extent to which human rights and constitutionalism were recognised in pre-Communist Hungary should not be exaggerated. See, generally, on this point the chapter in this volume by Istvan Pogany.

17 See e.g. on these developments, Holló 1993 pp. 13–22.

Saxon type of regulation should be followed ('you are allowed to do whatever is not expressly prohibited').

The Party (which was the only one at that time) argued in favour of detailed legal regulations even in cases (e.g. the freedom of assembly) where previously there had been no laws governing the matter at all. Some organizations (called 'alternative' at that time), on the other hand, argued that the detailed legal elaboration of those rights would have a potentially restrictive effect on the recognition of the basic rights in question. In the end, even the opposition did not advocate the idea of a total lack of legal regulation. What it boiled down to was that under the given conditions, when even institutional forms of the rule of law did not exist, a total lack of specific rules governing such rights would neither guarantee nor even facilitate their exercise.

The process of establishing a state governed by the rule of law began with the recodification, enacted in January 1989, of the rights of assembly and of association (see e.g. Halmai 1990 p. 167 *et seq*.). These rights must be understood in the context of the extremely rapid regeneration of civil society in Hungary at that time. Similarly to what Habermas wrote about the emergence of civil society in Europe, at first it was nothing more than non-political gatherings and associations, where one could spend one's leisure time. Later on, however – similarly to the 18th century transformation of political society – there was an increasing need for political meetings and demonstrations as well as for establishing trade and overtly political unions (See Halmai 1991).

This development, of course, made it necessary to conceive of the rights of assembly and association in a radically new manner; a conception not limiting these rights to politically neutral programs, festival marches, or the possibility of setting up associations (e.g. for stamp collecting), but including the freedom to conduct antigovernment demonstrations, to establish political parties and to create coalitions.

In March 1989, the Opposition Round Table (henceforth ORT) was formed by opposition groupings who wanted to concert their strategies with a view to reaching an agreement with the Communist Party about the contents of the so-called fundamental laws that should guide the democratic transition in Hungary.

In the subsequent tripartite Round Table talks, which began in June 1989, the opposition groupings and representatives of the ruling Communist Party were joined by a third negotiating partner, delegates from various social organizations which had, throughout the socialist era, been subject to overview by the Party. These talks concluded in mid-September with agreement on six bills of constitutional significance that would be presented to Parliament.   These bills dealt, respectively, with the proposed Constitutional Court, with the operating and financing of political parties, with the election of Members of Parliament, with the Penal Code and with criminal procedure.   However, the most significant, without any doubt, contained major revisions of the 1949 'Soviet-type' Constitution, pending the adoption of a new Constitution which was to be enacted by the first democratically elected, post-Communist Parliament.   Elections were scheduled for the spring of 1990.

According to the preamble of the considerably amended Constitution, which was approved during the course of the Round Table talks and which was adopted by Parliament on 18 October 1989, the revisions were necessary 'in order to promote the peaceful political transition to the rule of law realizing the multiparty system, parliamentary democracy and a social market economy'.

The intention of distancing the revised constitution, and the political process of which it was an expression, from the socialist era that existed for the previous forty years, is apparent in Article 1 of the amended Constitution, which proclaims that Hungary is a republic.   With this, Hungarian constitution-making has reverted to a number of legal principles incorporated in Act I of 1946, on the form of the state in Hungary, which had been adopted by the National Assembly which was formed after the first free elections to be held after World War II.[18]

Article 2 of the amended Constitution states the following about the basic structural principles characterizing the new Hungarian Republic: 'The Hungarian Republic is an independent, democratic state governed by the rule of law'.[19] This wording replaced the earlier provisions of the Constitution which had stated that Hungary was a socialist state.

There was no longer any doubt at the start of the tripartite Round Table talks that paragraph 3 of the 1949 Constitution, which had declared the leading role of the Marxist-Leninist party of the working class, would be replaced by a provision guaranteeing the freedom to establish political parties.   According to Article 3(1) of the revised text, 'parties in the Hungarian Republic can be freely formed and can freely operate provided they respect the Constitution and constitutional laws'.   The Ministerial explanation which accompanied this draft amendment stated that even if such parties advocated in their manifestos a political direction contrary to socialist development, this could not prevent them from being registered

---

18 On the historical and political background of constitution-making in Hungary see Paczolay op. cit., Ch. 2.

19 'State governed by the rule of law' is a somewhat infelicitous translation of the Hungarian 'jogállam' which corresponds to the German 'Rechtsstaat'.

and from functioning. Subsection 2 of Article 3 states as a basic task of the parties, the formation and articulation of the will of the people. Subsection 3 – in order to avoid the emergence of another 'party state' – prohibits parties from exercising public power directly and from running any type of state organ. However, it is the rules of incompatibility that are destined to separate parties and public power. These rules can be found – as in the case of judges and justices of the Constitutional Court – in other chapters of the Constitution and in the law on parties. Thus, Article 20(5) of the revised Constitution sets out those official positions which a parliamentary deputy cannot occupy, while noting that statutes may establish additional cases of incompatibility.

During preparatory work on the amendments to the Constitution, the Opposition Round Table proposed that changes to the structure of the Constitution should reflect the belief that human rights are henceforth to be regarded as basic values. According to this conception, such rights are not privileges granted by the state in the exercise of its discretion but – on the contrary – they are the very limits of state power. According to the Opposition Round Table, it was still acceptable that rights which were 'secured' by the state should be put in a chapter *after* a chapter dealing with the organs of the state. However, basic rights, which limited state power, should *precede* those parts of the constitution dealing with state organs. In the end, however, the view which was supported by the Hungarian Socialist Workers' Party (henceforth: HSWP) and by the third negotiating party in the tripartite talks prevailed. This was that such a modification of the very order of the subjects dealt with in the Constitution was not permissible because it would have gone beyond a simple amendment of the Constitution.

At the same time – as proposed by the Opposition Round Table – the amended text of the Constitution includes among its general provisions in Chapter 1 the principle that, 'the Hungarian Republic recognizes the inviolable and inalienable rights of man, and that their respectful observance and protection is the first and foremost duty of the state' (Article 8(1)). This human rights approach replaces the earlier 'socialist conception' of rights characterized by three types of restrictions which annulled their very essence.

The first type of restrictions were when rights could only be exercised in the interests of the Socialist system. In the constitutions of the various socialist countries, this was phrased differently. However, the values which had to be defended included Socialism, society, the people, the community, the state etc. But in every case, behind all these values stood the interests of the Party which was in power. Another typical form of restriction made the exercise of the rights dependent on the citizen satisfying his constitutional obligations. The third type of restriction can be summed up by saying that those rights which were not guaranteed legally in the constitutions were not recognised as human rights at all. In the first period of Socialist constitution-drafting, only the workers were recognised as possessing rights. Even after other social categories were given the same rights, the basic rights contained in most of these constitutions were still exclusively the rights of the citizens of the given state. By using phrases to the effect that the rights were 'ensured' by the state, the constitutions reflected the typical Socialist attitude according to which basic rights are not limits upon state power; on the contrary, they are merely benefits which may be allocated by the state in accordance with its discretion. According to this peculiar form of Socialist legal positivism, the regulations in the constitutions governing rights and fundamental freedoms did not have to satisfy any moral obligations. At all times the 'basic laws' were considered those ephemeral laws which were 'ensured' at a particular moment.

Having placed Hungary on the path of constitutionality, the comprehensive constitutional amendments which were enacted in 1989 stated that any restrictions in the exercise of the basic rights could only be introduced by so-called constitutional laws adopted by a qualified majority in Parliament, and with a view to protecting national security, internal order, social security, social health, social morals and other people's basic rights and freedoms.

In the spring of 1990, as a result of a pact between the largest government and opposition parties, restrictions reminiscent of those found in certain international human rights agreements were omitted from the modified Constitution; in their place it was decided to insert a formulation found in the German Basic Law prohibiting the restriction by law of the essential content of the human rights. According to the Hungarian constitutional system, the Constitutional Court is authorized to intepret the scope of the basic rights found in the Constitution.

The Constitutional Court and the very idea of judicial review were previously unknown in the Hungarian constitutional tradition. The most important features of the court's jurisdiction are the authority to review acts of Parliament and other legal rules, the authority to review unconstitutional omissions by the legislature, and the authority to hear so-called 'constitutional complaints' alleging the violation of an individual's constitutional rights as the result of the application of an unconstitutional law. The decision of the Constitutional Court is final and without appeal and is binding on everyone. If the Court finds a legal norm unconstitutional, it declares it wholly or partly null and void.

In order that legislative restrictions on basic rights should not become autocratic, the Constitutional Court has stated that the following conditions must be met. In order to introduce a restriction there must be some very strong compelling reason, such as the enforcement of another basic right. This objective must be proportionate to the injury to the basic right brought about by its restriction. The legal restriction must be adequate for attaining its objective. At the same time, the legislation must embody the mildest of the possible restrictions necessary for accomplishing the intended objective. These principles can be seen most clearly in a decision of the Constitutional Court (20/1990. X.4.), in which the Court abrogated a provision in a law which compelled the leaders of parties and of social organizations to provide information about the extent of their personal assets. The court declared that this statutory provision was against the Constitution because it restricted the essential contents of the right to protect one's private secrets and personal data. Similar to this concept is the scholarly opinion that the restriction of our rights is in itself autocratic if all four of the following criteria are not met: the restriction must have an equally important, rational motive; the restriction must be relevant from the point of view of the motive; the restriction must be necessary for all means; the restriction must be proportionate.

From the viewpoint of guaranteeing fundamental rights the introduction of the Constitutional Court is of outstanding significance in Hungarian constitutional practice. In the event of the violation of one's rights as guaranteed in the Constitution, one can directly turn to the Court if the violation was due to the application of an unconstitutional legal rule.[20]

The amended Constitution also introduced the institution of the 'ombudsman', which is of Scandinavian origin and which was previously unknown in the Hungarian legal system. It is the duty of this official, who is responsible for citizens' rights, to investigate irregularities in connection with procedures concerning constitutional rights, or to get them investigated, and to take measures to remedy them. Anyone can ask the ombudsman to act on his behalf. The text of the Constitution makes it also possible to elect a special parliamentary official, besides the ombudsman, who has general powers and duties – to protect particular constitutional rights, such as the protection of minorities, the environment, data, consumers, etc. Unfortunately, Parliament has not yet elected an ombudsman or special officials of the type described above.

---

[20] On judicial review by the Hungarian Constitutional Court see Klinsberg 1992 pp. 41–144.

As I have already mentioned, those participating in the tripartite Round Table Talks agreed upon the extensive amendments to the Constitution, and also to certain draft statutes dealing with major issues (these latter laws were termed 'fundamental' by the Opposition Round Table) – which were also instrumental in effecting the democratic transition. Among these 'fundamental' statutes were laws on the operation and financing of parties and on the election of Members of Parliament.

As a result of the tripartite talks, and following a proposal to this effect by the ORT, the bill on political parties only dealt with the operation and financing of such parties. By contrast, the original draft had contained special rules about establishing, registering and supervising political parties as well.

As regards the operation of political parties, the most heated debate was sparked off by the issue of what should happen to party cells in factories and offices. During the tripartite Round Table talks, the HSWP only wanted to ban the establishment and operation of party cells in the Constitutional Court, in other courts, in the administrative offices of Parliament and of the President of the Republic, in the State Audit Office, and in the prosecutors' offices, in the organs of state administration, in the armed forces and in the police. In offices other than the above, as well as in factories, the HSWP did not support the view that all parties should dispose of their cells as long as they observed the following restrictions: that during office hours they should not perform any political activity, that parties should not be incorporated into the administrative system of the office, and that parties should not control any important professional decisions taken by the office. This position was not modified by the Hungarian Socialist Party, which was established as the successor of the HSWP in early October of 1989. The ORT, on the other hand, argued in favour of a general ban on party cells in order to make offices free of politics.

In the end the negotiating parties involved in the tripartite talks agreed to submit both proposals to Parliament. With an overwhelming majority, Parliament ruled that all party cells should be abolished no later than 90 days prior to the forthcoming general elections. Career soldiers and policemen were also banned by law from occupying leading positions in the political parties.

On the road towards democracy it was essential to transform the system of representation and electoral law according to the requirements of pluralism. The political mechanism of the one party system had been based almost totally on the principle of regional representation. The individual constituency system best suited this purpose.

However, the law shaped during the tripartite Round Table talks and adopted by Parliament in October 1989 introduced a mixed electoral system aiming at achieving proportional representation. Under this system one can get a seat in Parliament in three different ways:

1. In an individual constituency with an absolute majority of the votes achieved in the first round or a relative majority in the second round. In constituencies, citizens and social organizations have the right to nominate candidates if they meet the requirements of the law on parties, i.e. that they are registered members of a party. A nominee needs at least 750 signatures of support.
2. Candidates on the fixed lists of the parties in the different counties and in the capital may be elected in proportion to the votes cast. Regional lists are fielded by parties that nominated candidates in one quarter of all the constituencies in the given county or in the capital, or in at least two constituencies. No seats are awarded, however, to candidates on the regional lists of parties that did not attain more than five per cent of the valid votes cast nationally for the regional lists. This clause received fierce attacks from some smaller parties that could not find a seat at the '(round) table of law'.
3. Finally, seats can be awarded to those on the national lists of parties on the basis of wasted votes cast in constituencies or for regional lists. National lists can be fielded by a party that had a list in at least seven out of the 20 regional constituencies (19 counties and the capital). However, wasted votes cast for regional lists or in individual constituencies are, of course, only taken into consideration if the candidates for whom these votes were cast belonged to a party. Thus, these constituencies are based on parties as well as on individual candidates.

The constitutional developments that occurred in both Poland and Hungary in 1989, as outlined above, were aimed at the restoration of the constitutional state governed by the rule of law. However, this process cannot be regarded as complete.

It seems that many Eastern European governments, attracted by traditional 20th century étatism, have not only failed to dismantle over-strong governments but have actually tried to strengthen them with the help of 'new–old' ideologies.

This tendency can also be felt in Poland and Hungary and is indicative of the attitude of the political leadership i.e. that democracy comes before a political constitutionalism based unconditionally on Human Rights. The same attitude is behind the idea that parliamentarianism may be equated with unrestricted parliamentary sovereignty. This is why there have been attempts to remove certain institutions of constitutionality which could guarantee the existence of political and civil rights. The majority vote cast during elections is the rather trite concept behind this idea of an omnipotent parliament and underlying this notion of democracy.[21] This conscrvative attitude could be seen, for instance, in Hungary when parliamentary deputies attacked the Constitutional Court for daring to characterise a politically important law, which had been voted for by a majority in Parliament, as unconstitutional. (See e.g. the Compensation Law or the Law concerning the right to prosecute serious criminal offenses committed between December 21, 1944 and May 2, 1990 that had not been prosecuted for political reasons.)

European history has shown some sad examples of the consequences of sacrificing rights and freedom on the altar of democracy. In the concept of freedom expounded by Rousseau in the 'Social Contract', the freedom of the citizen of the republic can only mean agreeing to the wish of the public (volonté générale). In order to enforce this, the executive power has the right to interfere in every way with the lives of the citizens. The 6th and 3rd paragraphs of the Declaration of the Rights of Man and of the Citizen (of 26 August 1789), are based on Rousseau's concept: 'Law is the expression of the public will' and that 'The nation is the source of sovereignty. No association or person may exercise power which does not originate from this.' In my opinion, even the already mentioned and frequently quoted 16th paragraph of the Declaration ('A society where rights are not guaranteed institutionally ... has no constitution') can only be understood as meaning that the 'guarantee' of rights does not mean that the government cannot interfere in the individual's life. This is hinted at in Benjamin Constant's criticism of Rousseau's antique concept of freedom, according to which a democracy may get rid of an oligarchy, of a privileged person or of a group of people, but may still rule as mercilessly over individuals as a previous ruler would have done. Therefore, argues Constant, the principal question is not in whose hands lies the power, but in how much power resides in one person or body. John Stuart Mill's caution, in his famous work 'On Liberty', is similar to Constant's observation: the tyranny of the majority can ruin the sovereignty of the individual because rule by the people does not necessarily mean freedom; it does not exclude the possibility of the tyranny of the majority, of the prevailing feelings and opinions.[22]

---

[21] For a critique of this majoritarian concept see Habermas 1992b and Arato 1994.

[22] The expression 'tyranny of the majority' is taken from the already mentioned work of Tocqueville.

The Jacobinus French constitution, which is associated with Robespierre and which is based on Rousseau's ideals is 'only' democratic; and by equating the revolutionary government with the power of the people, it finally results in an autocratic restriction of the personal freedoms of the citizens.

The Weimar era, when democracy was considered everything and was constitutionalized, nevertheless finally allowed Hitler to come to power. It can also be described as a period when the people could decide anything, even the elimination of democracy. But we do not even have to go so far back, since the socialist constitutions of the last four decades – including the Hungarian one – were all based on the concept of unrestricted parliamentary sovereignty, of course without such sovereignty ever having been real.

There is no doubt that the balance between democracy and constitutionality can also be overturned if the legal system is reduced to one single value. This idea is characteristic of the 19th century German concept of the constitutional state, described by Laband as follows: 'Justice is what Law is. Law is what has been pronounced during formally correct procedures' (Laband 1876–1882 p. 63). This formal approach to the constitutional state obviously creates dangers for democracy. However, this danger is presently slight in Poland and Hungary and many of the other countries of the region.

Nevertheless, it is especially important for the governments of the Central and Eastern European countries to take Isaiah Berlin's caution, given in 1958, very seriously: the rule of the majority leaves little scope for individual freedoms; democracy, as such, is not tied to it logically. That is, the concept of individual freedoms, as an essential part of constitutionality, should not be pushed into the background of democracy.

This makes it important to build a constitutional structure in which the legal system guarantees the citizens, and others living in the territory of the country, their basic rights, in such a way that at the same time it restricts interferences by state power (including by parliament) into an individual's rights. In other words, this is a legal system which allows the citizens to do everything apart from what has been proscribed by laws encated in accordance with a proper legal process. In contrast, government bodies should only be permitted to do what has been actually allowed to them by laws. The goal of constitutionality as described here is to ensure individual freedoms. The most important way of achieving this is to believe in the power of Laws and of legal institutions, since all states which consider themselves constitutional must abide by the principle that everybody, including the legislature and the judiciary, are bound by the law.

On the other hand, the Hungarian legal philosopher Barna Horváth, who left for New York in 1949 when the Constitution of the Hungarian party-state was adopted, astutely summed up both the noble potentialities and limitations of law in the process of democratic transformation: 'It is the most wonderful task of lawyers to seek new techniques of democracy ... The limits of the performance of law warn us that one cannot expect law alone to realize democracy. Law can always provide only a frame, patterns, ways and methods, [law can only] carve the bed of the river.'[23]

---

23 Barna Horváth: 'Demokrácia és jog' ('Democracy and Law'). A lecture. First published by the Budapest University in 1945, later in *Medvetánc*, 2–3/1985 p. 320.

8. Human Rights: A Matter of Individual or Collective Concern?

Gábor Kardos[1]

I INTRODUCTION

The collapse of Soviet-type social and political systems in Eastern and Central Europe has significantly changed the agenda of international human rights debates. Issues related to the previously chronic East–West division over human rights have become obsolete. Economic, social and cultural rights are no longer championed by the states of Eastern and Central Europe, while these countries now participate in multilateral human rights conventions permitting individual complaints to international organs. As far as civil and political rights are concerned, the Western approach is now the only one that is recognised, as the rapid extension of the European Convention of Human Rights to Eastern and Central Europe illustrates.

The change in *the social role of law* presents a unique possibility for the 'socialisation' of human rights in the countries of Eastern and Central Europe. Formerly, in most of the countries in the region, human rights represented no more than empty declarations, having very little connection with reality. Therefore, for the governments concerned, there was little at risk if, in certain instances, such rights were phrased broadly. The rights would remain on paper only. However, as a result of the change in the political system brought about by the collapse of the communist regimes in 1989/90, the law is beginning to fulfil its social function. Today, the content of human rights legislation is no longer irrelevant in terms of actual political and social practice. Laws touching on certain human rights, an obvious example is the law on abortion, can provoke real social debate during the legislative process.

---

[1] This paper has been prepared in the context of a NATO Fellowship Programme.

However, *the manifest lack of a human rights culture* in the countries of
Central and Eastern Europe has unfortunately arrested this positive
development to a significant extent. As noted previously, during the
communist era, human rights represented little more than hortatory
declarations by the power elite. At the same time, political dissidents in
Eastern and Central Europe construed these declarations as if they
expressed genuine legal rights, or even tried to act as though such rights
truly existed. Today, at least in some countries in the region, human rights
are guaranteed by a framework of laws. In such states, the problem lies not
in the legal or political recognition of human rights themselves but in their
day to day enforcement. *People are not accustomed to having recourse to
the law as a means of protecting their human rights*, although this would be
entirely natural to them in other matters, such as disputes over the
inheritance of property. There is *an absence of test cases being pursued
through the courts*, while *the multi-party system has absorbed, and partly
factionalized*, a large part of the human rights movement. In the midst of the
disintegration of civil societies, all these manifestations can be taken as a
matter of course. However, they are clearly detrimental in terms of the
protection of human rights.

The prospect of a forty party European Convention on Human Rights
could prompt structural or other changes in this system. For example, new
human rights themes could become dominant. The freedom of the press and
the protection of national, ethnic and religious minorities are prominent
examples of issues which could become increasingly important in the future
(see Kay, 1993 p. 221).

A lot of effort has been expended to elaborate a new protocol to the
European Convention on Human Rights on the rights of national
minorities.[2] The UN has also given significant attention to this question, as
the General Assembly's Declaration on the Rights of Persons Belonging to
National or Ethnic, Religious and Linguistic Minorities, demonstrates.[3] The
UN Secretary-General's report, 'An Agenda For Peace', also underlines the
importance of the protection of minorities:

> Yet if every ethnic, religious or linguistic group claimed statehood, there would be no
> limit to fragmentation, and peace, security and economic well-being for all would become
> ever more difficult ... One requirement for solutions to these problems lies in commitment
> to human rights with a special sensitivity to those of minorities, whether ethnic, religious,
> social or linguistic. (*'An Agenda For Peace'*, UN doc. A/47/277 (1992))

---

2 See, first of all, Parliamentary Assembly of the Council of Europe, Forty-Fourth
   Ordinary Session, Recommendation 1201 (1993) on an additional protocol on the rights
   of national minorities to the European Convention on Human Rights.
3 UN General Assembly resolution 47/135 of 18 December 1992.

With this strong emphasis on the protection of minorities, the familiar debate over individual *versus* collective rights has gained a fresh impetus. Moreover, this apparently theoretical discussion has important political implications. Would the recognition of the collective rights of minorities lead to the resolution of ethnic conflicts in Eastern and Central Europe or, as most observers think, is the opposite true? Would the recognition of the rights of minorities merely feed the fires of nationalism?

II THE COLLECTIVE DIMENSION OF INDIVIDUAL RIGHTS

A strong objection to collective rights stems from security considerations. Robert Cullen in 'the Advice for President Clinton' issue of *Foreign Affairs* expresses this widely shared view:

> Now that the artificial order of Soviet power has vanished, the unbridled assertion of collective rights, most often expressed as an aspiration to national self-determination, has become a major threat to global stability. (Cullen 1992–3 p. 79)

Later on the author enumerates those *individual* rights which are 'pillars of the American democracy' and which the US should support through her foreign policy: freedom of religion, freedom of speech and press, freedom to travel and settle wherever one's means will allow and freedom from discrimination (Cullen 1992–3 pp. 82–3).

If one were to analyze carefully the individual rights listed above, particularly the first two rights, one could not avoid the conclusion that even these rights have a collective dimension. In a society which consists of related not isolated individuals, the repeated exercise of *individual* rights has the consequence that *collective* actions occur, and that social institutions are created whose existence cannot be separated from the very essence of these rights. Perhaps the best illustration of this is the freedom of religion, whose collective dimension is expressly recognised, for example, in Article 9(1) of the European Convention on Human Rights:

> Everyone has the right to freedom of thought, conscience and religion, this right includes freedom to change his religion or belief and freedom, either alone or in community with others and in public or private, to manifest his religion or belief, in worship, teaching, practice and observance.

The social institution which is associated with the freedom of religion is, of course, the church. Indeed, 'the entire functioning of churches depends on respect for this right' (van Dijk and van Hoof, 1990 p. 405). The European

Commission on Human Rights clearly recognised this fact in its report in the case of *Pastor X and the Church of Scientology*, where it stated that:

a church body is capable of possessing and exercising the rights contained in Article 9(1) in its own capacity as a representative of its members.[4]

As far as freedom of expression is concerned this right could hardly function without the freedom of the press, radio, television, cinema, etc. to work without interference by public authorities because, in modern societies, these institutions are responsible for the dissemination of information on a massive scale. Freedom of expression concerns, in part, the *content* of the opinion that is expressed. However, this right should logically protect the *means* of expression as well (van Dijk and van Hoof, 1990 p. 407). These means, i.e. the press and the electronic media, are social institutions whose rights must be protected as an essential part of the freedom of expression.[5] The European Court of Human Rights has not yet gone this far. However, in the *Müller* case the Court stated that the Convention protects a person who has provided the means to express an opinion, although he has not been the holder of the opinion himself.[6] It is true that the recognition of the provider's rights preserves the *individual* character of freedom of expression. However, it is also true that the protection given to the person who furnished the means to express an opinion amounts to indirect protection for the means themselves, which are generally corporate bodies rather than natural persons.

In the case of discrimination, the collective dimension is obvious. Discrimination generally takes place because somebody belongs to a racial, political, social or linguistic community. Consequently, in most cases, discrimination presupposes the existence of a minority community and the victim's membership of that group. Furthermore, the victims of discrimination can be either individuals or groups of individuals, as recognised for example in Article 14(1) of the Convention on the Elimination of All Forms of Racial Discrimination, which provides that, '[a] State Party may at any time declare that it recognises the competence of the Committee to receive and consider communications from individuals or

---

4   Appl. 7805/77, *Pastor X and the Church of Scientology v. Sweden*, as quoted in van Dijk, van Hoof 1990 p. 405.

5   This conclusion has been reinforced by the Hungarian 'media-war' over public service radio and television (1991–3). For an analysis of the decisions of the Constitutional Court in the 'media war' see Arato 1994 p. 3.

6   Judgment of 24 May 1988, E.C.H.R. Series A., Vol. 133 (1988) p. 19.

groups of individuals'.[7] Against the most extreme form of discrimination, the denial of a group's right to existence, the Genocide Convention protects groups themselves. In 1948, when the text of the Genocide Convention was adopted by the UN General Assembly,[8] one might have been forgiven for thinking that this treaty was a 'backward looking' agreement which had little relevance to the future. Unfortunately, just the opposite has proved to be true. Genocide has occurred in many places in the world, from East Timor to the former Yugoslavia, while the targets have generally been ethnic groups. Tibor Várady, an ethnic Hungarian and a professor of international law, served as Minister of Justice in the Panic government of the 'small' Yugoslavia. He correctly observed that:

> During the ongoing conflicts in the former Yugoslavia and in certain parts of the former Soviet Union, real or imaginary atrocities are being ascribed to ethnic collectivities, and vengeance is also aimed at ethnic groups. ... It is abundantly clear that the *targeted victims are precisely minority groups*, rather than citizens as individuals. *One cannot have a viable system of protection while ignoring the target of the attack.* (Várady, Tibor 1993 p. 10)

Consequently, Robert Cullen has not furnished the best examples of truly individual rights. Even the freedom to travel has a collective dimension and has produced social institutions such as travel agencies. Of course, the importance of such commercial institutions, in terms of fundamental human rights, is not comparable with that of the churches in the context of freedom of religion.

As we have seen, the collective dimension of individual rights has a specific form when the right-holder is a member of a community. In such cases, an individually held right implies a special status for every person who is a member of a certain group (Lindholm 1991 pp. 94–5). Such rights are enshrined in Article 27 of the International Covenant on Civil and Political Rights: 'persons belonging to such minorities shall not be denied the right, in community with the other members of their group, to enjoy their own culture, to profess and practise their own religion, or to use their own language.' As far as such minority rights are concerned, a good example to illustrate the interdependence of the individual and collective elements is the right to use one's own language, especially the right to be educated in one's own language. If the minority community is poor and not able to maintain its own schools the general educational system should

---

[7] For the text of the Convention, which entered into force on 4 Jan. 1969, see e.g. *Human Rights: A Compilation of International Instruments* (1988), UN Doc. ST/HR/1/Rev. 3, p. 56 (hereafter cited as '*Human Rights*').

[8] For the text of the Convention on the Prevention and Punishment of the Crime of Genocide see e.g. ibid., p. 143.

satisfy this need. The need is *individual*, but a minimum number is required in order to arrange a specific class having minority language instruction or to establish a separate school for this purpose. Consequently, the implementation of a person's right to study in his own language within the educational system cannot be done individually. There is an analogy with the right to freedom of association; to establish an association obviously requires more than one individual. In Hungary, for example, ten persons are needed to form an association. Furthermore, the free operation of an association cannot be separated from the right of its members to freedom of association, just as the enjoyment of the right to study in one's own language cannot be separated from the existence and undisturbed work of minority schools.

However, it should be emphasised that the collective dimension of individual rights, touched upon in the previous pages, does *not* lead to two things. It never removes the individual's right to have recourse to the courts in defence of the given right. Nor does it divide the right into two parts, producing separate rights for the individual and for the collectivity. Of course, it is possible to confer separate rights on a collectivity, but this is a different matter. According to Pieter van Dijk and G.J.H. van Hoof, a church has its own right to manifest its religion, which is separate from the rights of the believers (van Dijk and van Hoof, 1990 p. 405). This would mean the recognition of a collective right, a right held by a collective entity. Additionally, certain rights are reserved exclusively to a collective subject. This is true, for example, of self-determination which belongs to peoples rather than to individuals. Thus, common Article 1 of the UN Covenants on Civil and Political Rights and Economic, Social and Cultural Rights states that, '[a]ll peoples have the right of self-determination'.[9]

III THE PROBLEM OF COLLECTIVE SUBJECTS

When a community is the subject of rights, this gives rise to a host of problems. In certain cases, it may be difficult to decide whether a community exists or not. Another important issue is that of representation: who can claim the right to act on behalf of a community? A logical answer to this second question is that a corporate body established by the community itself can do so. This answer leads to further knotty problems which must be resolved. How should one proceed if the community has more than one such organisation? Even if there is only one representative

---

[9] For the texts of the Covenants see *Human Rights*, op. cit., pp. 7, 18.

body, how can one ensure that democratic processes are observed *within* the corporate entity? Other questions also present themselves – how can one establish the boundaries of a community? Who is entitled to claim membership of a community? How can one avoid members of a community having to register their minority affiliation? This is particularly important in Eastern and Central Europe because of the long shadow of the past. Millions of people were persecuted or killed during the course of this century in Eastern and Central Europe because they openly belonged to a particular community. Jews and Gypsies were notable victims of the Nazis and their allies during and immediately before the Second World War. However, ethnic Germans and Hungarians were subject to systematic persecution in certain states in the region immediately after the War.[10] Thus, hard questions must be answered.[11]

As far as the existence of a community is concerned, the Permanent Court of International Justice elaborated the concept in the *Greco-Bulgarian Communities* case:

> By tradition ... the 'community' is a group of persons living in a given country or locality, having a race, religion, language and traditions of their own and united by this identity of race, religion, language and traditions in a sentiment of solidarity, with a view to preserving their traditions, maintaining their form of worship, ensuring the instruction and upbringing of their children in accordance with the spirit and traditions of their race and rendering mutual assistance to one another.[12]

In the *Lovelace* case, the UN Human Rights Committee set out certain principles in connection with the boundaries of an ethnic community. As far as a Canadian woman's membership of an Indian tribe was concerned, for the purposes of Article 27 of the International Covenant on Civil and Political Rights, the Committee stated:

---

[10] These successive 'waves' of persecution are examined in Pogany 1996, forthcoming.

[11] During the preparation of the recent Hungarian Act on the Rights of Minorities all of these problems emerged. The Act, which was passed in 1993, tried to provide answers to these questions. The Act includes a list of minorities; however one thousand people can claim that they constitute a minority. Each minority can have only one national representative body and complicated rules exist to guarantee the internal democracy of such representative bodies and to protect the anonymity of those who have registered themselves as members of a minority. The result is an intricate construction of norms and, at the time of writing, the minority associations have not yet come into existence.

[12] Advisory Opinion of 31 July 1930 in the *Greco-Bulgarian Communities* case, P.C.I.J., Ser. B, No. 17, p.21.

Persons who are born and brought up on a reserve, who kept ties with their community and wish to maintain these ties must normally be considered as belonging to that minority ...[13]

Consequently, the conditions to be taken into account are the following: birth, upbringing, ties with the community and the intention to maintain them. However, 'normally' suggests these criteria are not absolute (Thornberry 1993 p. 21). The principles set out by the Human Rights Committee can also be regarded as a clarification of the findings of the Permanent Court of International Justice in the *Rights of Minorities in Upper Silesia* case, where the Court stated:

the question whether a person does or does not belong to a racial, linguistic or religious minority ... is a question of fact and not solely one of intention.[14]

A further problem arising from collective rights is the fear that the rights of a collective subject may overshadow the rights of natural persons and that organisations exercising collective rights may take certain decisions instead of (but ostensibly on behalf of) individuals. Furthermore, such bodies may make their decisions on the basis of political abstractions. As Paul Sieghart suggests:

If any of the individual rights and freedoms protected by modern international human rights law ever came to be regarded as subservient to the right of a 'people' ... there would be a very real risk that legitimacy might be claimed on such a ground for grave violations of the human rights of individuals. (Sieghart 1983 p. 368)

I think Sieghart has a point; political abstractions can endanger individual rights, especially in those countries where the conditions securing the existence of human rights as positive law are missing. Besides, the realisation of these individual rights could never depend on the rights of a collective subject. It is clear that it is *political* abstractions which are truly dangerous. However, we should not lose sight of the fact that *legal* abstractions can serve as a basis for the restriction of individual rights, such as the highly debated public order (*ordre public*) concept, and other recognised legal qualifications on the exercise of individual rights (Triggs 1988 p. 144). In summary, a partial way out of this dilemma is the legalization of political abstractions. However, this solution brings us back to certain problems which have already been raised, especially the problem of who can claim the right to act on behalf of a community?

---

[13] Human Rights Committee, *Selected Decisions Under the Optional Protocol* (2nd to 16th session) UN Doc. CCPR/C/OP/1. Views of the Human Rights Committee, para 14.

[14] P.C.I.J., Ser. A, No. 15, p. 32.

IV THE RIGHT TO SELF-DETERMINATION

Self-determination is one of the leading political ideas of the twentieth century.[15] It has led to the fall of empires three times in our age – after the First World War, in the case of the Austro-Hungarian and the Russian Tzarist empires, after the Second World War, with the gradual dismantling of the British, French and other colonial empires and, finally, with the ending of the Cold War and of the bipolar world system, the dissolution of the Soviet empire. As we have seen from the quotation taken from the UN Secretary General's report, ethnic conflicts are occurring in many parts of the world today, particularly in Eastern and Central Europe, giving rise to a further problem of international relations wherever a people claims not only the right to democratic governance but independent statehood as well. Consequently, states interested in preserving their territorial integrity usually prefer to restrict the *right* of all peoples to self-determination, even if this is at the expense of democratic governance. It should be understood here that democratic governance means not merely majority rule but rather a political system which, while responsive to the wishes of electors, can also accommodate the rights of minorities.

A tactic applied by the international community, notably in the context of the United Nations, has been to restrict the right of self-determination to colonial situations and to foreign rule. This approach has been elaborated by Hector Gross-Espiell:

> The United Nations has established the right to self-determination as a right of peoples under colonial and alien domination. The right does not apply to peoples already organized in the form of a state which are not under colonial and alien domination, since resolution 1514 (XV) and other United Nations instruments condemn any attempt aimed at the partial or total disruption of the national unity and the territorial integrity of a country. If, however beneath the guise of ostensible national unity, colonial and alien domination does in fact exist, whatever legal formula may be used in an attempt to conceal it, the right of the subject people concerned cannot be disregarded without international law being violated. (Gross-Espiell 1980 p. 10)

The last sentence in this quotation is very important because it opens up the possibility of regarding the 'refolutions' (reform + revolution, an expression of Timothy Garton Ash) of Eastern and Central Europe, even under this restrictive view of self-determination, as a genuine exercise of this right. J.E.S. Fawcett has already interpreted the Hungarian revolution of 1956 in this way (Fawcett 1971 p. 44). Furthermore, this type of legal characterisation of the dramatic events of 1989 in Eastern and Central Europe can be deduced indirectly from the reports submitted by the

---

[15] For a recent analysis see e.g. Koskenniemi 1994 p. 241.

socialist states to the Human Rights Committee, pursuant to Article 40 of
the International Covenant on Civil and Political Rights. For example,
Bulgaria declared:

> The existence of the People's Republic of Bulgaria as an independent State and its
> progress along the path of socialism and communism demonstrate the continuing exercise
> by the Bulgarian people of their right to self-determination in all its forms.[16]

Since progress down the road of socialism and communism was regarded as
the exercise of the right to self-determination, the events which marked a
deviation from this path cannot be interpreted differently. In other words,
the collective choice of peoples, at each stage and irrespective of the
content of that political choice, represents the exercise of the right of self-
determination.

Another tactic which has been employed to restrict the scope of self-
determination has been to equate a subject people with the population of a
state. This is the final result of applying those objective criteria used by
Aureliu Cristescu:

> (a) The term, 'people' denotes a social entity possessing a clear identity and its own
> characteristics,
> (b) It implies a relationship with a territory, even if the people in question has been
> wrongfully expelled from it and artificially replaced by another population.
> (c) A people should not be confused with ethnic, religious or linguistic minorities, whose
> existence and rights are recognized in Article 27 of the International Covenant on Civil
> and Political Rights. (Cristescu 1981 p. 41)

As far as the first restrictive formulation of self-determination is concerned,
to confine the right of self-determination to colonial situations and to
foreign rule is clearly contrary to common Article 1 of the two UN human
rights covenants which state: 'All peoples have the right to self-
determination.' The second of the above-mentioned restrictive
formulations, which refers to the inclusion of all peoples living on a defined
territory in the democratic process, generalises the Western European form
of social development where territorial self-determination has been typical.
In other parts of the world where the foundation of the political system has
not been the *demos* but the *ethnos*, a claim for *ethnic* self-determination has
emerged. Moreover, Judge Dillard correctly observed in his separate
opinion in the *Western Sahara* case: 'It is for the people to determine the
destiny of the territory and not the territory the destiny of the people'.[17]
This viewpoint seems to be consistent with Felix Ermacora's critical
comments concerning Cristescu's definition of self-determination: 'A
minority can well be considered a people if a given minority has the

---

[16] CCPR/C/1/Add. 30.
[17] *Western Sahara Case*, ICJ Reports 1975, p. 122.

elements of a people' (Ermacora 1988 p. 328). Unfortunately, this approach could lead to a highly subjective debate in specific cases as to whether this or that minority community can be characterised as a people.

V HOW SHOULD THE RIGHT TO SELF-DETERMINATION BE INTERPRETED IN EASTERN AND CENTRAL EUROPE?

Interpretations of the right to self-determination in Eastern and Central Europe should meet the following requirements: they should not reward secessionism and irredentism, while at the same time they should accommodate the legitimate expectations of minority communities. As I see it, there are a number of possible interpretations which could serve these purposes. All of them have advantages and disadvantages, while none of them can avoid including restrictions in connection with the subject or the content of the right to self-determination, or both.

a) The Right to Self-Determination as a *Pacta de Negotiando*

This interpretation results in a minimalist concept of the right to self-determination by confining the content of the right to self-determination to *pacta de negotiando*. Consequently, as Kamal S. Shehadi states, the right to self-determination:

> means negotiating with the state(s) concerned about how best to promote their national identity and their political aspirations. This can only be achieved with the active engagement of international organisations. (Shehadi 1993 p. 31)

As it is generally conceived, the content of *pacta de negotiando* is not more than an obligation to negotiate in good faith, and does not mean that the parties have to reach an agreement. Even the active participation of international organisations could not necessarily achieve more. Such negotiations between a state and minority communities can occur at any time in the political process and in general they are problematic only in the worst cases. The new elements in Shehadi's concept are the engagement of international organisations and of other state(s) who may be involved. Unfortunately, the participation of international organisations in the deliberative process may give rise to serious political conflict and the involvement of another state, for example of a state whose population has ethnic ties with the minority community may also be problematic, because the idea of a protective state, and past efforts to apply such a principle, have not generally been welcomed by the international community.

b) The Right to Self-Determination as a Sanction

The UN Declaration on Principles of International Law concerning Friendly Relations includes a passage which can be interpreted this way:[18]

> Nothing in the foregoing paragraphs shall be construed as authorizing or encouraging any action which would dismember or impair, totally or in part, the territorial integrity or political unity of sovereign and independent States conducting themselves in compliance with the principles of equal rights and self-determination of peoples as described above and thus possessed of a government representing the whole people belonging to the territory without distinction as to race, creed or colour.

If the government represents all of the peoples living on the territory of a state without discrimination, the whole population is the subject of the right to self-determination. If the government discriminates between the different ethnic groups, those minority communities which have been discriminated against can claim the right to self-determination. In this way, governments may be subject to a sanction because of their behaviour. However, this solution raises the difficult question of who can decide whether discrimination has taken place? States would inevitably be biased because of their geopolitical interests, even if such decisions were taken under the auspices of international organisations. However, objective, balanced information is generally available in the reports of non-governmental organisations. If the minority community itself can decide, the content of the right to self-determination must be restricted. This conception, i.e. the right to self-determination as a sanction, restricts the application of the principle because the right to self-determination is not provided to 'all peoples'.

c) The Right to Self-Determination as a Right to Autonomy

This approach construes the *internal* aspect of the right to self-determination as a right to autonomy. You can arrive at this interpretation from an analysis of paragraph 4 of the relevant part of the UN Declaration on Principles of International Law concerning Friendly Relations. As Gaetano Arangio-Ruiz states:

---

[18] The Declaration is contained in the Annex to Resolution 2625 (XXV) of the UN General Assembly, adopted without vote on 24 October 1970. For the text of the Declaration see e.g. Brownlie 1983 p. 35.

Paragraph 4 of the relevant section of the declaration wisely indicates that the exercise of self-determination may bring about not only 'establishment of a sovereign and independent State' but 'free association with an independent State' (existing or to be created) or the 'emergence into any other political status freely determined' by the people concerned. (Arangio-Ruiz 1979 p. 137)

This freely determined 'any other political status' can readily be interpreted as autonomy. Manfred Nowak, in his commentary on the UN Covenant on Civil and Political Rights, also considers the right to internal self-determination as implying a right to autonomy (Nowak 1989 p. 24). As far as the definition of autonomy is concerned certain guidelines can be found in the Document of the Copenhagen Meeting of the Conference on the Human Dimensions of the CSCE:[19]

The participating States note the efforts undertaken to protect and create conditions for the promotion of ethnic, cultural, linguistic and religious identity of certain national minorities by establishing, as one of the possible means to achieve these aims, appropriate local or autonomous administrations corresponding to the specific historical and territorial circumstances of such minorities and in accordance with the policies of the State concerned.

Article 11 of the draft additional protocol to the European Convention on Human Rights, on the right of minorities (see note 2), uses similar but more explicit language and sets out clearer conditions:

In the regions where they are in majority the persons belonging to a national minority shall have the right to have at their disposal appropriate local or autonomous authorities or to have a special status, matching the specific historical and territorial situation and in accordance with the domestic legislation of the state.

The three possible interpretations of the right to self-determination outlined above can be combined and in this way you can arrive at the following variations:

Subject	Content
all communities which claim to be a people	– right to pactum de negotiando
all communities which can objectively qualify as a people	– right to autonomy
all communities which are discriminated against	

---

[19] For the text of the Document of the Copenhagen Meeting see e.g. (1990) *International Legal Materials* XXIX (5), p.130.

VI CONCLUSIONS

The 'short' twentieth century (1914–1989) and especially its end has demonstrated that Wilsonianism, the idea of national self-determination, has much more strength and potency than Marxist-Leninism, the competing ideology (Lukacs 1994 pp. 14–17). The return of former communists to power in Lithuania, in Poland or in Hungary does not contradict this thesis as they have not come back *as* communists, but rather as socialists. Thus, while the process of marketisation may slow down, the political system based on Marxist–Leninism has no chance of returning.

The aspiration for self-determination in Eastern and Central Europe comes not only from ethnic nationalism or the uncertain situation of ethnic communities in the new states, but also from the lack of internal mechanisms to settle inter-communal disputes. Ethnic communities are frequently in a weak position and they feel they need international legitimacy to improve their position *vis-á-vis* the central authorities of the state. The right to autonomy has a very vague legitimacy in international norms, in contrast to the right of self-determination. Consequently, various ethnic communities may believe that the right to self-determination can improve their position rather more than the more uncertain concept of autonomy. Besides, the idea of self-determination can elevate the spirit of a community, strengthening the bonds of the group (Shehadi 1993 p. 41). That is precisely why it can easily be misused by politicians from ethnic minorities who aspire to become prime ministers, ambassadors, etc. of sovereign states. Understandably, they present independent statehood as the only true form in which the right of self-determination can be realized. The other side of the coin is that if any reference has been made by an ethnic group to self-determination, even if the community has clearly stated that they don't need *external* self-determination, such a proposition is always interpreted by the central authorities of the state as a sign of secessionism. As far as the legal implications are concerned, the central authorities of a state could claim that once an ethnic group has been recognized as a 'people' subject to the right of internal self-determination, they could subsequently extend their demands to the whole content of this right, i.e. to sovereign statehood. So, the term self-determination can be problematic.

For myself, I believe that the solution lies not only in the realisation of minority rights whose subject is the individual belonging to a community, but also in the strengthening of the constitutional status of such communities themselves, which will involve a kind of self-administration in harmony with the local circumstances. This is the true meaning of the right to autonomy and of the right to self-determination in Eastern and Central Europe.

9. Changing Trends, Enduring Questions Regarding Refugee Law in Central Europe

Boldizsár Nagy

I INTRODUCTION

Refugee law, as well as human rights, is concerned with the distribution of wealth and income, relates to entitlement and access to tangible and non-tangible goods such as land and safety, to means of survival and to human dignity. In a pessimistic mood – which is the natural attitude in Central Europe – one could say that both relate to the maximum level of suffering and deprivation that the individual can endure, without revolting against her fate. Refugee law is widely understood as a subsidiary tool to provide a remedy for the most flagrant violations of the individual's basic political and economic rights, to be used when normal routes of human rights protection are inaccessible. There is a kind of circularity in the logic of thinking about the relationship between human rights and refugee status: although refugee status may provide protection against human rights violations, it is precisely the improvement of the human rights record of countries which produce asylum seekers that is frequently thought of as a solution for the refugee problem. Refugee law corrects human rights abuses,[1] human rights development remedies the refugee situation. The United Nations High Commissioner for Refugees, in speaking of her strategy, is very clear when she states that:

Conditions of economic decline are among the most conducive to displacement, as conflict breaks out among social classes, regions or ethnic groups trying to preserve or

---

[1] As expressed by one of the major supporters of reconceiving refugee law as human rights law, if that was achieved then 'refugee law would allow people to become directly and immediately involved in the process of calling attention to affronts to human dignity in their home state. By "voting with their feet", refugees deny a state's abuse of sovereignty to oppress.' (Hathaway 1991b p. 120).

advance their positions, if necessary at the expense of others ... Respect for human rights in general and minority rights in particular, are fundamental to the establishment and continued development of democratic states (Ogata 1993 p. 19)

This study provides a review of the fundamental changes concerning asylum seeker movements affecting East-Central Europe in the last decade and of the enduring problems the Czech Republic, Hungary, Poland and Slovakia encounter. When analysing these developments parallels will be drawn with the most recent Western European trends.

II THE CHANGING TRENDS IN EUROPE, WEST AND CENTRAL

1. Western European Trends:

Since 1983 when 15 countries of Western Europe had altogether 68.7 thousand new asylum seekers requesting refugee status (People 1992 p. 195) (the two most preferred countries being Germany with almost 20 and France with almost 15 thousands applications) most of the West European States have experienced the multiplication of new arrivals, the peak being reached in 1992 when the number of applications reached 685,700 (Salt et al., 1994 p. 209). In 1993 more than a 25 percent decrease in the figures could be observed.[2] If one compares the arrival data of the late eighties with

---

2   *Number of persons requesting asylum:*

Country	1991	1992	1993
Belgium	15173	17647	26882
Denmark	4609	13876	14347
Finland	2137	3634	2203
France	46545	28873	27564
Germany	256112	438191	322842
Greece	2572	1972	789
Ireland	31	39	91
Italy	26472	2600	1646
Luxembourg	238	120	225
Netherlands	21615	20346	35399
Norway	4569	5238	12876
Portugal	233	688	1659
Spain	8140	12000	12615
Sweden	26500	84018	37581
Switzerland	41600	17960	24739
United Kingdom	44840	24600	22370
Total:	501386	671802	506294

that of the mid-nineties and disregards the unprecedented flow of asylum seekers from the Southern Slav states, then it is clear that less asylum seekers are managing to reach Western Europe, especially the traditional receivers. (Note the stabilisation and/or decline in numbers in France, Germany, Switzerland, Sweden and the UK.)

This cannot be because less persecution occurs in the world. The number of displaced persons outside their country in a refugee-like situation is 23 million and those who are internally displaced is above 26 million.[3]

Rather one could speculate that the restrictive tendencies both at the national and the international levels have produced this result. It would be beyond the scope of this paper to review the new legislation adopted in Austria (1992) France (1993), Germany (1993) the UK (1993) and in other Western European countries.[4] However, the trend is unequivocal:

> The widespread perception that the asylum channel is being abused by would-be economic migrants, and the spectre of virtually unlimited numbers of people in need of international protection because of violence and chaos at home, inspire fear in many industrialised countries ... Domestic pressures create a political imperative for the governments of receiving countries to be seen to be in control of the asylum process.[5]

Such controls seem to be achieved by measures to prevent the *physical* access of the asylum seekers or by measures preventing *legal* access.[6] The two most conspicuous tools to prevent the arrival of the asylum seeker are visas and carrier sanctions. More and more countries have reintroduced the visa requirement, including a transit visa for an increasing number of countries, which means that potential asylum seekers simply do not get access to the authorities of the target country, because they are not allowed to enter the territory. Only a few countries have counterbalanced this measure by allowing refugee status applications from abroad, handed in at consulates, embassies or other representative offices in or close to the

---

Source: ECRE, (1994c) p. 1. The discrepancy between ECRE's figure for 1992 and Salt's may be explained both by the statistical difficulties and by the exclusion of Austria from the ECRE figures.

[3] For a comparison: The number of refugees (in a broad sense)

In

1970	2.5 million
1983	11 million
1993	18.2 million
1995	23 million

Source: UNHCR 1993a p. III and Refugees, 1994, no. 98, p. 31. The number of internally displaced persons appears in: UNHCR at a Glance 10 November 1994, p. 1.

[4] An excellent review is provided by Widgren 1994. Further insights can be gained from UNHCR 1994b.

[5] UNHCR 1993a p. 38.

[6] This categorisation is derived from ECRE 1994a p. 7–11.

persecuting country.[7] The tools for preventing legal access to the country's determination procedure include the operation of the 'safe country of origin' and 'safe third country' concepts.[8]   They also encompass the detention of asylum seekers in territories which are considered as legally outside the national jurisdiction where domestic law, including human rights standards and their enforcement mechanisms, is not applied.

These steps on the national level correspond to efforts on the international plane to limit the number of refugee status determination procedures and to curtail the time devoted to them.[9]   In 1990 the then twelve EC members adopted the Dublin Convention[10] outside the legislative mechanism of the EC to identify one single state responsible for the investigation of an application for asylum status, with the effect of a binding decision on the other eleven.   The same purpose motivated relevant parts of the Schengen agreements of 1985/1990.[11]   Although at present none of these agreements is effective,[12] they deeply influence the practice of Western European states.[13]   In order to avoid the substantive evaluation of the asylum seeker's application, Western European states endorse several concepts not to be

---

7   Someone who grew up in Central Europe and remembers how closely every person who entered a Western embassy up to the eighties was watched and recorded by the secret police, can clearly understand how seeking refugee status within one's home country may increase (not without grounds) fear of persecution.

8   The content and origin of these concepts as understood by the ministers responsible for immigration matters of the (then) EC member states is described in Joly 1994 p.166–71.

9   The goal of cutting back on resources invested into decision-making concerning asylum seekers is not unjustified. 'It is estimated that Western European countries alone spend the enormous sum of $7 billion a year on their asylum systems' (footnote omitted) (UNHCR, 1993b, p. 37), when the total budget of the UNHCR including the general programs and the special programs and emergencies is below $1.3 billion (UNHCR at a Glance 10 November 1994, p. 2).

10 See: International Journal of Refugee Law, vol. 2 1990 No. 3, p. 469.

11 The Schengen Agreement on the Gradual Abolition of Controls at the Common Frontiers of 14 June 1985 and the 19 June 1990 Convention Applying the Schengen Agreement of 14 June 1985 were concluded by France, Germany and the Benelux countries see ILM, vol. 30 (1991) p. 68. Greece, Italy, Portugal and Spain adhered later (Greece: 6 November 1992, Italy: 27 November 1990, Portugal: 25 June 1991, Spain: 25 June 1991).   They include provisions on control at outer frontiers, a common visa policy, carrier's sanctions, responsibility for dealing with requests for asylum and establish the Schengen Information System.

12 The Dublin Convention is still awaiting a number of ratifications, the Schengen Application Convention of 1990 legally entered into force on 1st September 1993 but according to the most recent reports the Executive Committee of the Schengen Group decided in Berlin on 22 December 1994 that 'irreversible implementation of the Convention' would take place on 26 March 1995. Migration News Sheet, No 142, January 1995, p. 1.

13 For a balanced analysis of the situation see Joly 1994.

found in the 1951 Geneva Convention. Resolutions of the Ministers of the Member States of the European Communities responsible for immigration, adopted at their meeting in London between 30 November and 1 December and confirmed by the European Council in Edinburgh on 12 December, 1992, legitimise the use of categories such as 'manifestly unfounded claim', 'deliberate deception or abuse of asylum procedures' and 'host third country'.[14] For 'manifestly unfounded claims' an accelerated procedure is foreseen which 'need not include full examination at every level of the procedure [of] those applications which fall within the terms of paragraph 1'. That paragraph identifies three kinds of manifestly unfounded claims: where there is no substance to the claim, where the claim is based on deliberate deception or is an abuse of asylum procedures, and finally when the asylum seeker comes from a host third country.

The claim has no substance when it does not invoke Convention grounds for persecution, when it is presented in a non-credible way and also if the applicant refers to persecution which allegedly took place in a country where, according to the authorities of the country deciding on the refugee status, 'there is in general terms no serious risk of persecution'.

The request for recognition of refugee status qualifes as manifestly unfounded if it represents an abuse of the asylum procedure which, according to the resolution, includes applications based on false identity, forged documents, false representations or the destruction of the ticket or of other relevant documents.

The other decision adopted at the same meeting, the 'Resolution on a Harmonised Approach to Questions Concerning Host Third Countries', plainly states that '[t]he principle of host third country is to be applied to all applicants for asylum, irrespective of whether or not they may be regarded as refugees.' In order to qualify as a host third country, modest requirements are to be met. The life and freedom of the asylum applicant must not be threatened, (s)he must not be exposed to torture or inhuman or degrading treatment, and must be afforded effective protection against refoulement. If these conditions apply and the person at least 'has had an opportunity at the border or within the territory of the third country to make contact with that country's authorities in order to seek their protection', then the case will not be examined on the merits.

These tendencies reveal that the Western European asylum system is in a crisis (Ogata 1993 p. 7; Arboleda and Hoy, 1993 p. 73). No wonder. The 1951 Convention definition was:

---

[14] For a brief, critical analysis of these terms see ECRE 1994b pp. 4–7.

carefully phrased to include only persons who have been disfranchised by their state on
the basis of race, religion, nationality, membership of a particular social group or
political opinion, matters in regard to which East bloc practice has historically been
problematic. ... By mandating protection for those whose (Western inspired) civil and
political rights are jeopardised, without at the same time protecting persons whose
(socialist inspired) socio-economic rights are at risk, the Convention adopted an
incomplete and politically partisan human rights rationale. (Hathaway 1991a p. 8)

The East bloc and the Cold War are gone, the Convention cannot promote
the political purpose of protecting ideological dissidents from Communist
Europe. It ought to serve as a vehicle for burden-sharing on a global scale
and as an instrument which could function as the legal basis for protection
of victims of civil strife who are – collectively – deprived of basic human
(not necessarily political) rights.

2. East-Central European Trends:

a) General remarks:

More than half a decade of transition is over and few observers in early
1990 would have forecast that Hungary, Poland and Slovakia would be
governed in 1995 by coalitions in which socialist or postsocialist parties
have a leading role. In other words, the fast and unequivocal switch of
political camps has not come about. East-Central Europe is still somewhere
'between'; it has retained specific features.

Part of that picture is the self-image in these countries which seems to be
confused. Leading politicians hardly miss an occasion to declare that these
countries are either already part of the Western system or that only a few
last steps, such as joining the EU and NATO as full members, are missing,
but that *essentially* the countries have already acquired the attributes of the
developed West. However when it comes to behaving as developed
industrialised states are expected to behave, then they contend that the
resources available do not permit the provision of assistance to those who
are poorer. The donor role, that of the provider, still seems to be alien to
these states,[15] although they all belong to the top third of all states in terms
of *per capita* income.

---

[15] Mr. G. Debnár, a senior official in the Ministry of the Interior in the Slovak Republic
complained of the fact that Slovak 'pensioners do not get an increase in their pensions
whereas refugees cost thousands' and he claimed that 99 per cent of the asylum seekers
were economic migrants who live in worse conditions in Slovakia than they had lived in
at home. Speech delivered at the training workshop: Refugee Law and Human Rights,
organised by UNHCR and the International Helsinki Federation at Stupava, 24–25
June 1994. Notes of this author.

This economic fact contributes to their specific role among the former socialist states. Around 1989 it was still usual and justified to speak about Eastern Europe (with or without the Soviet Union) as a single geopolitical unit which was to share a common future, for good or bad. The five years which have elapsed since then have clearly revealed that a dividing line across Central and Eastern Europe is in the making. The Czech Republic, Hungary, Poland and Slovenia definitely, Slovakia and Croatia most probably, and the Baltic states eventually, belong to that group which – albeit after a harsh period of economic recession and political tensions – will emerge as firm parliamentary democracies with social behavioural patterns comparable to the lesser developed Western European states. This 'northern tier' took shape with the formation of the Visegrád group in 1991 comprising (then) Czechoslovakia, Hungary and Poland. The dividing line within Central and Eastern Europe is reinforced by the reluctance to extend the Central European Initiative[16] to Romania, Bulgaria or to the successors of the former Soviet Union.

b) Similarities:

The four countries show a number of features which are similar and which influence their approach to the refugee movements of our day.

The 1951 Geneva Convention Relating to the Status of Refugees is binding in all the four states: Between 1951 and 1989 among the countries of Central and Eastern Europe only Yugoslavia was a party to the 1951 Convention Relating to the Status of Refugees and its 1967 Protocol, expanding the Convention's application to events after 1951 and beyond Europe. East European countries did not participate because they perceived the convention – not unjustifiably – as a Western tool in the ideological battle between the two camps.[17]

The scene only changed in March 1989 when the – still socialist – leadership of Hungary decided to adhere to the 1951 Geneva Convention.[18]

---

[16] Established in 1989 by Austria, Hungary, Italy and Yugoslavia, enlarged in 1990 with Czechoslovakia and in 1991 with Poland. Four successor states of Yugoslavia (except for rump Yugoslavia) and the other six states make up the membership now.

[17] As Gil Loescher explains in 1992: 'For most of the past four decades, the West has seen refugees as symbols of foreign policy. The term "refugee" and "defector" became synonymous, particularly during the height of the Cold War. A 1953 National Security Council Paper entitled *Psychological Value of Escapees from Soviet Orbit* stated explicitly that it was American policy to "encourage defection of all USSR nationals as well as of 'key' personnel from the satellite countries" as this would inflict "a psychological blow on Communism"' (Loescher 1992 p. 36).

[18] On the motives of, and false assumptions behind, this step see Nagy 1991 p. 531–2.

The Convention became effective with regard to Hungary on 12 June 1989, the Protocol three months earlier on 14 March 1989. The Czech and Slovak Republic ratified the 1951 Convention and its Protocol on 10 July 1991. However the dismemberment of the federation necessitated renewed action on behalf of the two successor states. Whereas Slovakia thought to resolve the issue by declaring on 25 January 1993 that it was bound by these treaties, the Czech Republic formally acceded to them on 11 May 1993. Poland was the last to adhere to both instruments on 27 September 1991.

Council of Europe membership achieved: The Council of Europe is based on the 'spiritual and moral values which are the common heritage of' the peoples of the Member States, values which are the 'true source of individual freedom, political liberty and the rule of law, principles which form the basis of all genuine democracy'.[19]   Therefore, joining this organisation had more than practical value, it symbolically expressed the return of the East-Central European countries to the community of European States.   Membership in the Council of Europe not only presupposes the adoption of the European Convention on Human Rights and Fundamental Freedoms, but also integration into that web of international instruments which embody much of that heritage referred to in the Statute's preamble.[20] In addition to the formal legal instruments affecting asylum seekers and refugees,[21] the Council of Europe has adopted many important soft law instruments[22] affecting the perception of solutions to problems outside the scope of the 1951 Geneva Convention, the last being the Recommendation adopted on 21 June 1994 by the Committee of Ministers 'On Guidelines to inspire practices of the Member States of the Council of Europe concerning the arrival of asylum seekers at European airports'.[23]

---

[19] Statute of the Council of Europe as amended, preamble third paragraph, Council of Europe, Strasbourg, 1992.

[20] The number of international treaties adopted under the auspices of the Council of Europe was around 150 by 1994.

[21] Like the European Agreement on the Abolition of Visas for Refugees, adopted in 1959 E.T.S. no 31, or the European Convention on the Transfer of Responsibility for Refugees concluded in 1980 E.T.S. no. 107.

[22] Between 1961 and 1984 the Committee of Ministers or the Parliamentary Assembly adopted 11 resolutions or recommendations relating to persons in danger of persecution, including such important ones as those on granting asylum (Resolution 14 [1967] of the Committee of Ministers), on *de facto refugees* (Recommendation 773 [1976] of the Assembly) and the Declaration on Territorial Asylum of the Committee of Ministers, adopted in 1977. The texts of these documents are reproduced in Plender, 1988 128–51.

[23] Recommendation No. R.[94] 5.

Hungary was the first to become a full member of the organisation on 6 November 1990, while Czechoslovakia was the next a few months later (21 February 1991) and Poland became the 26th Member State on 26 November 1991. After the dissolution of the Czechoslovak Federation both successor states were admitted as new members.[24]

Ready to adhere to human rights standards /the European Convention, the Helsinki process: The Czech Republic, Hungary, Poland and the Slovak Republic are parties to a great number of human rights instruments[25] which are of paramount importance also in the context of refugee law. The principle of non-refoulement and obligations such as the prohibition of subjecting someone to cruel, inhuman or degrading treatment or punishment, are safeguarded by several documents which bind these countries.[26] Because of their strong emphasis on Europe the uniform participation of the four states in the (European) Convention for the Protection of Human Rights and Fundamental Freedoms, (including the optional clause on individual petition) and its first, fourth and seventh Protocols should be mentioned.

---

[24] Both the Czech and the Slovak Republics are members as of 29 July 1993.

[25] It would be too lengthy to quote the participation data for all the four countries in respect of all the relevant human rights instruments. It may serve as a useful summary if one mentions that on 1 January 1992 Czechoslovakia was party to 19 out of the 25 universal human rights texts listed in Human Rights, Status of International Instruments, UN, 1987, with updated charts on participation. The exceptions relate to the Second Protocol to the International Covenant on Civil and Political Rights abolishing the death penalty, the amendment of the 1926 Slavery Convention and the two Conventions on stateless persons as well as the recent Convention on the rights of migrant workers. Hungary has a similar record (20 out of 25), with the same exceptions, but is a party to the instruments on slavery, whereas Poland's participation in the 25 human rights instruments, on 1 January 1992, had *precisely* the same pattern as that of Czechoslovakia.

[26] Article 7 of the International Covenant on Civil and Political Rights became part of Hungarian law on 22 April 1976, promulgated as Law-decree No. 8 of 1976. Article 3 of the 1984 UN Convention against Torture and Other Cruel Inhuman or Degrading Treatment or Punishment expressly prohibits refoulement or extradition of a person 'to another State where there are substantial grounds for believing that he would be in danger of being subjected to torture' became part of Hungarian law in 1988 as Law-decree No. 3 of 1988. Hungary is bound by the Convention for the Protection of Human Rights and Fundamental Freedoms and its Protocols which she signed on November 6, 1990. Certainly the recent practice of the Strasbourg institutions concerning articles 3, 5, 8 and 13 are more than relevant. See e.g. *Bozano* 12 December 1986, Series A vol. 111; *Söering* 7 July 1989 Series A vol. 161; *Djeroud* 23 January 1991 Series A vol. 191-B; *Moustaquim* 18 February 1991, Series A vol. 193; *Cruz Varas and Others,* 20 March 1991 Series A vol. 201; *Vilvarajah and others* 30 October 1991, Series A vol. 215.

What used to be the CSCE process and in 1994 became the Organisation for Security and Cooperation in Europe has had an important role in guiding these countries to accept more and more requirements relating to the human dimension. Although earlier documents, with the exception of a few lines,[27] do not explicitly speak of refugees, the concluding document of the Helsinki Summit in 1992, 'The Challenge of Change', clearly established the linkage between the violation of human rights and the displacement of persons.[28]   The follow up of the Helsinki Meeting, the CSCE Human Dimension Seminar on Migration including Refugees, held in Warsaw, revealed that the role of the CSCE with regard to migration and refugees is disputed.   Whereas members of the European Union were reluctant to discuss these issues in the CSCE framework, Central and Eastern European states saw an opportunity in trying to enhance burden sharing.[29] It remains to be seen whether the OSCE will strengthen its position in the European decision-making process relating to refugees, but it is likely that the Council of Europe, with its well developed organisational system and long tradition,[30] will remain the major all-European organisation.

Long term objective: membership in the European Union: The long term objective of the four countries is to join the European Union, which will have serious repercussions on their freedom of action with regard to the movement of persons. Whereas the existing agreements on association with the EU do not limit the competence of these states to regulate issues relevant to migration as they wish, membership in the Union will subject their competence in regulating migration to the decisions of the Union taken in accordance with Article 100c of the Rome Treaty establishing a common visa policy and Title VI of the Maastricht Treaty declaring asylum policy and immigration policy to be matters of common interest.

Growing number of return agreements: East-Central Europe is frequently seen as a wide corridor for regular and irregular migrants heading for the affluent West. In a paradoxical way, two contradictory processes unfolded

---

[27] See the Concluding Document of the Vienna Follow up Meeting, 19 January 1989, paragraph 22 on the principles securing the return of refugees to their home country.

[28] Paragraph 42 of Decision VI, 'The Human Dimension'.

[29] ECRE 1993 p. 41–2.

[30] The Parliamentary Assembly of the Council of Europe is assisted by the Committee on Migration, Refugees and Demography (CDMG), the Committee of Ministers by the Ad Hoc Committee on the Legal Aspects of Territorial Asylum, Refugees and Stateless Persons (CAHAR).

after 1989. While Central and Eastern Europe was euphoric about its newly gained human rights and freedoms, including the much yearned for freedom of travel, the West, which had criticised the East for keeping its subjects behind closed borders,[31] was starting to erect ever higher barriers against the entry of those deprived subjects. Visa requirements were reinstated, material conditions of entry, such as financial resources, were scrutinised more thoroughly.

The price for keeping Western Europe's borders open for citizens of the East-Central European states became more and more identifiable: a deal concerning asylum seekers and other potential immigrants into the West. The deal took and is still taking the form of return agreements, guaranteeing that persons who illegally crossed the borders of a Western state, or who are found to be staying or residing there unlawfully, can be deported back to the other contracting party and that they will be taken back.

The web of return agreements is expanding. On 29 March 1991, Poland concluded a much commented on agreement with six states,[32] parties to the Schengen Agreement and the Convention Applying that Agreement. This agreement between Poland and the six Schengen states, which could provisionally be applied from 1 April 1991,[33] guarantees that Poland (and the six West European States) shall take back without specific formal procedures not only their own citizens but also citizens of third states. Poland is therefore obliged to readmit not only Polish citizens, but also citizens of third states if they had (legally or illegally) crossed the external frontier of Poland before travelling to the Schengen states and if their stay on the territory of those states is illegal. That illegality may arise either because they crossed the border illegally or because their permission to stay has expired or has been terminated for any other reason. Poland is only exempt from the readmission obligation if the citizen of a third state had a visa or residence permit from the state in which his stay became illegal or if there is another contracting state which has issued a valid visa or residence permit for the person to be removed.

Although Article 5 of the Agreement declares that the Agreement is without prejudice to the application of the 1951 Convention relating to the Status of Refugees and its 1967 Protocol, it has been noted that in practical terms it serves as a measure deterring potential asylum seekers from

---

31. One may think of the long fights, over two decades, in the Helsinki process concerning freedom of travel.

32 The Agreement Concerning the Readmission of Persons in an Irregular Situation between the Schengen States and Poland was published in Hailbronner 1992 pp. 208–13.

33 Article 6, para 2.

crossing Poland[34] and that it makes Poland the border-guard of the six Schengen States, obliged to scrutinise each transit passenger for her ability to fulfill the requirements of entry and sojourn in each of those countries. If Poland wants to avoid the readmission of 'illegal aliens' from the territory of those six states, including asylum seekers who fail to become recognised as refugees, and if Poland does not want to finance the eventual return of these persons to their country of origin, then it has to stop them at its borders, before entering Poland. This would force its neighbours (the Czech Republic, Slovakia, Ukraine, Belarus, Lithuania) to either permit the stay of those potential migrants or to send them back at their expense. The only alternative to closing Poland's eastern and southern borders is for it to conclude readmission agreements with its neighbours. This process seems to be under way.[35]

Although the 1991 Agreement between Poland and the six Schengen states allows for the accession of other states upon invitation by consensus of all Contracting States (Art. 7), parties to this agreement seem to be striving for bilateral agreements with other Central-European states. After the adoption of the new German Asylum regulations,[36] Germany initiated negotiations on a readmission agreement with the Czech Republic because the smooth operation of the new system, declaring the Czech Republic both a safe country of origin and a safe third country, was only viable if Germany could transfer to the Czech Republic those persons – including asylum seekers – who, because of coming from or through the safe Czech Republic, are excluded from the protection offered for refugees by Article 16a of the Grundgesetz. After prolonged negotiations the agreement was concluded on 3 November 1994, providing also for 60 million DM financial support from Germany to the Czech Republic.[37]

---

34 [Dutch] Standing committee of experts on international immigration, refugee and criminal law: 'Readmission agreement between the Schengen States and Poland' undated photocopied note, p. 2.

35 Poland has concluded readmission agreements with Slovakia, the Czech Republic, Ukraine (Lemay, 1994, p. 18) and in order to guarantee the direct return of persons removed to Poland from Germany, with Bulgaria and Romania (ibid.).

36 Gesetz zur Änderung des Grundgesetzes vom 28 Juni 1993, BGBl I p. 1002 and Gesetz zur Änderung asylverfahrens-, ausländer- und staatsangehörigkeitsrechtlicher Vorschriften vom 30 Juni 1993, BGBl.,Teil I 1 Juli 1993, p. 1062, point 20 inserting § 29a into the Asylverfahrensgesetz vom 26 Juni 1992 (BGBl. I. p. 1126) on safe country of origin and point 17 inserting § 26a into the same statute on safe third countries, together with annexes I and II listing both the Czech Republic and Poland as a safe country of origin and a safe third country but excluding Hungary and Slovakia from the safe third countries' list, only mentioning them as safe countries of origin according to § 29.

37 Migration News Sheet, No. 141 December, 1994, p. 10.

The Czech Republic has further readmission agreements in force with Austria, Slovakia, Poland and Romania and plans to conclude such agreements with Bulgaria, the Ukraine and Russia.[38]

Hungary was also active in building its own network of readmission agreements.[39] Although the pressure from Austria to conclude one was fairly palpable it had to wait until the continuity of the chain in the direction of the countries of origin, that is the readmission agreement with Romania, was signed. At present Hungary has signed readmission agreements and executive agreements for their implementation with all of its neighbours, and also with a non-neighbour state, Switzerland. Although most of them are still awaiting the expression of consent to be bound and although they have not been published in the Hungarian Official Journal, nevertheless most of them, including their provisions on transit, have great influence on actual practice. It is a characteristic feature of the readmission agreements that they not only prescribe an obligation to readmit their own nationals or foreigners residing or lawfully staying in the requested state, but that they ensure the possibility of transportation through the requested state by the requesting state with a destination in a third state. All the agreements contain a formal possibility of denying this transit if the requested state fears that the principle of *non-refoulement* may be violated, but none of these agreements enables an impartial body or public opinion to determine whether persons transited by its readmission partners through Hungary to a third state do not fear threats to their life or freedom on account of their race, religion, nationality or political opinion there.

Slovakia is also active in securing that it becomes part of this European web formally aimed at removing irregular migrants but practically threatening asylum seekers as well. It has concluded readmission agreements with Austria, the Czech Republic, Croatia, Hungary, Romania, Slovenia and the Ukraine.[40]

A reservoir for those in front of whom the gates of Western Europe have closed? One of the major concerns of these countries is that they might

---

[38] Budapest Group (1994) p. 4 of the Czech answer to the questionnaire. To illustrate the difficulties in acquiring reliable data let it be mentioned that IGC (1994) indicates that the Czech Republic is negotiating with Belgium and has an existing agreement with Hungary.

[39] The agreement with Austria was signed on October 9, 1992, with Romania on September 1, 1992 and with Slovenia on October 20, 1992. They were followed by the readmission agreement with the Ukraine signed on 26 February 1993, with Switzerland signed on 4 February 1994 and with Slovakia signed on 5 August 1994.

[40] Budapest Group (1994), Slovak answer, p. 4, with Hungary added on the basis of Hungarian information.

become surrogates to Western Europe, a reservoir for all unsuccessful asylum seekers and other migrants who try to settle in the affluent West, but fail.

The bureaucracies of these countries, frequently less sensitive to nuances, devote a minimal effort to keeping different issues apart and to not mixing up illegal and irregular migrants on the one hand, pursuing strictly private benefit, with asylum seekers on the other, fleeing from individualised persecution or other events seriously disturbing public order, such as civil war or open violent ethnic conflicts. Therefore the administrations of these countries were and are active in the 'Vienna/Berlin process', the series of intergovernmental conferences and meetings aimed at responding to irregular and/or mass migratory flows.

The meeting in Vienna on 24–25 January 1991 was organised for an 'ad hoc' group of states[41] which were perceived as having a specific interest in the then expected mass emigration from the Soviet Union. The Final Communiqué[42] of the Ministerial Conference was a typical mix of refugee related pronouncements and envisaged steps to curb illegal migration.[43] With the passing of time and the absence of mass emigration from the successor states of the USSR, the emphasis gradually shifted from asylum seeker flows to voluntary migration and within that to illegal migration of individuals or small groups. Thus the Final Communiqué of the Ministerial Conference for Checking Illegal Immigration from and through Central and Eastern Europe, held in Berlin on 30–31 October 1991,[44] and the documents of its follow up meeting, held in Budapest on 15–16 February 1993, had hardly anything to say about helping asylum seekers or

---

[41] 31 European States, including Czechoslovakia, Hungary, Poland and their neighbours plus Canada, participated as full members, together with observer delegations from Albania, Australia and the US.

[42] Reproduced as Council of Europe Document MMP (91) 7.

[43] The noble invitation to consider accession to the 1951 Geneva Convention relating to the Status of Refugees and to the two Covenants on Human Rights and the recommendation to take into account specific needs of countries of first asylum were followed by suggestions to pursue 'active collaboration to promote those development policies and measures which would help prevent disorderly migration' and to consider the conclusion of readmission agreements.

[44] The document was adopted by the competent ministers of Albania, Belarus, Belgium, Bulgaria, Czechoslovakia, Denmark, Estonia, France, Germany, Greece, Hungary, Ireland, Italy, Latvia, Lithuania, Luxembourg, the Netherlands, Poland, Portugal, Romania, the Soviet Union, Spain, Switzerland, Ukraine, the United Kingdom, and Yugoslavia in Berlin on October 31, 1991.

reinforcing the freedom of travel, but were quite detailed on how to curb illegal migration in the short and long term.[45]

The Ministers of the Interior of the Czech Republic, Hungary, Poland, Slovakia, and Slovenia gathered in Prague on 16 March 1993 to negotiate 'Measures to Regulate the Migration influx into the Territories of States in the Central European region', as the title of the Closing Communiqué[46] puts it. They acknowledged the recommendations adopted in Budapest two months before, and agreed on the following: to propose to their own governments not to readmit asylum seekers from Germany who had arrived there before the amendment of the German law on asylum; to consider the possibility of allowing the transit of returned persons by another state signing the communiqué to the country of origin; to exert efforts 'towards completing mutual standardised readmission agreements' and towards a harmonisation of the asylum procedures. Finally, they noted that they '[c]onsider[ed] the issue of European migration a serious security problem'. This blunt and voluntaristic condemnation of European migration as a problem reflects a one-sided view of the complexities of the free movement of persons, neglecting its benefits and over-emphasising its – undeniable – potential for negative impacts.

This process of transforming an articulated response to different kinds of migratory waves into a simple defensive action against illegal migration led to the disappearance of the Vienna group[47] whereas the Berlin process is

---

[45] A list of working groups set up in Berlin and presenting their recommendations in Budapest is more than telling:

harmonising sanctions against smuggling illegal immigrants,

mutual legal assistance in prosecuting smugglers of illegal immigrants,

establishment of special forces to combat clandestine immigration networks,

exchange of information about illegal immigration,

procedures and standards to improve frontier controls,

readmission agreements,

implementation of readmission,

securing the external borders away from authorised crossing points,

obligation of carrier companies to prevent illegal entry.

This list was produced in: Commission of the European Communities: Communication from the Commission to the Council and the European Parliament on Immigration and Asylum Policies COM (94) final, Annex IV *Recent Developments in International Fora*, p. 2, 23 02 1994, Brussels. The texts adopted at the Budapest Conference were reproduced as Council of Europe document MMG-5 (93) 5.

[46] Unpublished document on file with the author.

[47] At its 7th meeting in Strasbourg, Senior Officials of the Vienna group came to the conclusion that '[t]he Vienna Group should cease to meet as an independent body and its mandate and mission should be entrusted to the Council of Europe and where relevant to other appropriate bodies such as the Budapest Group.' Conclusions of the group of senior officials responsible for the follow-up to the Conference of Ministers on

continuing. On 18–19 November 1993, ministers responsible for migration of the 32 members of the Council of Europe, together with their colleagues from Canada, the US, Russia, Ukraine, Albania, Latvia and the Holy See, met in Athens, declaring themselves the successors of both processes[48] and focusing their discussions on '[w]ays of moderating migration flows [and] [r]racism, xenophobia and intolerance'.[49] They declared that '[w]hen the national interest leads to restrictions on immigration, which may particularly be the case in certain economic circumstances, such restrictions must be applied fairly, with respect for human dignity and without infringing international legal obligations concerning the protection of refugees and family life'.[50] They then turned to the condemnation of racism, xenophobia and intolerance which – one could add with some scepticism – was evoked precisely by that mentality which was not altogether absent from some earlier documents emanating from the same ministers.

  If all these steps to limit migration are seen in conjunction with the continued efforts of the Western European states to minimise the number of asylum seekers in respect of whom they have responsibility for determining whether the applicant is a refugee or someone not under the protection of the 1951 Geneva Convention, then it is understandable that the East-Central European countries feel threatened that they will become a reservoir of the rejected. This is especially so if one takes into account those procedural innovations[51] which serve as a basis for not proceeding even if no doubt concerning the probability of recognising the person as a refugee arises.

c) Differences:

In respect of the role of the Czech Republic, Hungary, Poland and Slovakia in the international migratory process, similarities and differences can be observed against the background of changing trends over time.

Movements of Persons from Central and Eastern European Countries (Vienna Group), 13 September 1994.

[48] Therefore the meeting was designated the Fifth Conference of European Ministers responsible for migration affairs, the previous four meetings having been the ones in Vienna, Berlin, Budapest, and the European Population Conference in Geneva, in March 1993.

[49] Fifth Conference of European Ministers responsible for migration affairs, Athens, 18–19 November 1993, Conclusions, para 1.

[50] Ibid., para 5.

[51] An analysis of both the safe country of origin and the safe country of asylum (as Hailbronner puts it) can be read in Hailbronner (1993), a more critical view of these instruments is published in Amnesty (1992).

However, before trying to identify these differences with numerical, statistical methods a very serious word of caution has to be said, directly in the text, not relegated to a footnote; it is impossible to establish final, verifiable figures in most cases. The range of error may even be in one order of magnitude, without any fault on the part of the data collector.

The most frequent mistakes to be found in the sources are: mixing up the flow and the stock data, confusing asylum seekers with recognised refugees, not determining whether temporary protected persons should come under the heading of refugees, uncertainty as to whether cases involve individuals or groups of persons. The most common mistake is that the numbers of new arrivals are faithfully added up, but changes to another status (e.g. naturalisation and therefore loss of refugee status), or departure for another country – frequently illegal crossing of the border – is not – or cannot be – followed. Sometimes the data given by the competent authority simply do not correspond to the facts or are inconsistent.[52] As one of the most competent commentators noted:

> It is thus not surprising that much of the current debate about actual and potential international migration in Europe, especially from East and South, has throughout the field of study been limited by the patchy availability of up-to-date, unambiguous and consistent data on stocks of foreign population and flows of international migrants ... (Salt 1993 p. 10)

In historic terms, Czechoslovakia, Hungary and Poland were all countries of origin. Legal emigration and illegal emigration ('denial of return to home', as it was called) were characteristic of these communist party ruled states. Each of them has produced at least one large wave of migrant population,[53] besides the constant flow of legal and illegal emigration.[54] Poland and Czechoslovakia, and to a lesser degree Hungary, were also a

---

[52] To give an example: the Hungarian Office for Refugee Affairs in a document distributed in February 1993 (Refugees in Hungary 1988–92, mimeo) stated that in those years 5,305 persons were recognised as refugees according to the 1951 Geneva Convention. The same office states in January 1995 that the total number of recognised refugees (from 1989 up to 1 January 1995) is 4,102 out of which exactly 600 was recognised in 1993 and 1994.

[53] Czechoslovakia in 1968, Hungary in 1956, Poland in 1956, 1968, 1981.

[54] 'Between 1968 and 1989 244,597 people left Czechoslovakia' (Joly et al., 1992 p. 75). Poland had a yearly net loss of around 20,000 in the 1960s and 1970s and lost another 250,000 between 1981 and 1990, all in terms of legal emigration (Salt et al. 1994 p. 198). Unofficial emigration is estimated at 533,000 between 1981 and 1988 (Okolski 1992 p. 95). With regard to Hungary, approximately 50,000 persons emigrated legally and an estimated 70,000 illegally between 1963 and 1988 (SOPEMI 1992 p. 99 and Table 37).

source of large numbers of 'Aussiedler' (ethnic Germans) resettling in Germany.[55]

The difference between these states arose in the late eighties. Whereas Hungary ceased to be a country of emigration and quickly became a target country for asylum seekers, Czechoslovakia and Poland maintained their pattern of producing emigrants and asylum seekers and practically not receiving victims of persecution. The approximate number of citizens of these countries applying for asylum in the three years 1989–91 is as follows: Czechoslovakia, 12 thousand; Poland, 62 thousand; Hungary, 6.5 thousand.[56] The number of incoming asylum seekers is best illustrated by the following table:

Table 9.1 Summary data on asylum seekers in East Central Europe, 1989–93

Country	1989	1990	1991	1992	1993	total
Czechoslovakia		1.000*	1.948	816	–	3.764
Czech Republic					3.800 (with Y)	3.800
Hungary	17.448 + 13.173 (for 1987 and 1988)	18.283	53.359 (with Y)	16.204 (with Y)	5.366 (with Y)	123.833 –
Poland		1800	2.433	592	2.250 (with Y)	5.570
Slovakia	–	–	–	–	151+ 2.000* Y	2.151

Y = including temporarily protected persons from the former Yugoslavia
* = approximate figure

Source: Author's calculations based on UNHCR (1993b), on SOPEMI 1992 and on other unpublished sources

---

[55] Poland alone was the country of origin for 400,000 Aussiedler in 1989 and 1990 (SOPEMI 1992 p. 93). Between 1970 and 1989, 800,000 ethnic Germans left Poland for West Germany (Salt 1993 p. 35).

[56] Author's calculations based on Salt et al. (1994) pp. 213–4.

This table clearly indicates that there was a significant time-lag between Hungary and the other countries. The first signs of the potential for refugees coming from another socialist country were to be felt in Hungary in 1987 (Sik 1992 p. 16). Although, in order not to offend 'brotherly Romania', the term 'refugee' was not used until 1989, already in 1988 a special fund for the support of ethnic Hungarians and others escaping from Romania was set up. The large-scale constant flow of desperate Romanian citizens crossing the Romanian-Hungarian border, in most cases illegally, because before 1990 they could not get a passport to leave the country, lasted till 1991.

Table 9.2 The number of asylum seekers arriving in Hungary in the first wave

		Until the end of 1988	1989	1990	1991, until June 1, 1991	Total until June 1, 1991
Total		13,173	17,448	18,283	2,629	51,533
	From Romania	13,098	17,171	17,416	2,103	49,788
Formally recognised as refugees		0	185	2,561	149	2,895

Source: Author's calculations based on data of the Office of Refugee and Migration Affairs

The second wave, lasting from the Summer of 1991 till the end of 1992, is characterised by a totally different composition of asylum seekers. The number of arrivals in the second half of 1991 once again increased radically. Whereas until 1 June, a mere 2629 persons had come, of whom 80 per cent were Romanian citizens almost exclusively of Hungarian origin and a further 16 per cent were Soviet citizens, after the outbreak of war in Croatia an estimated 35,000 persons fled to Hungary between 1 June and 30 September. Most of these were Croats (67.7 per cent of the registered asylum seekers). By the end of the year the proportion of Yugoslav citizens among the total of 54,693 asylum seekers had reached 87 per cent and that of Romanian citizens had dropped to 10 per cent. In 1992, 92.7 per cent of the 16,204 asylum seekers came from Yugoslavia, 5.2 per cent from Romania, 1.5 per cent from the former Soviet Union and 0.6 per cent from other countries.[57] The arrival of Croats, Serbs, Bosnian Muslims, Albanians and Russians meant that, for the first time, the state organs were confronted with a real refugee flow, calling for rapid reactions and brave emergency solutions. They had to deal with asylum seekers who came from genuine nightmares, often only hours before crossing the Hungarian border. All in all the support system functioned quite well and many civil servants of the Office of Refugee Affairs[58] proved to be ingenious in solving acute problems which they had never experienced during the far more balanced previous phases. Contrary to the ethnic Hungarians who had come from Romania with a view to settling here, the refugees from Croatia and Bosnia were, and are, awaiting the end of hostilities when they can voluntarily return. This was even reflected in the fact that they were unwilling to leave the close vicinity of the Southern border of Hungary (facing Croatia and Serbia) and move into the middle or Northern part of the country. The only alternative to voluntary return in their eyes was resettlement in the West.

Table 9.3 The number of asylum seekers arriving in Hungary in the second wave

		June 1, 1991– December 31, 1991	1992	Total
Total		52,064	16,204	68,268
	From (the former) Yugoslavia	approx. 48,000	15,021	approx. 63,000
	From Romania	1,791	844	2,635
Formally recognised as refugees		285	472	757

Source: Data of the Office of Refugee and Migration Affairs

As the centre of the conflict moved away from the Hungarian border to Bosnia-Herzegovina and as a growing number of European states became unwilling to receive asylum seekers transiting through Hungary, Hungarian

---

[57] All the data in this paragraph stem from mimeographed fact sheets of the Office of Refugee and Migration Affairs.

[58] The Office of Refugee Affairs was renamed the Office of Refugee and Migration Affairs by Government Decree 43/1993 (III. 3) on 3 March 1993 without any visible change in its activites. I use the denomination corresponding to the moment of action under discussion.

admission policy has changed somewhat, reinforcing the already existing trend of a decreasing number of asylum seekers. Therefore data for the last two years shows a convergence of the four countries in terms of aggregated numbers of persons in need of protection. This process is sustained by the fact that most of the ethnic Hungarians who came from Romania in 1988–1991 have in the meantime integrated into Hungarian society by way of acquiring formal immigrant status or becoming naturalised, and a few thousand have either resettled in third countries or have decided to return home voluntarily. The majority of the victims of the Serb-Croat conflict of 1991 also managed either to return to Croatia (even if not to their original place of residence but to other, safe parts) or to resettle.

Therefore the official statistics indicated that, at the end of 1994, 1693 persons were taken care of in reception centres maintained by the Office of Refugee and Migration Affairs and that a further 6045 registered persons, who lived either with Hungarian hosts or on their own, were financially assisted.

The Czech Republic, Poland and Slovakia offer protection to significantly smaller numbers of persons, in the range of 1000–3000 each.[59]

---

[59] Various data for these countries:
  Stock data:
  Czechoslovakia:
      as of 31 December 1992: 2,200 (World Refugee Survey, 1993, p. 50).
  Czech Republic: ⸴
      'Convention refugees': at the end of 1993: 1,211 IOM (1994b), p. 6.
      'Refugees from former Yugoslavia with temporary asylum status': 2,415 IOM (1994b) p. 6.
  Poland:
      as of 31 December 1992: 1.500 (World Refugee Survey, 1993, p. 50).
      'number of foreigners covered by full assistance', 'in the spring of 1993': 1600 (Kozlowski 1994, p. 6).
      'Political refugees maintaining asylum' at the end of 1993: 800 (Weydenthal 1994, p. 40).
  Slovakia:
      'As of 1 April 1993: 91 asylum seekers and 60 recognized refugees were staying in the territory of the Slovak Republic' + 1983 temporary protected persons from Yugoslavia (UNHCR 1993b, p. 46).
      Approximately 1500 persons including temporary protected persons. Oral communication to this author at the training workshop: Refugee Law and Human Rights, organised by UNHCR and the International Helsinki Federation at Stupava, 24–25 June 1994.
  Flow data:
  The Czech Republic:
      In 1993: 1700 foreigners 'applied for political asylum' (Pehe, 1994, p. 31).
  Poland:

II LEGAL ISSUES

1. Substantive Law

a) Definitions

The Czech law underwent substantive restrictive changes in three years. Act No. 498 Concerning Refugees, adopted on 16 November 1990, not only contained a simplified version of the 1951 Convention definition[60] but also extended to forcibly displaced persons who did not qualify as political refugees in the spirit of the 1951 Convention as reflected in section 2 of the Act.[61] An amendment introduced in 1993 removed the 'B status' from the Act.[62]

The Hungarian law on refugee procedure and status[63] does not incorporate a specific definition, but refers back to the 1951 Geneva Convention as part

---

Between '1989 and 1993: 110 persons have been given refugee status excluding former Yugoslavs' (IOM 1994a, p. 33).

'In 1993 applications for awarding the status of refugees concerned 830 persons' (Kozlowski, 1994, p.6).

Slovakia:

'In 1993 ... only two people were granted political asylum' (Fisher 1994, p.43).

[60] Section 2 para (1): 'The status of refugee shall be granted to an alien who has a justified fear of being persecuted in the country whose citizenship he or she possesses for reasons of race religion, ethnic origin, membership in a particular social group, or political belief.' Paragraphs (2) and (3) make arrangements for refugees with multiple citizenship, and those being stateless.

Quotes from the Act concerning refugees stem from a widely circulated mimeographed translation of the Czech text by Dr Ivo Dvorak.

[61] Section 3: 'The status of refugee may be granted for reasons of protection of human rights or humanitarian reasons to an alien who does not meet conditions specified in Section 2, par. 1.'

[62] Act No. 317 adopted on 8 December 1993 and in force since 1 January 1994. Section 3 of Act No 498 (16 November 1990) recognising refugees on humanitarian grounds was replaced by a section actually undermining the principle of the unity of the family declaring that refugee status '*may* be granted to the spouse or the minor children of an alien who has been granted refugee status'(emphasis added). One would think that this is a weakening of the idea already incorporated in recommendation B on the principle of the unity of the family, unanimously adopted by the Conference adopting the Convention relating to the Status of refugees in 1951. (The recommendation is reproduced in *Collection of International Instruments Concerning Refugees*, Geneva, UNHCR, 1988, p. 37.) The English text of the Czech Act was provided to this author by Organizace pro Pomoc Uprchlikom, Prague.

[63] The Convention and the Protocol together became Law-Decree No. 15 of 1989 (1989. évi 15. tvr.) see Magyar Közlöny (Official Gazette) 1989 No. 60, p.1022 entering into force on 15 October, 1989. The Cabinet-Decree (101/1989. Mt. rend.) on the procedure was published in Magyar Közlöny (Official Gazette) 1989 No.66., p. 1090. An unofficial and inaccurate translation of it can be read in the Report of the ECRE

of the Hungarian law – albeit with a geographic reservation[64]. The Polish solution is the same, but without a geographic reservation.[65]

The Slovak Republic has also continued the application of federal Act No 498 of 1990. As of June 1994 the plans to introduce a restrictive modification have not materialised, which means that in principle Slovakia can still apply section 3 of that Act, recognising refugees on humanitarian grounds.

b) Collective temporary protection, individual B status

It is the conviction of this author that the prevailing trend favouring a restrictive interpretation of the 1951 Convention relating to the Status of Refugees, together with the disquieting 'new' pattern of persecution aimed at whole groups, especially at minorities and in civil war situations, necessitates the introduction of legal categories of protection which reflect the fact that most forced migrants do not flee individualised persecution for political reasons, but because of other existential threats.[66] Recent pronouncements of the United Nations High Commissioner for Refugees confirm the need for a revision of the system of protection with a view to exploring the possibilities of temporary protection.[67]

Biannual General Meeting, Budapest, 1991, Appendix 14, which reproduces the Council of Europe, European Committee on Migration document (CDMG) 'Information on the main features of the situation with regard to refugees in Hungary'. The Law-Decree on the status of refugees (1989. évi 19. tvr.), see Magyar Közlöny (Official Gazette) 1989 No 66, p. 1090, like the Cabinet-Decree on the recognition procedure, has entered into force on 15 October 1989. Law No. XXXI of 1989, radically reshaping the Constitution and enacting the new rules on asylum, was promulgated on 23 October 1989. Magyar Közlöny, (Official Gazette) 1989. No. 74, p. 1244.

[64] The technical solution is as follows:
Cabinet-Decree 101/1989 (IX.28) in Art. 2 states that a person is 'entitled to be recognised as a refugee' if he qualifies as a refugee according to Art. 1 B) para (1)(a) of the 1951 Geneva Convention or according to Art. 1, paras. (2) and (3) of its Protocol, and that the exclusion grounds incorporated in Art. 1 C), D), E) or F) of the Convention do not apply. It is a further requirement that the stay of the person 'does not prejudice national security, public order or public health'.

Law-Decree No. 19 of 1989, on the status of persons recognised as refugees, does not give any definition but speaks of 'persons recognised as refugees'.

[65] 'A foreigner may be granted the status of refugee under the Convention Relating to the Status of Refugees, adopted in Geneva on 25 July, 1951, and its additional Protocol Relating to the Status of Refugees, adopted in New York on 31 January, 1967.' Uniform text of the Act on Foreigners as published in the Polish Journal of Laws, 1992, No. 7 item 30, Quoted in English by Galicki (1993) p. 8.

[66] See e.g. Nagy 1991 p. 537; Nagy 1994b p. 132.

[67] The Statement by Ms Sadako Ogata, United Nations High Commissioner for Refugees, to the Forty-fifth Session of the Executive Committee of the High Commissioner's

Clear rules should be formulated in the countries of the region according to which the victims of civil wars and of other man-made catastrophes are exempted from the usual requirements that foreigners are supposed to meet if they want to stay temporarily or reside in these states. An 'asylee'[68] status, something similar to the temporary protected status established by US legislation[69] or to the practice of several European states in connection with Southern Slav victims of the Bosnian war[70] should be introduced, where it has not happened yet, which would unambiguously determine whether the temporary protected person has a right to work, or to set up a business venture, to what level of state assistance (s)he is entitled, whether (s)he is allowed to return briefly to her/his home country to check if the house has not been destroyed and whether family members are still alive. The determination should extend this form of protection to a whole group or class of persons and it would explicitly have a temporary character, not – or at least not necessarily – furnishing a basis for claims for extended residence, immigration or naturalisation.

The second 'asylee' situation to be regulated would refer to cases where an individual who, for one or more reasons, does not meet the criteria of the 1951 Convention but who, for humanitarian reasons to be determined on a case by case basis, would be allowed to remain for a reasonably long or an unlimited period. Such an individual should enjoy full protection from the persecuting state and against refoulement; moreover he should enjoy part of the benefits offered to Convention refugees. A decision would be needed to regulate their position if the grounds for flight ceased to exist. It is crucial that procedural rules on the recognition of asylees (group or individual) be elaborated.

Programme, referring to the safe haven granted to Haitian asylum seekers and to victims of the conflict in former Yugoslavia, included the following words:
'Asylum is not necessarily synonymous with an enduring solution. More often than not, it is a measure of interim protection, which buys time for solutions. ... I believe we must debate the wider and more consistent application of temporary protection. As we mark the twenty-fifth anniversary of the OAU Convention and the tenth anniversary of the Cartagena Declaration, it is opportune to examine the lessons of the broader protection offered by these regional instruments.' Mimeographed text, distributed by UNHCR, p. 3.

68 I use this term to comprise both temporary protected status recognised on the basis of group determination and de facto or B status recognised in individual procedures.

69 See Section 302 of the Immigration Act of 1990 which became Section 244A of the Immigration and Nationality Act of 1952, 8 USC 1254A.

70 See: (UNHCR) Comprehensive Response to the Humanitarian Crisis in Former Yugoslavia, Survey of Implementation of Temporary Protection, 16 July 1993; see also Kjaerum (1994).

Hungary, host to the greatest number of temporary protected Southern Slav asylees, has not adopted rules concerning the procedure for their recognition or their status and everything has been left to low level, non-public circulars and to similar ad hoc decisions. Slovakia, by contrast, has adopted a government resolution fixing the basic terms of the temporary protected status.[71] According to this resolution, the Government agrees:

1. to extend residence and assistance to such citizens from former Yugoslavia until 31 December 1994, who either at the time of entry or after entry to the territory of the Slovak Republic apply for the temporary protection ...
2. to provide social benefit payments and social service care to those 'de facto' refugees who are accommodated with private persons and comply with the conditions for the provision of the above ...[72]

The above quoted government resolution incorporates a group decision, concerning victims of the (civil) wars in former Yugoslavia. However, it may be noted[73] that the Law on the Stay of Aliens in the Territory of the Czech and Slovak Federal Republic, dated 4 March 1992 (which is still applied in both successor states) provides in Article 7 that refuge may be given to asylum seekers who do not qualify as Convention refugees. Notably, it declares that permission for permanent stay may be granted to an alien not only in the event of family unification, but also 'in other humanitarian cases'.[74]

Poland has no legislation either on collective recognition of temporary protected status or on individual 'de facto' status. Nevertheless Poland, just like Hungary, does extend temporary protection to victims of civil wars by way of extending the visa of the person requesting it. Poland also invited Bosnian children and offered protection for 1,000 ex detainees.[75]

c) Incomplete legislation

It is a general feature of the countries of the region that legislation, i.e. the web of legal norms concerning asylum seekers, temporary protected

---

[71] Resolution of the Government of the Slovak Republic of 11 January 1994, No. 12. Mimeod English text distributed at the training workshop: Refugee Law and Human Rights, organised by UNHCR and the International Helsinki Federation at Stupava, 24–25 June 1994.

[72] Ibid.

[73] See e.g. Lemay 1994 p. 43.

[74] The *Survey of the Implementation of Temporary Protection* produced by UNHCR on 30 April 1993 notes that 'Temporary refuge for citizens of former Yugoslavia was provided until 31 December 1992 by a decree of the authorities of the Czech and Slovak Federal Republic. The Czech republic, after the dissolution ... extended the time period for temporary refuge until 1993.' Unfortunately the legal nature of this 'decree of the authorities' is not explained by the UNHCR and could not be established.

[75] UNHCR: *Survey of the Implementation of Temporary Protection* 30 April 1993, p. 14.

persons and recognised refugees, is and remains incomplete and uneven. Incompleteness refers to the fact that major segments of life remain unregulated, unevenness is used to point out that some rules appear in acts of parliament, while others, eventually no less important from the protected person's point of view, appear only in ministerial decrees, or even in unwritten 'gentlemen's agreements'.

Without listing all the major gaps in the legislation one may refer to the non-existence of regulations in all the four countries describing the rights and duties of temporary protected persons, at least in the same detail as the 1951 Geneva Convention provides in respect of refugees, to the lack of specific procedural rules for any determination procedure in Poland, or for temporary protected status in Hungary.

With regard to the varied level of right-determining authorities, it may serve as an illustration that in Hungary, notwithstanding the Constitution according to which basic rights have to be regulated by Acts of Parliament, the status determination procedure is regulated by a government decree and the rights of persons recognised by the UNHCR branch office in Budapest are only based on a gentlemen's agreement between the UNHCR representative and the Hungarian authorities.[76]

d) Differences between Constitutions and the Convention

In several Central European countries the provisions of the constitution concerning refugees and the Convention definition do not coincide. It has been pointed out[77] that, for example in Hungary, the Constitutional amendment adopted in October 1989, eight days after the text of the 1951 Convention became part of Hungarian law, did not, and still does not, precisely reflect the Convention's approach. Amongst the grounds of persecution, membership in a special social group is *not* accepted in the Hungarian Constitution while 'language' is *added* to the acceptable

---

[76] The unresolved status of persons escaping non-European persecution has been frequently highlighted by authors writing on Hungarian law. See e.g. Nagy 1992 p. 37, and Tóth 1994 p.111.

[77] Nagy, 1994a, describing in detail the differences between the Hungarian Constitution and the 1951 Convention.

The text of Section 65 of the Hungarian Constitution is as follows:

'(1) The Republic of Hungary – in accordance with the provisions of law – grants asylum for those foreign nationals, who in their country of nationality, or for those stateless persons who in their residence, were persecuted for racial, religious, national, linguistic or political reasons.

(2) A person granted asylum cannot be extradited to another state.

(3) The adoption of the law on asylum requires the votes of two thirds of the Members of Parliament who are present.'

grounds. A well founded fear of persecution is replaced simply with the term 'persecution', which would mean a substantive shift if interpreted literally, not allowing for the mere probability of persecution but requiring past persecution or the certainty of persecution in the future.

A specific difficulty, characteristic only of the Hungarian situation, arises from the fact that in 1989 Hungary had adhered to the 1951 Geneva Convention and its 1967 Protocol relating to the status of refugees, with a geographic reservation excluding victims of non-European events from the protection offered by the Hungarian authorities.[78] Since the Constitution does not contain any formal restriction on the application of Section 65 granting asylum 'in accordance with the law' for the persecuted, the question arises whether this incorporates – according to the dualistic tradition of Hungary – the 1951 Convention *as incorporated into Hungarian law*, that is with the geographic reservation. It seems that neither of the possible answers to this question leads to a satisfactory outcome. If one says yes, then an unresolved contradiction between the two definitions arises, if the answer is negative then not only the practice of the last half decade, which has been tolerated by the international community, must be found to have been illegal, but major problems would arise in connection with the status of international conventions, including the covenants on human rights, in Hungarian domestic law.

Section 53 of the Constitution of the Slovak Republic similarly simplifies the Convention language. It declares that: '[t]he Slovak Republic grants the right of asylum to foreigners persecuted for the exercise of their political rights and freedoms. Those who acted in contradiction with the basic human rights and freedoms may be refused asylum.'[79] However, since according to Section 11 of the same Constitution international agreements on human rights and basic freedoms take precedence over Slovak law, it may be presumed that the Convention definition would have priority over the Constitution's much more restrictive definition.

2. Procedural Aspects

a) Eligibility (preliminary screening, fast procedures)
The Czech Republic was the first among the four countries to institutionalise an accelerated procedure. Law No. 317 of 8 December 1993 has amended the 1990 regulation by introducing into section 11 two

---

[78] Other European states maintaining a geographic reservation are Malta, Monaco and Turkey, but none of the Central and Eastern European states.

[79] Blaustein, Albert P. and Flanz, Gisbert (1993) *Constitutions of the Countries of the World.*

new paragraphs on manifestly unfounded claims. According to the amendment the Ministry of the Interior 'will decide about [the] refusal within seven days of the application'.[80] This will happen if the applicant does not cooperate to establish his identity, if he is a citizen or resident of 'a state in which there exists no threat of persecution ... on the grounds of generally known facts',[81] or if there are reasons which would *ab initio* exclude recognition as a refugee, or if the applicant justifies his application exclusively by reference to economic needs.

In contrast to the general rule of 15 days' leave for appeal, an appeal against the speedy decision of the Ministry for the Interior must be brought within three days.

One wonders if the tough but controllable rules of the Czech Republic are better (i.e. less bad) than those of the other states analysed here. While the latter may be softer, they are also difficult to identify since they cannot be found in statute books, only in practice. A careful scrutiny of the statistics will immediately reveal that there is a huge gap between 'new arrivals' and 'procedures started'. Even if those – usually Southern Slav – asylum seekers are deducted, who do not start a formal procedure for recognition as refugees because they have received temporary protected status without recourse to a full scale procedure, there remains a difference between the new arrivals and the procedures set into motion. As an example the Hungarian data can be used. According to the official statistics[82] there were 5,366 new arrivals in 1993. Of these, 3,721 persons have received asylee (temporary protected) status, which means that 1,645 had to enter by another process. However, only 468 procedures for recognition of refugee status had been started in 1993. Since, according to the procedural rules, the determination procedure must start within six days from arrival it is fair to assume that more than a thousand persons belong to the category which was screened out. Many of them may have been potential immigrants who were confused about the procedure and who, on a 'trial and error' basis, went to see the local authority of the Office of Refugee and Migration Affairs to ascertain whether they could be exempted from the rather onerous requirements set for immigrants. However, another subgroup of those who were among the 'new arrivals' but who do not show up either under the heading 'temporary protected' or under 'status determination

---

80 The English text of Law No. 317/1993 , changing and amending Law No. 498/1990 on refugees, is available from the UNHCR database. The quote comes from Art. I modifying Section 11.

81 Ibid.

82 Menekültügyi és Migrációs Hivatal (Office of Refugee and Migration Affairs) Menekültügyi Statisztika (Refugee Statistics), Budapest, 1994, mimeo.

procedure started' may have been genuine refugees entitled to protection who did not manage to convince the authority about the solid basis of their case. Since the decision to start the procedure rests with the authority and since no formal decision on the refusal to start the procedure has to be taken it may be assumed, without undue cynicism, that a few of that roughly 1,000 persons who disappeared from view, as a consequence of the informal preliminary screening, may have been persons entitled to protection according to the 1951 Geneva Convention.

b) Some other procedural insufficiencies

A lively bunch of critical remarks concerning the determination procedure in these countries can easily be collected. To follow the eventual route of such applicants either appearing at the border crossing point or at the 'green border', and wishing to cross the 'magic' line illegally, many of them will face a border guard not speaking any language they understand, and with minimal or no specific education in refugee issues. Although it has been a long-standing requirement that decisions – even on eligibility – be taken by competent, specially trained officials,[83] one has the impression, after conversations with men in the field, that the goodwill or even apathy of a border guard can decide the fate of a busload of Bosnian asylum seekers.

The next group of problems relates to the role of NGOs and public opinion in the process. Societies of East-Central Europe have a much less developed 'civil society' network of charitable and voluntary assistance organisations than the Western democracies. Therefore, international NGOs active in the refugee field, like ECRE, Interights or Amnesty International, have difficulty in establishing a solid local network of volunteers who are sufficiently numerous and powerful to provide, for example, an around-the-clock consulting service at the major border crossing points or at the international airports. Therefore, the legal entitlements incorporated in the procedural rules – for example to have a legal counsel – remain hollow words if the asylum seeker – especially ones not speaking any of the very few languages spoken by the competent officials – have no chance to use the mediating services of NGOs. The weakness of the NGO network exacerbates the fact that decisions in individual cases, just as decisions on policy issues and legislative dilemmas, remain hidden from the broader public.

If the asylum seeker manages to observe the tough deadlines and submits his application, then the next major problem of communication is confronted. Very few professional and impartial interpreters of non-

---

[83] Recently reaffirmed – in respect of Western states as well – in ECRE 1994b, p. 8.

European languages are available, so authorities frequently work with the help of other asylum seekers and refugees, who may not be professional interpreters, and sometimes through the medium of a third language. There is no need to emphasise the extent to which this method may influence the subsequent analysis of the brief record of the personal interview, when e.g. the issue of credibility arises.

Long periods of confinement in reception centers (even if formally the asylum seeker or refugee is allowed to leave, (s)he has nowhere to go and no funds with which to liven up an outing) may lead to infringements of behavioural rules which, in the Czech republic, Hungary and Slovakia, may lead to a refusal to recognize her status. One commentator has rightly noted that termination of the procedure for grounds unrelated to the substance of the claim and not incorporated in the 1951 Geneva Convention is, at the very least, problematic.[84]

The list of procedural problems could be extended further and that would still leave untouched the no less important substantive issues of integrating recognized refugees and of deciding about the maximum possible extent of temporariness.

III CONCLUSION

It is the conviction of this author that migratory waves, encompassing people escaping harsh political, environmental or economic conditions, will emerge as one of the most pressing issues of the medium term future, eventually requiring more scholarly and political attention than habitual topics of learned debate, such as power relations. The disparity between the sophisticated North and the struggling South will take forms which will not be susceptible to containment with the methods and techniques presently preferred by Western European states. Exclusion and defense are not a solution in the long run. Voluntary and involuntary migration are in a dialectical relationship. Confusing them is as great a sin as treating them as fully separate. This is the delicate task the East-Central European countries should master. Immigration policy may be selective, national-interest maximising and own-ethnicity oriented. However, refugees are entitled to be treated without discrimination, to be protected and assisted not because of the benefit which they bring to the receiving society[85] but because of the

---

[84] Lemay, 1994 p. 66 referring also to a UNHCR commentary related to the proposed amendments of Act No 498/1990 of Czechoslovakia.

[85] Although as we all know, at least from the UNHCR poster, 'Einstein was a refugee, too'.

underlying idea of, yes, global solidarity. East-Central European states should identify their immigration policy as well as confirm their commitment to refugee law principles, keeping in mind that regular, voluntary migration is not a danger but the most natural process, which they themselves have contributed to. This requires 'courage and vision'.[86]

Therefore, simply copying the Western European patterns as a recipe for East-Central Europe won't help, especially since the OECD states are also undergoing a period of new target-setting, building new mechanisms to respond to events not adequately contemplated in the 1951 Geneva Convention. The United Nations High Commissioner for Refugees has recently proposed a five element strategy in response to the actual crisis (Ogata 1993 pp. 14–20). First, protection, eventually a reformulated temporary protection to be granted to victims of war and generalized violence. Second, a clear distinction between refugees and migrants. Third, greater assistance to poorer asylum countries and countries where large scale repatriation takes place. Fourth, prevention, including not only economic assistance but also increased respect for human rights. Fifth, sound public information on migration and refugee affairs to deflate unrealistic expectations. This, together with the serious self control and intensive human rights checks advocated by ECRE and other NGOs on the micro level, constitute viable alternatives to the never-ending spiral of restrictive innovations.

---

[86] Words of the UN High Commissioner for Refugees, Ms Sadako Ogata, used in connection with the 'dilemma that confronts Europe in preserving the fundamental principles of human rights and humanitarianism while resisting threats to the security and stability of European societies' (Ogata 1993 p. 11).

10. A New Constitutional (Dis)Order for Eastern Europe?

Istvan Pogany[1]

I INTRODUCTION

Constitutions, by their very nature, cannot be neutral.[2] Of necessity, they purport to embody the key political, moral and economic values of the societies in which they function.[3] Thus, the transition from Communism to democratic, market-oriented societies in Eastern Europe – seemingly a region-wide phenomenon – has been accompanied by fundamental changes in constitutions.[4]

---

[1] I am grateful to Dr. Boldizsár Nagy, of the Eötvös Loránd University, Budapest, for his helpful and insightful comments on an earlier draft of this chapter. While I know he would vigorously dissent from many of my conclusions, I greatly appreciated discussing the contents of this chapter with him. All translations from Hungarian-language texts are mine.

[2] Of course, the principle of neutrality, or equality, may itself be a constitutional norm, such as the principle of equality before the law. However, this is scarcely ideologically-neutral.

[3] In certain instances, constitutions do not reflect the actual political or economic realities of a society. Rather, they function as an instrument of foreign policy (and domestic legitimation) by giving an appearance of concern for human rights, the rule of law and democratic government. See e.g. the 1946 Constitution of Albania, as revised through to 1958. The Constitution 'guaranteed' Albanian citizens various human rights including, in Article 20, 'freedom of speech, of the press, of organization, of meetings, of assembly and of public manifestations' (See Peaslee 1968, p. 6).

[4] For the consolidated text of the 1949 Hungarian Constitution, as amended through to 1990, see Blaustein and Flanz, Binder VIII, issued Oct. 1990; for the text of the Constitution of the Czech Republic of 16 December 1992, see ibid., Binder V, issued June 1993; for the text of the Constitution of the Slovak Republic of 1 September 1992, see ibid., Binder XVII, issued June 1993; for the consolidated text of the Constitution of the Republic of Poland as of 1 May 1990, see ibid., Binder XV, issued August 1991. See, also, the text of the 'Little Constitution', ibid., issued Oct. 1993. For the text of the Constitution of Romania of 21 November 1991, see ibid., Vol. XV, issued March

In essence, the new constitutional order that has been proclaimed by (and for) the states of Eastern Europe enshrines three complementary principles. These are democratization, the recognition of individual and minority rights and constitutionalism. 'Constitutionalism' is to be understood here as the imposition of constitutional constraints on either executive or legislative discretion, even if the government or legislature appears to have strong electoral support.[5]

In terms of democratization, the new or revised constitutional texts provide for the establishment of political parties, for periodic parliamentary elections, and for the right of adult citizens to participate directly in public affairs and to vote in elections by means of secret ballot. For example, Article 29(2) of the Constitution of the Slovak Republic states that '[c]itizens have the right to establish political parties and political movements and to associate in them', while Article 30 provides:[6]

(1) Citizens have the right to participate in the administration of public affairs either directly or through the free election of their representatives.
(2) Elections must be held within deadlines that do not exceed the regular electoral period as defined by law.
(3) The right to vote is universal, equal and direct and is exercised by means of secret ballot.

The recognition of human rights has been of central importance in the new or revised constitutional texts adopted throughout Eastern Europe.[7] In general, the rights included emphasise those civil and political freedoms which were denied (in practice if not always in theory) during the Communist era. Significantly, these rights are compatible with the market economies which the post-Communist states have pledged themselves to

---

1992. For the text of the Constitution of the Republic of Bulgaria of 12 July 1991, see ibid., Binder III, issued May 1992.

5 See e.g. J. Elster, 'Introduction', in Elster and Slagstad 1988 p. 2, who states that 'Constitutionalism refers to limits on majority decisions; more specifically, to limits that are in some sense self-imposed.' Constitutionalism is sometimes understood in more general terms. Thus, according to a recent definition, constitutionalism 'enshrines respect for human worth and dignity as its central principle. To protect that value, citizens must have a right to political participation, and their government must be hedged in by substantive limits on what it can do, even when perfectly mirroring the popular will' (See Murphy in Greenberg et al, 1993 p. 3).

6 For the text of the Constitution of the Slovak Republic, of September 1, 1992 see Blaustein and Flanz, Binder XVII, issued June 1993.

7 The novelty does not lie simply in the fact that human rights are included in the new or revised constitutional texts as many rights, albeit often in a qualified form, were enshrined in the constitutions that were in force up to 1989. Rather, perhaps, the novelty of the new or revised constitutional texts lies in the fact that the enumerated rights are not, for the most part, intended to be merely of rhetorical significance.

construct.[8] In addition, in view of the existence of linguistic, ethnic or religious minorities in virtually all of the states of Eastern Europe (and a long regional history of problems in accommodating minorities), minority rights also feature prominently in these constitutional texts.[9]

In the Czech Republic, for example, Article 1 of the Charter of Fundamental Rights and Freedoms, which is considered to be part of the constitutional order of the state, affirms that, '[h]umans are free and equal in their dignity and in their rights. The fundamental rights and freedoms are inherent, inalienable, nonprescriptive'.[10] The Charter enumerates various civil and political rights in Chapter Two. These include, for example, the 'right to life' (Article 6(1)), the prohibition of torture and 'of inhuman or degrading treatment' (Article 7(2)), '[f]reedom of movement and settlement' (Article 14(1)), '[f]reedom of thought, conscience and religious confession' (Article 15(1)), '[f]reedom of expression and the right to information' (Article 17(1)), the 'right of petition ... to organs of the State or of territorial self-government' (Article 18(1)), the right of peaceful assembly (Article 19(1)), and the right of citizens 'to participate in the administration of public affairs either directly or through the free election of their representatives' (Article 21(1)).

Social and economic rights, which featured prominently in the communist constitutions adopted by the Eastern European states after the Second World War,[11] are relegated to Chapter Four of the Charter. They are limited in extent and are largely confined to the barest essentials of a welfare state rather than the familiar precepts of a socialist economy. Thus, in place of a right *to* employment, the Charter guarantees the right of everyone 'to acquire the means of his livelihood by work', i.e. that no one's right to obtain and to engage in work shall be impeded. In the event that citizens 'are unable without their fault to exercise this right', the state 'shall provide appropriate material security' (Article 26(3)).

The rights of national and ethnic minorities are provided for in Chapter Three of the Charter. These include the principle that a person's 'national or ethnic identity' may not be 'used to his detriment' (Article 24), and that

---

8 By contrast, social and economic rights may make material demands upon governments which, in a market economy, the state is powerless to fulfill (whether from practical or ideological considerations)

9 The problems of minorities and of minority rights are discussed more fully *infra*, Part II.

10 In accordance with Article 3 of the Constitution of the Czech Republic, the Charter of Fundamental Rights and Freedoms is 'part of the constitutional order of the Czech Republic'. For the text of both the Czech Constitution of 16 December 1992 and of the Charter of Fundamental Rights and Freedoms see *supra* n. 4.

11 For a discussion of the communist constitutions see *infra*, Part III.

citizens belonging to 'national and ethnic minorities' have the right to 'education in their language' and to 'use their language in official contact' (Article 25(2)(a),(b)).[12]

In terms of constitutionalism i.e. the imposition of constitutional constraints on executive or legislative discretion, the most significant innovation has been the establishment of constitutional courts in the post-Communist states of Eastern Europe.[13] While there are significant variations between individual courts in terms of subject-matter jurisdiction, rights of access or judicial assertiveness, there are important unifying elements. In essence, these courts are separate from the ordinary judicial structures and are mandated soley to secure the constitutionality of laws, and to otherwise ensure that the constitution is respected.[14] For example, Article 83 of the Czech Constitution states '[t]he Constitutional Court is the judicial organ protecting constitutionality'. Similarly, the Preamble of Act XXXII of 1989, adopted by the Hungarian National Assembly, states that the Hungarian Constitutional Court was established:[15]

> to realise the rule of law, constitutional order, the protection of fundamental rights guaranteed in the Constitution, to ensure the separation of powers and the balance of power between the branches of government ...

Thus, these courts have been entrusted with responsibility for safeguarding the new constitutional order mapped out for Eastern Europe.[16] In this daunting enterprise, their ability to resist encroachments on the various constitutions, by either the legislature or the executive, will be of paramount importance.

---

[12] See, similarly, Article 34(2)(b) of the Slovak Constitution. However, the Slovak text adds, somewhat ominously, '[t]he enactment of the rights of citizens belonging to national minorities and ethnic groups that are guaranteed in this Constitution must not be conducive to jeopardizing the sovereignty and territorial integrity of the Slovak Republic or to discrimination against its other inhabitants'. For the text of the Slovak Constitution see *supra* n. 4.

[13] Of the Eastern European states only the former Czechoslovakia possessed a Constitutional Court with powers of review over primary legislation during the inter-war period. During the Communist era, Poland established a Constitutional Tribunal in 1985, while Hungary instituted a somewhat less powerful Constitutional Law Council in 1984. See Schwartz 1993a p. 28. See also Schwartz 1993b Ch. 6. On the German Constitutional Court, which has been an important model for the Constitutional Courts established in Eastern Europe see e.g. Kommers 1976.

[14] On the significant differences in subject-matter jurisdiction between these courts see e.g. Schwartz 1993b at pp. 167–70.

[15] See 1989: XXXII tv., in *Magyar Közlöny*, No. 77, 30 October 1989, p. 1283.

[16] In addition to the sources cited *supra* n. 13, see e.g. Brzezinski 1993a p. 673; Pogany 1993 p. 332; Paczolay 1993 p. 21.

However, in considering whether a new constitutional order has truly been inaugurated in Eastern Europe and whether such an order enjoys reasonable prospects of permanence, it should be borne in mind that, despite a shared history of Communism in the post-War era, the countries of Eastern Europe are by no means uniform. Indeed, viewed historically, Eastern Europe has never been remotely monolithic.[17] Whether in terms of economic development, political culture, religion, language, national and ethnic composition, or historical experience, the states of the region have a richly diverse heritage. These elements may yet prove decisive in determining the extent to which the new constitutional structures, grounded in an apparent commitment to democratic government, the rule of law and the protection of human rights, take root within particular states in Eastern Europe. A degree of diversification, whether in terms of constitutional arrangements or political culture (and of course in matters of economic policy) is probably inevitable now that the countries concerned (or political elites within these countries) are 'free' to determine for themselves their institutions and principles of government.[18]

Moreover, Eastern Europe, before its enforced sovietization, was not simply an extension or continuation of Western Europe (other than geographically). Thus, not only was Eastern Europe characterised by internal variations of every kind, it was also *different*, in certain fundamental and loosely unifying respects, from Western Europe.[19] Of course, these differences were neither absolute nor uniform. Thus, the 'differentness' of any individual East European state depended on its particular historical experience. Nevertheless, the differences between East and West Europe were real and important, whether in matters of economic development, political culture or social stratification. Therefore it should not be assumed (as has sometimes appeared to be the case) that the existence of Soviet-type communist regimes was the *sole* obstacle to the establishment of pluralistic, liberal democracies in Eastern Europe, committed to the rule of law and the protection of human rights. Any real

---

[17] Eastern Europe appeared monolithic during the period of Communist rule, when economic, political and constitutional structures were, of necessity, modelled to a significant extent on those of the Soviet Union. Nevertheless, even during this period of enforced conformity substantial differences emerged, notably in economic policy. See Swain and Swain 1993 Ch. 6.

[18] Of course, freedom is relative. Thus, it is doubtful whether the countries of Eastern Europe would be free to choose 'unfreedom' through a return to either unreconstructed Communism or some other form of totalitarianism. Such a choice, even if *freely* exercised, would undoubtedly result in economic and political sanctions.

[19] See Schöpflin 1993 Ch. 1; Polonsky 1975 Ch. 1; Rothschild 1974 Ch. 1. For an excellent historical overview see Okey 1986.

understanding of the prospects of an enduring constitutional transformation of the region must be informed by a knowledge of its history and particularities. (See, also, on this point, Lewis 1993 p. 262, at pp. 264–5.)

II EASTERN EUROPE BEFORE THE COMMUNIST ERA

Eastern Europe did not *become* different from Western Europe as a result of sovietization. Rather, the differences were transformed and accentuated as a consequence of sovietization. Thus, important dissimilarities between Eastern and Western Europe were apparent long before the Commmunist era.[20] These were in part *material* and in part *social* and *political*. In material terms, the 'otherness' of Eastern Europe was reflected in the region's relative poverty and economic backwardness (Rothschild 1974 pp. 14–15):

> By virtually every relevant statistical index ... East Central Europe was less productive, less literate, and less healthy than West Central and Western Europe. A potentially rich region with poor people, its interwar censuses record not so much a distribution of wealth as a maldistribution of poverty.

The 'differentness' of Eastern Europe was also apparent in the overwhelmingly agrarian character of the region's economies, with significant industrialization having occurred only in Poland, Hungary and Czechoslovakia (Polonsky 1975 pp. 9–10).   Of these states, only Czechoslovakia possessed a broadly-based manufacturing sector comparable to those of the major Western economies.[21] Moreover, the more productive Czechoslovak industries were concentrated, overwhelmingly, in Bohemia and Moravia in the Czech part of the republic (Rothschild 1974 pp. 87–8). Lack of industrialization was compounded by the relative backwardness of agricultural production in Eastern Europe (Rothschild 1974 p. 15):

> Interwar East Central Europe was preponderantly unproductively agricultural. While far higher proportions of its population were engaged in farming than was the case in Western Europe, the productivity of its agriculture in terms both of yield rates per unit of agricultural area and of yield rates per agricultural worker was far lower. The result was a vicious cycle of rural undercapitalization, underproductivity, underconsumption, underemployment, overpopulation, and pervasive misery.

---

[20] See references *supra* n. 19. Okey suggests that '[i]t was in the sixteenth and seventeenth centuries, the period beginning with the Renaissance and the Reformation, that the crucial change occurred that made Eastern Europe thereafter a land apart ... remote from West European experience' Okey 1986 p. 17.

[21] However, even Czech industry was not uniformly advanced by the standards of the day. See e.g. Rothschild 1974 pp. 87–8.

The economic plight of the bulk of the peasants was due, in part, to the fact that they were either landless or owned 'dwarf-holdings' too small to be economically viable.[22] Post World War I efforts at land-reform, such as in Poland and Hungary, were generally half-hearted and failed to materially improve their condition.[23] Against this background of rural poverty and deprivation,[24] the existence of large estates, occupying a substantial proportion of the agricultural land, engendered considerable bitterness.[25]

The *material* underdevelopment of Eastern Europe went hand in hand with a range of social and cultural characteristics markedly at variance with the experience of the West. In particular, the survival of feudalism in Eastern Europe until as late as the middle of the nineteenth century (it was abolished in Austria-Hungary in 1848 and in Russia in 1861) left a pervasive and socially conservative legacy. Thus, many of the states in the region were characterised by a high degree of social stratification, by limited social mobility and by the existence of a property-owning class with a pronounced aversion to involvement in either commerce or manufacturing.[26] In the absence of a 'native' class able or willing to engage in these activities, 'foreign' elements, generally ethnic Germans or Jews, tended to predominate (Polonsky 1975 p. 5; Schöpflin 1993 p. 20). The social stratification, referred to above, reproduced itself in the political sphere with the formation of peasant parties throughout Eastern Europe affirming the interests of their class and often characterised by a

---

[22] Polonsky 1975 p. 7. On the general backwardness of agricultural production, particularly in Eastern (as distinct from East Central) Europe see Gunst, in Chirot 1989 Ch. 3. By the beginning of the twentieth century in Hungary, 'the agrarian society ... had been significantly proletarianized due to the principle of equal inheritance. Since industry could not absorb the agrarian labor, about half the agricultural population consisted of totally destitute agrarian proletarians or dwarf holders who subsisted by wage labor'. ibid., p. 80. On the various categories of peasants in Eastern Europe see e.g. Schöpflin 1993 pp. 25–9.

[23] Polonsky 1975 p. 8. By contrast, land reform in Czechoslovakia, in 1920, was more far-reaching. ibid., pp. 119–20. In Romania, radical land reforms failed to alleviate the economic plight of the peasants due, in the main, to significant population growth. See e.g. Stokes, in Chirot 1989 p. 210, at p. 233.

[24] For an interesting autobiographical study of the condition of agricultural labourers living and working on the large estates in South Western Hungary in the '20s and '30s see Illyés 1967. The book was originally published in Hungarian under the title of *Puszták Népe* in 1936.

[25] Polonsky 1975 p. 7. On the distinctive position of both Serbia and Bulgaria, where no real landowner class existed (and consequently no large estates) see e.g. Stokes 1989 pp. 234–6.

[26] See Schöpflin 1993 pp. 15, 19, 24. Such social stratification, which was particularly pronounced in Poland and Hungary, was largely absent in Serbia and Bulgaria where the Ottoman Turks had liquidated the nobility. See Stokes 1989 pp. 234–6.

pronounced distaste for the towns and for supposedly 'urban values' (Polonsky 1975 p. 11; Rothschild 1974 pp. 16–18).

Politically, inter-war Eastern Europe differed fundamentally from Western Europe in terms of its historical experience and (consequently) its political consciousness. As late as the beginning of the nineteenth century, Eastern Europe remained subsumed within various Empires, in contrast to the modern nation states that had emerged as the primary political unit in the West (see e.g. Rothschild 1974 p. 3). Many of the states which were subsequently created in Eastern Europe only gained their independence in the general political settlement following the First World War,[27] a settlement which also produced substantial increases in the size of certain states and corresponding contractions in the proportions of some of their neighbours.[28] The prolonged colonization of Eastern Europe tended to inhibit both the development of a democratic political culture and modern, industrial economies.

The states established after the First World War adopted broadly democratic constitutions. Thus, Czechoslovakia adopted a constitution in 1920 which conferred extensive powers upon the presidency, created a bicameral legislature, and introduced compulsory universal adult suffrage in parliamentary elections (see e.g. Rothschild 1974 pp. 93–94). In addition, as noted above, Czechoslovakia was the only state in the region to establish a Constitutional Court during the inter-war period. Poland adopted a democratic constitution in March 1921 which, in contrast to the Czech model, limited the authority of the presidency and concentrated ultimate power in the Sejm (Davies 1986 p. 121). Hungary, which emerged from the First World War as a defeated power, did not follow this trend. In contrast to Czechoslovakia and Poland, where the post-First World War settlement resulted in genuine efforts to democratize the political process and to create a modern constitutional structure, Hungary experienced, in rapid succession, a short-lived government under Count Mihály Károly, established on 31 October 1918 after a bloodless revolt, a Soviet government headed by Béla Kún, formed in March 1919, and a repressive and reactionary regime installed in August of the same year (Rothschild

---

27 This was true of Czechoslovakia, Yugoslavia (formerly only Serbia had achieved statehood), Poland (an example of the restoration of sovereignty) and the Baltic states.

28 The principal 'winner', apart from the newly-established states (whose borders were often drawn with considerable generosity at the expense of neighbouring states) was Romania. The principal 'loser' was Hungary, which was left with 'only one-third of her historic territory, two-fifths of her prewar population, and two-thirds of her Magyar people'. Rothschild 1974 p. 155. Other 'losers' included Bulgaria (to Greece), Germany (to Poland) and Austria which, to quote Clemenceau, became 'what is left over'. See Polonsky 1975 p. 63.

1974 pp. 139–53). Constitutionally, Hungary remained an anomaly. Unlike either Poland or Czechoslovakia, Hungary did not adopt a written constitution. Instead, the country continued to be governed, as in centuries past, by an unwritten constitution composed of custom and a series of basic laws (Paczolay 1993 pp. 22–3). Thus, Hungary lacked 'a real constitutional moment' (see Paczolay 1993 p. 23).

The democratic 'experiment' in inter-war Eastern Europe was generally unsuccessful. In Poland, a military coup in May 1926 returned Marshall Pilsudski to power (Davies 1986 pp. 123–5). Although the subsequent Polish regime can scarcely be described as *totalitarian* – the press enjoyed relative freedom and most political parties were permitted to operate – it was nevertheless, and to an increasing extent, *authoritarian*.[29] In 1935, a new Constitution was adopted providing for a massive extension of presidential powers (Rothschild 1974 p. 61).

In Hungary, the democratic 'experiment' had been notably circumscribed. Despite a system of government which was, in broad terms, parliamentary, Hungary lacked the universal adult suffrage which is an indispensable adjunct of democracy. In 1920, the proportion of the adult population entitled to vote was actually *reduced* while the secret ballot was removed in country areas. This was accomplished under the premiership of the 'liberal' and relatively enlightened Count Bethlen (Rothschild 1974 pp. 160–1).

Of course, it would be unfair and pointless to apply contemporary standards of democratic entitlement to inter-war Hungary. Thus, one should not lose sight of the fact that universal adult suffrage was only achieved gradually (and often painfully) in the 'developed' democracies of Western Europe. Nevertheless, the principle of universal adult suffrage in the modern sense, i.e. of a secret ballot in which all citizens enjoy a vote of equal weight (irrespective of property, wealth or other considerations) was generally accepted in Western Europe either before, or immediately after, the First World War. Apart from France, which recognized the principle of universal adult suffrage as early as March 1848, Sweden adopted the principle in 1909, Italy in 1912, the Netherlands in 1917, Great Britain in 1918, Germany in 1919 and Belgium in 1921.[30] Thus, in actually *reducing* the proportion of the adult population entitled to vote in 1920, and in

---

[29] Rothschild suggests that this quasi-constitutionalism was due to the contradictions in Pilsudski's own personality, which united a craving for constitutional legitimacy with the assertion of his personal will. See Rothschild 1974 pp. 55–6.

[30] See Chantebout 1986 pp. 202–4. However, as the author notes, these dates apply to the recognition in each state of the principal of universal adult suffrage for *men* aged twenty one or more. A later date would be required, 'si l'on s'attache à d'autres critères: le vote des femmes et celui des jeunes' ibid., p. 204.

removing the secret ballot in country areas, Hungary was moving against the tide of European political and constitutional practice at that time. In truth, Hungary was 'an authoritarian state which remained parliamentary, but not democratic, in the old eighteenth century oligarchic sense' (Hobsbawm 1994 p. 113).

In Czechoslovakia, the introduction of democratic institutions was more successful than elsewhere in East Central and Eastern Europe. This can be explained, at least in part, by reference to *social* and *economic* factors. Thus, it has been widely acknowledged that the relatively successful adoption of democratic practices in inter-war Czechoslovakia owed much to the *embourgeoisification* of the state, particularly of the Czech lands, by the time of the First World War. Thus, the emergence of a large and self-confident middle class with strong democratic aspirations, a process coinciding with (and owing much to) the industrialization of the Czech provinces, provided a receptive environment for democratic institutions (Stokes 1989 pp. 212–19). By contrast, Hungary remained a predominantly agrarian society on the eve of the First World War, with a powerful and politically ascendant land-owning aristocracy (Stokes 1989 pp. 219–26).

The failure of the Czech model was due, ultimately, to external factors, notably the territorial claims of Nazi Germany, which culminated in the dismemberment of Czechoslovakia and the establishment of a German Protectorate over Bohemia and Moravia (Rothschild 1974 pp. 132–4). However, despite its democratic successes, Czechoslovakia had largely failed to accommodate the increasingly strident nationalist claims of its Slovak and ethnic German populations (Polonsky 1975 pp. 122–5). Slovakia had entered the union with the Czech provinces with a sense of frustrated nationalism and an ingrained feeling of inferiority. The Czech authorities proved incapable of assuaging these feelings.

However, the nature or genuineness of the democratic and constitutionalizing experiment in inter-war Eastern Europe also calls for comment. Thus, it has been suggested that, despite an appearance of democratization and of constitutionalism in certain states in the region, the realities of power had altered only slightly, if at all.[31] George Schöpflin has

---

[31] The limits of constitutionalism in inter-War Eastern Europe were stark. Thus, in neither Poland nor Hungary was judicial review of primary or secondary legislation recognized in the pre-Communist era. On Poland see e.g. Rapaczynski, in Howard 1993 p. 93, at pp. 104–5. On Hungary see Paczolay 1993 pp. 43–4.

characterised this as a form of 'facade politics' in which an illusion of democratic and constitutional propriety was tolerated or even cultivated:[32]

> This had two aspects. On the one hand it involved a measure of outward and occasionally genuine respect for constitutional proprieties ... .Hence some real autonomy could and did exist ... On many occasions the courts delivered politically uninfluenced verdicts, the press could and did print criticism of the state, and interest protection organisations, like trade unions, could work for the benefit of their members. On the other hand, the system was equally evidently guided by the power elite, which tended to regard constitutional and legal procedures as an inconvenience and a facade, behind which it was free to defend its positions and interests unhindered by other forces. An external appearance of an institutional framework to provide for mass participation in politics existed, but in real terms political participation remained the privilege of the elite.

Some support for this argument can be found in the fact that, throughout the inter-war period, only one government in Eastern Europe apparently lost an election.[33]

The nature of constitutionalism as understood in inter-war Eastern Europe also merits analysis. Modern theories, as noted above, tend to associate constitutionalism with *both* the participation of citizens in the political process (generally through exercising the vote at periodic elections) *and* with curbs on the power of the majority so as to protect minorities and basic human rights (see the sources cited *supra*, n. 5). However, constitutionalism (where practised) in inter-war Eastern Europe was often understood in a more narrowly formalistic sense. Thus, the requirements of constitutionalism in Hungary in the late '30s and early '40s were apparently satisfied by a series of progressively more draconian anti-Jewish laws adopted by the Hungarian Parliament.[34] In introducing the 'Second Jewish Law' in the Chamber of Deputies, on behalf of the government,[35] Deputy János Makkai stated, '[w]e are obliged to solve this problem [the Jewish question] with parliamentary means which are the result of our present

---

[32] Schöpflin 1993 pp. 12–13. Even Czechoslovakia has not been exempt from such criticism, despite its undoubted position as the most democratic state in pre-War Eastern Europe. Thus, Schöpflin has commented:
'In the interwar period Czechoslovak politics were unquestionably pluralistic and a very wide range of interests was able to participate in the political process. Parliamentary sovereignty, however, was not the reality of the system and global strategy was determined by the various interpenetrating Czech elites (political, administrative, economic, commercial, trade union, military), as articulated through the petka, the group of five parties permanently in office and guided by the presidency.' (ibid., p. 16.)

[33] This occurred in Bulgaria in 1931. See Rothschild 1974 pp. 346–7.

[34] For a summary of these laws see e.g. Rothschild 1974 pp. 197–9.

[35] The 'proper' name of the Second Jewish Law, which entered into force in 1939, was the Law 'On the Restriction of the Expansion of the Jews in Public and Economic Affairs'.

constitutional system ...'[36] The irony of this conundrum was apparently lost on the Deputy.

A further distinguishing feature of Eastern Europe before the communist era was that, almost without exception, the states of the region achieved independence within borders that contained substantial minorities.[37] Such minorities were distinguishable from the majority population not only by their ethnicity, race, language or religion, but also by their predominant modes of employment, their general socio-economic position, or their (sometimes presumed) political allegiances. Thus, there were over twelve million ethnic Germans in Eastern Europe and six million Jews. The latter, in particular, were strongly represented in the liberal professions, in commerce and in industry (Polonsky 1975 p. 5). The former came increasingly to identify with (or to be indentified with) the resurgent nationalism of Hitlerite Germany (Polonsky 1975 p. 15; Rothschild 1974 p. 14). Ethnic Hungarians also constituted a significant minority in various states in Eastern Europe following the shrinkage of the Hungarian state after the First World War. Thus, Hungarian landowners found themselves a minority in both the Slovak portion of Czechoslovakia and in the Transylvanian region of Romania, resented by the indigenous peasant population. In Western Poland, the bulk of the landowners were ethnic Germans while the peasants were Polish; in East Galicia, Polish landowners coexisted uneasily with Ukrainian peasants (Polonsky 1975 p. 15).

Without doubt, the existence of these minorities tended to exacerbate the problems of orderly political and constitutional development. Thus, both Poland and Czechoslovakia experienced recurrent problems with minorities throughout the inter-war period.[38] The Hungarian dilemma was the mirror-image of this minorities problem. The climate of political extremism and revisionism which characterised inter-war Hungary was induced, at least in part, by the post-First World War settlement which resulted in the territorial and demographic shrinkage of Hungary and in the incorporation of substantial Hungarian minorities in Czechoslovakia, Romania and the Kingdom of Serbs, Croats and Slovenes (Yugoslavia) (Rothschild 1974 p. 155).

---

[36] 372nd session of the Chamber of Deputies (24 February 1939), in Az Országgyülés Képviselöházának Naplója, Vol. 22, p. 2.

[37] The exclusion of such minorities from the new states of Eastern Europe would have been a cartographic impossibility.

[38] In Czechoslovakia, the principal minorities, apart from the Slovaks, were the Sudeten Germans and the substantial Magyar community in Slovakia. The new Polish state, whose Eastern borders were settled by the 1921 Treaty of Riga, incorporated substantial minorities of Germans, Ukrainians, Belorussians and Jews. See Rothschild 1974 pp. 38–45.

Thus, throughout the inter-war period, economic, social and political conditions in much of Eastern Europe were not conducive to the establishment of stable, democratic systems founded on respect for the rule of law, fundamental freedoms and minority rights.[39] Most notably, the elements of regional stability, national cohesion or continuity, a democratic political culture, a sense of the naturalness (or immutability) of national borders, as well as a general aura of civic tolerance were conspicuous by their absence. It is unsurprising therefore (at least in retrospect) that the liberal constitutional structures with which many of the East European states were invested after World War I gradually foundered.[40]

The erosion of democratic institutions and of liberal constitutional processes in pre-Communist Eastern Europe (with the partial exception of Czechoslovakia) owed much to the catastrophic effects of the economic depression of the early 30s,[41] to Nazi German diplomacy and to a pervasive fear throughout the region of the Soviet Union and of Bolshevism (Rothschild 1974 pp. 4–7, 22–3). However, at bottom, democracy and constitutionalism had shallow roots in pre-War Eastern Europe.

Thus, the 'differentness' of the East European experience *before sovietization* lay in the absence of effective constitutional constraints (notably judicial review) over the executive or legislative branches of government, in the lack of a genuine democratic tradition,[42] in the fragility and controversiality of national borders, in the relative novelty of statehood as the dominant form of political expression, in comparative economic backwardness and lack of industrialization with concomitant poverty amongst both the rural population and the urban workforce, in generally high levels of social stratification, and in recurrent and mostly insoluble problems associated with national minorities. Such minorities were frequently perceived in largely negative terms as a threat to national values

---

[39] Overall, as noted above, Czechoslovakia constituted an exception to this pattern.

[40] See Okey 1986 Ch. 7. On the international legal regime established to protect minorities in the East European states following the First World War, see e.g. Thornberry 1991 Ch. 3.

[41] Rothschild comments that 'it is difficult even in retrospect to appreciate and impossible to exaggerate the tremendous impact of this experience on the peoples and governments of interwar East Central Europe', Rothschild 1974 pp. 22–3.

[42] One should perhaps distinguish from this the notion of a more limited democratic culture amongst a particular social class. This obtained, for example, amongst the nobility in both Poland and Hungary. On the democratic traditions of the Polish Szlachta see e.g. Davies 1986 pp. 333–4. On the rights of the Hungarian nobility see e.g. Okey 1986 p. 70.

and cohesion, and to the realization of national aspirations.[43] These perceptions were reflected, for example, in parliamentary discussions over the anti-Jewish laws enacted by the Hungarian legislature between 1938 and 1942. During discussion in the Chamber of Deputies, in July 1941, of the so-called 'third Jewish law' which provided, in part, for the prohibition of marriages between Jews and non-Jews,[44] Béla Várga, a Catholic priest and a member of the Independent Smallholders' Party, stated:[45]

> Don't let anyone think that I don't acknowledge the justness of antisemitism. I am a Hungarian, and as much a Hungarian as anyone. ... I recognise the justness of antisemitism since I saw in my youth and I see also now that they have occupied practically every position in economic life; I know their nature, their materialism, they themselves respect and value one another purely on the basis of their material wealth; so Jewish materialism is utterly remote from my nature, from that of Christianity and from the nature of the Christian Hungarian people.

Some months earlier, before the 3rd Jewish law was formally introduced in the Chamber of Deputies, Hungary's Prime Minister, László Bardossy, had informed the Chamber:[46]

> we must prevent the mixing of Jews with non-Jews by legal means. We must also provide for the complete exclusion of the Jews from the nation's social, cultural, political and intellectual life, from all those places where the direction of the nation's spiritual, moral, ideological and political orientation, as well as the formation of the character of the masses and the instruction of the next generation, proceeds.

Thus, economic backwardness in pre-War Eastern Europe went hand in hand with political, social, constitutional and perhaps even moral underdevelopment. It is against this background that the subsequent impact of sovietization and the current efforts at democratization and constitutionalization should be judged.

III THE SOVIETIZATION OF EASTERN EUROPE

The sovietization of Eastern Europe resulted from the German invasion of the Soviet Union in the Second World War. By the conclusion of hostilities,

---

43 This was true, for example, of attitudes towards the Sudeten Germans in Czechoslovakia, towards Magyars in Slovakia and Transylvania, towards Germans, Ukrainians and Belorussians in Poland and to Jews practically everywhere.

44 The third Jewish bill (Act XV of 1941) was in fact an amendment to the Act on the Law of Marriages (Act XXXI of 1894). The amending legislation provided, in s.9, for the prohibition of marriages between Jews and non-Jews.

45 204th session (1st July 1941), in Az Országgyülés Képviselöházának Naplója, Vol. X, p. 373.

46 192nd session (24 April 1941), in Az Országgyülés Képviselöházának Naplója, Vol. X, p. 5.

in May 1945, Soviet forces occupied much of Eastern Europe having driven Axis armies back from Soviet territory into Germany (Carr 1987 pp. 362–5). At the same time, the trauma of German aggression, with its incalculable destruction of Soviet lives and property, had left the Soviet leadership with a firm resolve to establish some form of control over Eastern Europe as a measure of security in the event of a future threat from the West (Rothschild 1993 pp. 76–8; Zeman 1991 Ch. 17). The War had also upset established patterns of economic and political life all over the region, enfeebling certain social classes which had previously been politically prominent, such as the gentry in Poland (Rothschild 1993 p. 79), and radicalising other classes such as the peasants.[47] Thus, far-reaching socio-economic change in Eastern Europe was inevitable. Indeed, the ravages of war positively 'ruled out a return to pre-war patterns' whether in economics or politics (Okey 1986 p. 191). Within three years, Communist governments came to power in all of the countries of Eastern Europe (Okey 1986 pp. 188–98; Rothschild 1993 Ch. 3).

The sovietization of Eastern Europe resulted in an unparallelled degree of economic, ideological and constitutional convergence for the states of the region. This was due, in no small measure, to Stalin's growing paranoia. As a noted historian of the period has commented (Zeman 1991 p. 244):

Little scope was to be allowed to individual Communist parties to adapt socialism to different national requirements. From the end of 1948, Stalin pursued the campaign against bourgeois national deviation – to use the language of the time – with more vigour. A rigid discipline was imposed on the Communist parties, and Stalinist ways of enforcing it were employed.

In economic terms, sovietization entailed public ownership of manufacturing and other economically significant enterprises and assets, and the collectivization of agriculture.[48] However, these processes were not entirely a *product* of sovietization. For example, the nationalization of key manufacturing enterprises and fundamental land reforms featured prominently amongst the policies of the immediate post-war (and essentially pre-Communist) governments that were formed in both Hungary and Poland.[49] Sometimes these processes, notably land reform, developed

---

[47] For details see *infra*.

[48] The collectivization of agricultural land, a notoriously sensitive issue in the predominantly agrarian societies of Eastern Europe, was abandoned in Poland in the mid '50s, see e.g. Korbonski 1984 p. 54.

[49] In Hungary, the Communists constituted a minority in a coalition government formed after general elections held in November 1945. Further general elections were held in August 1947 and May 1949. Only after the last of these were the Communists left in undisputed power. See Rothschild 1993 pp. 99–102. In Poland, the immediate post-war administration represented a broad coalition in which the Communists were included.

in an organic, rather than an institutionalized, fashion as peasants and landless agricultural labourers spontaneously divided up large estates between themselves *prior to*, and *independently of*, the formation of Communist administrations. This occurred, for example, in both Romania and Poland during the autumn of 1944.[50]

The Communist governments, in nationalizing economic enterprises and in collectivizing agriculture, relied heavily on the law and on orthodox legal structures. Thus, the economic and social revolution was not pursued by revolutionary means; rather it was conducted, for the most part, using conventional legal forms.

In Hungary, for example, the Communist government formed after the elections of May 1949 continued the twin processes of industrial nationalization and agricultural collectivization initiated by earlier post-war administrations. The Communists, like their predecessors, relied on statutes and on ministerial and governmental decrees to carry out their policies which were pursued, very largely, on a piecemeal basis (Petö and Szakács, 1985 pp. 76–82, 95–103, 179 et seq.).

From a constitutional perspective, the sovietization of Eastern Europe resulted in the adoption of a series of constitutions closely modelled on the Soviet (or more properly 'Stalinist') Constitution of 1936.[51] In Hungary, for example, a Soviet-type Constitution was adopted in 1949.[52] In Poland, a very similar Constitution was enacted in 1952.[53] Comparable constitutions were adopted by Bulgaria in 1947 and by Romania in 1952 (Ádám 1987 p. 14). In the former Czechoslovakia, following the Communist seizure of power in February 1948, a new Constitution, embodying elements of federalism, was enacted in May of the same year.[54]

The essential uniformity of these constitutions is striking. For example, the 1949 Hungarian Constitution affirmed that '[t]he Hungarian People's Republic is the state of the workers and of the working peasants' and that

---

Although nominally in control of only six ministries, Communist power was actually much more extensive and pervasive. See ibid., pp. 81–82. For a more detailed discussion of the pre-Communist expropriations and land reforms in both Poland and Hungary see Pogany, 1996.

[50] On developments in Romania see e.g. Réti 1990 p. 18; on Poland see e.g. Davies 1981 p. 559.

[51] For details of these constitutions see e.g. Table 5.7, in Swain and Swain 1993 pp. 116–17.

[52] See Pogany 1993 at pp. 334–6; Paczolay 1993 pp. 23–4. For the text of the 1949 Constitution see 1949:XX tv., in *Magyar Közlöny*, 20 August 1949, No. 174, p. 1355.

[53] See e.g. Rapaczynski 1993 p. 94. For the text of the 1952 Constitution, as amended through to 1963, see Peaslee 1968 Vol. III, p. 709.

[54] For an excellent analysis of constitutional developments in the former Czechoslovakia see Mathernova, in Howard 1993 Ch. 3.

'all power belongs to the working people'.[55] The Constitution provided, in addition, that the state (Article 3):

safeguards the freedom and power of the Hungarian working people and the independence of the country, fights against every form of exploitation of man, organizes the forces of society for the construction of socialism.

In very similar terms, Article 1.2 of the 1952 Polish Constitution provided that '[i]n the Polish People's Republic the power belongs to the working people of town and country', while Article 3.1 stated that the Polish People's Republic:[56]

safeguards the achievements of the Polish working people of town and country and secures their power and freedom against forces hostile to the people;

Following certain amendments to the Hungarian Constitution adopted in 1972, Articles 2(1) and 3 stated, respectively, that '[t]he Hungarian People's Republic is a socialist state' and that '[t]he leading force of the society is the Marxist–Leninist Party of the Working Class'.[57] A similar evolution occurred elsewhere in Eastern Europe. Thus, following an amendment introduced in 1976, the preamble to the Polish Constitution recognized the 'leading role' of the Communist party (Kurczewski 1993 p. 447). In Czechoslovakia, the preamble of the Constitution adopted in 1960 recognized 'the leadership of the Communist Party', while Article 4 proclaimed:[58]

The guiding force in society and in the State is the vanguard of the working class, the Communist Party of Czechoslovakia, a voluntary militant alliance of the most active and most politically conscious citizens from the ranks of the workers, farmers and intelligentsia.

From a constitutional viewpoint the 'construction of socialism' entailed the abandonment (or non-introduction) of the principal features of Western liberal democracy. Thus, the rule of law, the separation of powers, political pluralism and democratic accountability (in any meaningful sense) became (or remained) alien concepts excluded by the advent of socialism. At least, such concepts, where recognized at all, were doomed to remain in the realm of abstract theorization with no bearing whatsoever on political or legal practice. Commenting on Poland's Communist Constitution of 1952, a leading specialist on Polish affairs has noted (Davies 1986 p. 7):

---

[55] Article 2(1), (2), Constitution of the Hungarian People's Republic (1949), *supra* n. 52.

[56] For the text of the 1952 Polish Constitution, as amended, see Peaslee 1968 Vol. III, p. 709.

[57] For the consolidated text of the Hungarian Constitution, adopted in 1972, see 1972:I tv., in *Magyar Közlöny*, No. 32, 26 April 1972, p. 257.

[58] For the text of the Constitution of the Czechoslovak Socialist Republic of 11 July 1960 see e.g. Peaslee 1968 Vol. III, p. 225.

The Constitution of the People's Republic was inaugurated on 22 July 1952, on the eighth anniversary of Soviet rule in Poland. For the most part, it appeared to introduce a model democracy, with guaranteed civil liberties, universal suffrage, parliamentary government ... and a Council of Ministers answerable to the Assembly. In practice, this 'People's Democracy' was a legal fiction ... All effective power lay in the hands of the Party's Political Bureau, in its First Secretary, and in the privileged elite of the *nomenklatura* whom he appointed.

The effects of the sovietization process on the separation of powers doctrine are illuminating. Constitutional theory in sovietized Eastern Europe elevated the legislature to a position of primacy, while constitutional practice deprived it of any genuine power or independence (Swain and Swain, 1993 pp. 115, 118). Thus, the Hungarian Constitution of 1949 declared that '[t]he National Assembly is the highest organ of state authority in the Hungarian People's Republic' and that it 'exercises all the rights resulting from the sovereignty of the people' (Article 10(1),(2)). Similarly, Article 15.2 of the Polish Constitution of 1952 provided that '[t]he Seym, which is the highest representative of the will of the working people of town and country, realizes the sovereign rights of the Nation'.[59] In reality, however, the 'sovereignty' of the legislature was little more than a legal fiction, crudely masking the unfettered power of the Party. Over the course of several decades during the post-war period the Hungarian Assembly met for only six to eight days per year and enacted a mere three to six statutes annually (Ádám 1991 p. 12). Thus, 'its role was restricted primarily to dressing up in statutory form the political decisions arrived at by the state party' (Ádám 1991 p. 12). The other legislatures functioning in Eastern Europe met with similar infrequency (Swain & Swain, 1993 p. 116).

At the same time as legislatures in Eastern Europe were divested of (or more frequently *not invested with*) meaningful powers, the role of the courts was severely restricted (or left undeveloped).[60] Judicial review of primary and secondary legislation or theories of constitutionalism,[61] whether based

---

[59] For the text of the 1952 Polish Constitution, as amended, see Peaslee 1968 Vol. III, p. 709.

[60] It may be useful at this juncture to remind ourselves that pre-War Eastern Europe was not, for the most part, a haven of liberal enlightenment characterised by the rule of law, the separation of powers and democratic government. As noted above, during the inter-war period Czechoslovakia was the only Eastern European state to possess a Constitutional Court with powers of review over primary legislation, see e.g. Schwartz, 1993a p. 28. By contrast, 'the very idea of judicial review' was alien to 'the Hungarian constitutional tradition' (Paczolay 1993 pp. 43–4).

[61] For a discussion of recent theories of constitutionalism see e.g. the sources cited *supra* n. 5.

on Anglo-American or Continental models,[62] found no place in the new constitutional order crystallizing in Eastern Europe.[63] Thus, the *separation* of powers, familiar to Western jurists, was rejected in favour of the *concentration* of power in the upper reaches of the Party. Only later, generally during efforts to liberalize and thus sustain the communist system, did elements of judicial review of legislation emerge.[64]

The extraordinary breadth of the discretionary powers wielded by the Party, with its capacity to determine almost every aspect of the citizen's material existence, must also be acknowledged in any account of the sovietization of Eastern Europe. As a distinguished Polish lawyer and parliamentarian has pointed out (Kurczewski 1993 p. 72):

> One needs to keep in mind that about two-thirds of Polish families were directly employed by the state, while the remaining one-third was under direct economic control by the government in the pursuance of their family, usually farming business; that the government was not elected but nominated by the ruling group of the Communist party; that all administrative agencies, officially recognized associations, industrial establishments, and the military and police were subordinated by force, by doctrine and by law, if there was a law at all, to the Communist party ruling bodies; that all the banking, medical, and social services were part of the government itself. The direct dependence of the atomized individual in all life functions upon the centralized and unresponsible government is the basic fact of social life under this type of social, economic and political organization.

Without doubt, post-War Eastern Europe was characterised by flagrant and pervasive human rights abuses during the Stalinist period, while the communist regimes in Romania and the former German Democratic Republic, for example, remained dependent to the very end on intimidation and coercion. However, we should not lose sight of the fact that the experience of communism in Eastern Europe varied significantly from country to country, particularly after the death of Stalin and the suppression of various anti-Soviet eruptions in the mid 50s.[65] Thus, in both Poland and Hungary a significant measure of intellectual freedom had emerged by the

---

[62] For a comparison of judicial review in the United States and the Continental system of review by Constitutional Courts see e.g. Schwartz 1993b pp. 164–7. On the German Constitutional Court, which has been an important model for the Constitutional Courts established in Eastern Europe see e.g. Kommers 1976.

[63] By contrast, the post-war period in Western Europe witnessed the gradual extension of the principle of judicial review of legislation. See Cappelletti 1989.

[64] Thus, a Constitutional Tribunal, with a limited jurisdiction, was established in Poland in 1985. See Brzezinski 1993b p. 38. In Hungary, a still more circumscribed Constitutional Law Council was created in 1984. The Constitutional Law Council, in contrast to the Tribunal established in Poland, lacked even the power to review legislative acts. See Paczolay 1993 p. 24.

[65] The most far-reaching of these was the Hungarian revolution of 1956. See Rothschild 1993 Ch. 5.

60s.[66] The distinctiveness of the Hungarian position was accentuated by the government's increasingly liberal and market-oriented economic policies, while in Poland the sense of pluralism was enhanced by the authority of the Catholic Church and by the relative freedom of the peasants, most of whom escaped collectivization.[67] These factors contributed in no small measure to the peaceful and negotiated transition in both Poland and Hungary from communist rule to democratic government (Sword 1991 pp. 112–13, 125–6).

IV CONCLUSIONS

This chapter has dwelt, very largely, on the history of Eastern Europe, both before and during the Soviet era. This emphasis on the past has been prompted by the conviction that these matters are not merely of historical importance, and that they remain relevant to contemporary constitutional and human rights issues.

The historical record suggests that there were relatively limited expressions of democracy and of constitutionalism in most of the states of Eastern Europe *prior to* the sovietization of the region. Instead, the dominant political traditions were authoritarian and, increasingly during the '30s and early '40s, fascist in character. Thus, sovietization did not so much interrupt a democratic evolution as represent another form of authoritarianism, albeit one with severely limited support amongst the local population.

This thesis may be open to at least partial challenge on the grounds that the withdrawal of Nazi forces from Eastern Europe, in 1944–45, was not followed immediately by the imposition of Soviet-backed Communist rule.

---

[66] Of course, such freedoms were not unlimited and were subject to reverses. Most notably, martial law was declared in Poland in December 1981 and was not removed until 1983. However, even the rigours of martial law were relative:

'The repression was highly selective, and strangely half–hearted. It lacked the gratuitous violence of Afghanistan or El Salvador ... It lacked the wholesale social terror which reigned in Kádár's Hungary after 1956, or the systematic purges of Husak's 'normalization' in Czechoslovakia after 1968. It did not resort to mass deportations ... and it lacked any note of urgency to restore the rule of the Party ... For some reason, which had not become entirely clear by the end of the State of War, the Military Regime did not feel inclined to exploit its new-found powers to the full. It was curiously inhibited, and by Soviet standards, unbelievably restrained.' Davies 1986 p. 28.

[67] On Poland see e.g. Davies 1986 at pp. 10–14; on Hungary see e.g. Rothschild 1993 pp. 204–7.

Thus, the newly-'liberated' states of Eastern Europe enjoyed a relatively brief period, of perhaps three or four years, in which *a degree* of political manoeuvre was possible and in which certain steps towards creating a truly democratic political system were taken.

However, it should be noted that the *degree* of political freedom exercised by each state during this transitional period varied significantly. Moreover, the ultimate decision as to the extent of political freedom permitted to each country rested with the Soviet Union, whose troops, security personnel and other operatives became increasingly active in the East European states during this period. Thus, Poland, which from the outset was deemed to be of vital importance to Soviet interests by Stalin, was only allowed limited and superficial expressions of democracy. In the general elections held in January 1947, even these were largely swept aside in an orgy of intimidation, abuse and outright terror, so that a coalition of parties headed by the Communists achieved 80.1 per cent of the votes cast (Rothschild 1993 pp. 79–84). At the other extreme, Hungary, towards whom Soviet intentions (and policy) seemed rather uncertain in 1945, enjoyed a brief period of democratic experimentation. Thus, in general elections held in November 1945, the Independent Smallholders won 57 per cent of the votes cast, while the Communists gained 17 per cent. However, the parliamentary elections of August 1947 were characterised by extensive abuse and intimidation, orchestrated by the Communists, while elections held in May 1949 resulted in the Communist-endorsed 'Government List' gaining 95.6 per cent of the votes (Rothschild 1993 pp. 97–102). Thus, the span of unfettered democratic experimentation in Hungary was extremely short while the principal or immediate beneficiary of this process, the Independent Smallholders' Party, could scarcely claim an unsullied democratic pedigree, not least because of its enthusiastic association with the anti-Jewish legislation of 1938–42 which divested some 5 per cent of the Hungarian population of their civil, political and other rights.[68]

---

68 During discussion of the Second Jewish Law in the Chamber of Deputies, on 28 February 1939, Tibor Eckhardt, one of the fourteen Deputies of the Independent Smallholders' Party, criticized the proposed law for its 'moderation', proposing additionally that Jews whose families had entered Hungary after 1914 should be expelled and that even Jews whose families had entered the country before 1867 should be subject to deportation – if they committed criminal acts, or seriously injured the economic or financial interests of the state:
   'such a solution would place the Jews under a permanent moral scrutiny, and a Jewish businessman would reconsider three times over an illegal financial transaction involving foreign trade, or other activities, if it had the consequence that he would be not only punished but that he would also be placed on the list of emigrants and that he

In addition to the lack of a strong democratic tradition in most of the states of Eastern Europe, nationalism and the coexistence of national groups has been a recurrent and frequently intractable problem in the region. The protracted denial of national self-expression, whether by imperial powers such as Austria-Hungary, Russia or the Ottoman Turks as late as the middle of the Nineteenth Century, or by the Soviet Union and its proxy Communist regimes in the post-Second World War era,[69] has no doubt contributed to the strength of nationalist sentiment. However, this problem has been aggravated by the sheer impossibility of drawing national borders corresponding to the distribution of national populations. Moreover, the nationalism of Eastern Europe has frequently been overlaid with religious elements. Thus, nationhood has sometimes been defined by reference to Christian values, or even by reference to membership of a specific Christian denomination.

History itself represents an obstacle to political stability and constitutional order in Eastern Europe. Thus, the peoples of Eastern Europe have a strikingly acute sense of their own national identity and history. This consciousness of the *particularity* of their national experience, with its inevitable litany of territorial losses, political subjugation(s) and economic exploitation, is scarcely conducive to a spirit of tolerance towards national minorities or to neighbouring states. This may explain, for example, the treatment of the Hungarian minority in both Romania and Slovakia by a resentful and suspicious majority population.

Finally, the history of Eastern Europe before the Communist era is the history not only of political, but also of economic, underdevelopment. The economic underdevelopment of Eastern Europe no doubt inhibited the formation of a genuine democratic tradition, aggravated social tensions and contributed to the politics of factionalism (such as the formation of peasant parties) and ultimately to the politics of Fascism. It is as well to recollect that the subsequent sovietization of Eastern Europe denied this relatively impoverished region the material benefits of Marshall Aid, and imposed on it an economic system incapable of producing sustained economic growth. Thus, an historical perspective is essential. As in the inter-war period, fragile democratic and constitutional structures may collapse in the face of

---

would have to turn his back on this beautiful country.' 373rd session (28 February 1939), in Az Országgyülés Képviselöházának Naplója, Vol. XXII, p. 42.

[69] Nor should one forget the impact of Nazi German policies on the attempts of the East Central and East European states to consolidate their (in most cases) newly-won statehood.

insoluble economic problems that threaten social stability and national cohesion.[70]

---

[70] At the time of writing, the Ukraine and Russia provide possible examples of this disturbing phenomenon.

References

Ackerman, Bruce (1992) *The Future of Liberal Revolution*, New Haven and London: Yale University Press.

Ádám, A. (1987) 'Az Alapjogok, Különösen a Szabadságjogok Alkotmányi Szabályozásának Fejlödési Irányairol', in XVIII *Dolgozatok az Állam és Jogtudományok Köréböl*, Pécs, Hungary: Janus Pannonius Tudományegyetem.

Ádám, A. (1991) 'A központi állami szervek rendszere Magyarországon', in A. Ádám and L. Kiss (eds), *Elvek és Intézmények az Alkotmányos Jogállamban*, Budapest.

Alekseyev, S. (1991) *Law and Legal Culture in Soviet Society*, Moscow: Progress Publishers.

Alekseyev, S. (1993) 'Ostrye Grani Svobody' ('Sharp Edges of Freedom'), *Rossiiski Vestnik*, 2 June 1993.

Amnesty International (1992) *Europe: Harmonization of asylum policy, Accelerated procedures for 'manifestly unfounded' asylum claims and the 'safe country' concept*, London, November.

Arangio-Ruiz, Gaetano (1979) *The United Nations Declaration on Friendly Relations and the System of the Sources of International Law*, Aalphen an den Rijn: Sijthoff and Noordhoff,.

Aráto, A. (1994) 'Az Alkotmánybíróság a Médiaháboruban', *Világosság* XXXV (2).

Aráto, A. (1994) 'Constitution and Continuity in the Transitions' 1 *Constellations*.

Aráto, Andrew (1994) 'Legitimation and Constitution-making in Hungary', *Tilburg Foreign Law Review*. (Forthcoming).

Arboleda, Eduardo and Ian Hoy (1993) 'The Convention Refugee Definition in the West: A Legal Fiction', *International Journal of Refugee Law*, Vol. 5. No. 1.

Arendt, H. (1951) *The Origins of Totalitarianism*, New York: HBJ Book.

Arendt, H. (1964) *On Revolution*, London: Penguin Books.

Arendt, H. (1970) *On Violence*, New York: HBJ Book.

Barány, Zoltán (1994) 'Mass-Elite Relations and the Resurgence of Nationalism in Eastern Europe', *European Security*, 1 (3).

Barbalet, J.M. (1988) *Citizenship*, Milton Keynes: Open University Press.

Benton, T. (1993) *Natural Relations: Ecology, Animal Rights and Social Justice*, London: Verso.

Berdyayev, N.I. (1989) 'Istoki i Smysl Russkogo Kommunisma' ('The Sources and Meaning of Russian Communism'), *Yunost*, No. 11.

Berlin, Isaiah (1969) *Four Essays on Liberty*, Oxford: Oxford University Press.

Blankenagel, A. (1992) 'Towards Constitutionalism in Russia', 1 *East European Constitutional Review*, 25.

Blankenagel, A. (1993) 'Where Has All the Power Gone?' 2 *East European Constitutional Review*, 26.

Blaustein, A.P. and G.H. Flanz (1990–) *Constitutions of the Countries of the World*, Dobbs Ferry, New York: Oceana Publications Inc.

Boles, Elizabeth (1988) *The West and South Africa: Myths, Interests and Policy Options*, London: Croom Helm.

Borinski, Philipp (1993) *Die neue NATO-Strategie. Perspektiven militärischer Sicherheitspolitik in Europa*, Frankfurt: HSFK Report, 1.

Brown, J.F. (1992) 'Crisis and Conflict in Eastern Europe', *RFE/RL Research Report*, 22 (1).

Brownlie, I. (1981, 2nd edn) *Basic Documents on Human Rights*, Oxford: Clarendon Press.

Brownlie, I. (1983, 3rd edn) *Basic Documents in International Law*, Oxford: Oxford University Press.

Brzezinski, M.F. (1993a) 'Toward "Constitutionalism" in Russia: The Russian Constitutional Court', in 42 *International and Comparative Law Quarterly*.

Brzezinski, M.F. (1993b) 'Constitutionalism Within Limits' in 2 *East European Constitutional Review*.

Budapest Group (Established by the European Conference on Uncontrolled Migration, 2nd meeting) (1994) *Survey (1) on the situation concerning the implementation of the European Conference's recommendations: The questionnaire and the answers*, BG (94) Doc. 9.

Butler, W. (1990) 'Towards the Rule of Law?' in Brumberg (ed.) *Chronicle of a Revolution: A Western-Soviet Inquiry into Perestroika*, London: Pantheon.

Capotorti, Francesco (1988) *Study on the Rights of Persons Belonging to Ethnic, Religious and Linguistic Minorities*, New York: United Nations.

Cappelletti, M. (1989) *The Judicial Process in Comparative Perspective*, Oxford: Oxford University Press.

Carment, David (1993) 'The International Dimensions of Ethnic Conflict: Concepts, Indicators, and Theory', *Journal of Peace Research*, 2 (30).

Carr, W. (1987, 3rd edn) *A History of Germany 1815-1985*, London and New York: Edward Arnold.

Chafetz, G. (1992) 'Soviet Ideological Revision and the Collapse of Communism in Eastern Europe', *International Relations*.

Chantebout, B. (1986, 7th edn) *Droit constitutionnel et science politique*, Paris: Armand Colin.

Chistyakova, A. (1993) 'The Russian Bill of Rights: Implications', 24, *Columbia Human Rights Law Review*.

Commission of the European Communities (1994): *Communication from the Commission to the Council and the European Parliament on Immigration and Asylum Policies* COM (94) final, 23 02 1994, Brussels.

Conquest, Robert (1971) *The Great Terror*, London: Penguin.

Cooke, K. (1993) 'Asians Challenge West on Human Rights', *The Financial Times*, 11 June.

Craig, Gordon (1978) *Germany 1866-1945*, Oxford: Clarendon Press.

Cristescu, Aureliu (1981) *The Right to Self-Determination: Historical and Current Development on the Basis of United Nations Instruments*, UN Doc./E/CN.4/Sub 404/Rev 1.

Cullen, Robert (1992-3) 'Human Rights Quandary', *Foreign Affairs*, 72 (5).

Czerwinska, Ewa (1993) 'Economy of Labour Force in Process of Systemic Transformation in Poland' in Jacek Glowacki (ed.), *Poland in Transition, 1989-1993*, Warsaw: BSE (in Polish).

Dahl, R. (1971) *Polyarchy. Participation and Opposition*, New Haven and London: Yale University Press.

Danilenko, G. (1991) 'International Jus Cogens: Issues of Law Making', 2, *European Journal of International Law*, 42.

Davies, N. (1981) *God's Playground: A History of Poland*, Oxford: Clarendon Press, Vol. II.

Davies, N. (1986) *Heart of Europe: A Short History of Poland*, Oxford: Oxford University Press.

Diablo, V. (1926) 'Burzhuaznaya zakonnost, sovetskaya zakonnost i revoliutsonnaya tseloobraznost' ('Bourgeois legality, soviet legality and revolutionary expediency'), 6 *Sovetskoye Pravo*.

van Dijk, P. and G.J.H. van Hoof (1990) *Theory and Practice of the European Convention on Human Rights*, Deventer: Kluwer.

Djilas, M. (1965) *The New Class. An Analysis of the Communist System*, New York: Praeger.

Dworkin, R. (1986) *Law's Empire*, London: Fontana Press.

European Consultation on Refugees and Exiles (1993) *Report of ECRE Biannual General Meeting, Berlin 23–25 April 1993*, London: European Consultation on Refugees and Exiles.

European Consultation on Refugees and Exiles (1994a) *Asylum in Europe Vol. II Review of Refugee and asylum laws and procedures in selected European countries*, Fourth Edition, London: European Consultation on Refugees and Exiles.

European Consultation on Refugees and Exiles (1994b), *A European Refugee policy in the Light of Established Principles*, London: European Consultation on Refugees and Exiles.

European Consultation on Refugees and Exiles (1994c), *Minutes and conference papers from the ECRE biannual general meeting, Amsterdam 15–17 April*, London: European Consultation on Refugees and Exiles.

Elster, J. and R. Slagstad (eds) (1988) *Constitutionalism and Democracy*, Cambridge: Cambridge University Press.

Ermacora, Felix (1988) *The Protection of Minorities Before the United Nations*, Wien: Braumuller.

Fawcett, J.E.S. (1971, 2nd edn) *The Law of Nations*, Harmondsworth: Penguin Books.

Feldbrugge, F.J.M. (1993) *Russian Law: The End of the Soviet System and the Role of Law*, Dordrecht: Martinus Nijhoff.

Feldman, D. (1989) 'Krestyanskaya Voyna' ('Peasants' War'), *Rodina*, No. 10.

Feofanov, Y. (1993) 'The Establishment of the Constitutional Court in Russia and the Communist Party Case', 19 *Review of Central and East European Law*.

Fisher, Sharon (1994) 'Immigrants and Refugees in Slovakia', *RFE/RL Research Report* Vol. 3 No. 24.

Fox, Lousie (1994) 'What To Do about Pensions in Transition Economies?', *Transition*, Vol. 5, No. 2–3.2

Fry, John (1993) *The Helsinki Process: Negotiating Security and Cooperation in Europe*, Washington D.C.: National Defense University Press.

Fukuyama, Francis (1989) 'The End of History?', *The National Interest*, No. 16 (summer).

Fukuyama, Francis (1992) *The End of History and the Last Man*, London: Penguin Books.

Fuszara, Malgorzata (1993) 'Abortion and the Formation of the Public Sphere in Poland' in Nanette Funk and Magda Mueller (eds), *Gender, Politics, and Post-Communism*, New York: Routledge.

Galicki, Zdsislaw (1993) *Protection of Refugees Under International Law and Polish Domestic Law*, mimeoed maunuscript.

Garlicki, Leszek (1990) 'Perspectives for Human Rights in Poland', in *For the Protection of Human Rights*, Tokyo: The Japanese Association of Comparative Constitutional Law.

Gerrits, André W.M. (1992) *Nationalism and Political Change in Post-Communist Europe*, The Hague: Clingendael Paper.

Gorbachev, M. (1987) 'Perestroika i Novoye Myshlenie dlja Nashei Strany i dlja vsego Mira' ('Perestroika and New Thinking for our Country and for the Whole World'), *Politizdat*, Moscow.

Gorbachev, M.S. (1988) 'On Progress in Implementing the Decisions of the 27th CPSU Congress and the Tasks of Promoting Perestroika', *Novosti*, Moscow.

Gross-Espiell, Hector (1980) *The Right to Self-Determination, Implementation of United Nations Resolutions* UN Doc. E/CN 4/Sub. 2/405/Rev. 1.

Gunst, P. (1989) 'Agrarian Systems of Central and Eastern Europe', in D. Chirot (ed.), *The Origins of Backwardness in Eastern Europe*, Berkeley, Los Angeles, Oxford: University of California Press.

Habermas, J. (1990) 'What does Socialism Mean Today? The Rectifying Revolution and the Need for New Thinking on the Left', 183, *New Left Review*, 3.

Habermas, J. (1992a) *Legitimation Crisis*, London: Polity.

Habermas, Jürgen (1992b) 'Volkssouveränität als Verfahren. Ein normativer Begriff der öffentlichkeit' in *Die Moderne – ein unvollendetes Projekt. Philosophisch-politische Aufsätze 1977–1992*, Leipzig: Reclam.

Habermas, J. (1994) 'Citizenship and National Identity', in van Steenbergen (ed.), *The Condition of Citizenship*, London: Sage.

Habermas, J. (1994a) 'Human Rights and Popular Sovereignty: The Liberal and Republican Versions', 7, *Ratio Juris*.

Hailbronner, Kay (ed.) (1992) *Asyl- und Einwanderungsrecht in europäischen Vergleich*, Trier: Schriftenreihe der Europäischen Rechtsakademie, Band 1.

Hailbronner, Kay (1993) 'The Concept of "Safe Country" and Expeditious Asylum Procedures – A Western European Perspective', *International Journal of Refugee Law*, Vol. 5, No. 1.

Halmai, G. (1990) 'The Freedom of Assembly and Association', in M. Soltész (ed.), *Human Rights in Today's Hungary*, Budapest: Mezon kft.

Halmai, G. (1990–91) 'The Re-establishment of the Rule of Law in Hungary', in *Cumberland Law Review*, Vol. 21.

Halmai, Gabor (1991) 'Regeneration of Civil Society in Hungary', *Law and Policy*, Vol. 13, No. 2.

Halmai, G. (1994) *A Véleményszabadság Határai (The Boundaries of Freedom of Expression)*, Budapest: Atlantisz.

Hassner, Pierre (1993) 'Beyond Nationalism and Internationalism: Ethnicity and World Order', *Survival*, 1 (35).

Hathaway, James C. (1991a) *The Law of Refugee Status*, Toronto: Butterworth.

Hathaway, James C. (1991b) 'Reconceiving Refugee Law as Human Rights Protection', *Journal of Refugee Studies*, 4 (2).

Hausmaniger, H. (1990) 'The Committee of Constitutional Supervision of the USSR', 23, *Cornell International LJ*, 287.

Hausmaniger, H. (1992) 'From the Soviet Committee of Constitutional Supervision to the Russian Constitutional Court', 25, *Cornell International LJ*, 305.

Hayek, F.A. (1944) *The Road to Serfdom*, London: George Routledge and Sons Limited.

Helsinki Watch Report 'Russian Residence and Travel Restrictions' (August 1992).

Hesse, K. (1990) *Grundzüge des Verfassungsrechts*, Heidelberg: Müller C.F. Jurist Verlag.

Hobsbawm, E. (1994) *Age of Extremes*, London: Michael Joseph.

Holló, A. (1993) *Az Államjogtól a Jogállamig (From state law to the rule of Law)*, Budapest: Alapitvány a Politikai Kultúráért.

Holmes, S. (1994) 'Superpresidentialism and its Problems', 3, *EECR*, 123.

Horowitz, Donald L. (1985) *Ethnic Groups in Conflict*, Berkeley: University of California Press.

Horváth, Barna (1985) 'Demokrácia és jog' ('Democracy and Law'). A lecture, first published by Budapest University in 1945, later in *Medvetánc*, 2–3/1985.

Hrynkiewicz, Jozefina and Teresa Krynicka (1993) 'Social Assurances', in Jacek Glowacki (ed.), *Poland in Transition, 1989–1993*, Warsaw: BSE.

Human Rights: A Compilation of International Instruments (1988) UN Doc. ST/HR/1/Rev. 3.

Huntington, Samuel P. (1990), 'Democratization and Security in Eastern Europe', in Peter Volten (ed.), *Uncertain Futures: Eastern Europe and Democracy*, New York: Institute for East-West Security Studies.

IGC (Inter–governmental Consultations on Asylum, Refugee and Migration Policies in Europe, North America and Australia) (1994) *Working Paper on Readmission Agreements*, Mimeo, August 1994.

Illyés, G. (1967) *People of the Puszta*, Budapest: Corvina.

IOM (International Organization for Migration) (1994a) *Transit Migration in Poland*, Budapest, Migration Information Programme.

IOM (International Organization for Migration) (1994b) *Transit Migration in the Czech Republic*, Budapest: Migration Information Programme.

Jeffrey, R. (1993) 'Social and Economic Rights in the South African Constitution: Legal Consequences and Practical Considerations', 27, *Columbia Journal of Law and Social Problems*.

Joly, Danièle (1994) The Porous Dam; European Harmonisation on Asylum in the Nineties *International Journal of Refugee Law*, Vol. 6, No. 2.

Joly, Danièle with Clive Nettleton and Hugh Poulton (1992) *Refugees Asylum in Europe*, London: Minority Rights Group.

Karol, K.S. (1993) 'After Perestroika', in Miliband and Panitch (eds), *Real Problems, False Solutions: Socialist Register*, London: Merlin Press.

Kay, Richard S. (1993) 'The European Convention on Human Rights and the Authority of Law', *Connecticut Journal of International Law* 2, (8), Spring.

Kazimirchuk, V. (1991) 'On Constitutional Supervision in the USSR', in Butler (ed.), *Perestroika and the Rule of Law: Anglo-Soviet and Soviet Perspectives*, London: I.B. Tauris.

Kelsen, H. (1991) *General Theory of Norms*, Oxford: Oxford University Press.

Kistjakovskii, B. (1909) 'V Zastsitu Prav: Intelligentsiya i Pravovoe Soznanie' ('In Defence of Rights: Intelligentsia and Legal Consciousness'), *Vekhi*, reprinted Moscow, 1991.

Kistyakovsky, B.A. (1990) 'Gosudarstvo Pravovoye i Sotsalisticheskoye' ('The Rule of Law State and The Socialist State'), *Voprosy Filosofii*, No. 6.

Kjaerum, Morten (1994) 'Temporary protection in Europe in the 1990s', *International Journal of Refugee Law*, Vol. 6, No. 3.

Klinsberg, Ethan (1992) 'Judicial Review and Hungary's Transition from Communism to Democracy: The Constitutional Court, the Continuity of Law, and the Redefinition of Property Rights', *Brigham Young University Law Review*, No. 1.

Kochan, L. and R. Abraham (1990, 2nd edn) *The Making of Modern Russia*, London: Penguin.

Kommers, D. (1976) *Judicial Politics in West Germany: A Study of the Federal Constitutional Court*, Beverly Hills and London: Sage Publications.

Korbonski, A. (1984, 2nd edn) 'Poland', in T. Rakowska-Harmstone (ed.), *Communism in Eastern Europe*, Manchester: Manchester University Press.

Koskenniemi, Marti (1994) 'National Self Determination Today: Problems of Legal Theory and Practice', *International and Comparative Law Quarterly*, (43) 2.

Kozlowski, Tomasz Kuba (1994) *Between Transit, Asylum Seeking and Immigration. Legal and Institutional Consequences of the Phenomenon of Involuntary Migration.* Paper for the seminar, Migration Issues in Poland Within the Context of European Integration, Warsaw 28 February – 1 March 1994.

Kozyrev, Andrei (1994) 'The Lagging Partnership', *Foreign Affairs*, 3 (73).

Kudryatvtsev, V. (1994) 'Pravovaya sityuatsiya i iuridicheskaya nauk' ('The legal situation and jurisprudence'), *Svobodnaya Misl*.

Kudryavtsev, V. (1988) 'Towards a Socialist Rule of Law State', in Aganbegyan (ed.), *Perestroika Annual*, London: Futura.

Kurczewska, Joanna (1989) *Nation in Polish Sociology and Ideology*, Warsaw: PWN.

Kurczewski, Jacek (1989) 'Rule of Law', *Res Publicata*, 12, reproduced in J. Kurczewski (ed.), 1993 *Democracy Under the Rule of Law*, Warsaw: ISSP PAN (in Polish).

Kurczewski, Jacek (1990) 'Carnal Sins and Privatisation of the Body. Research Notes', in Jacek Kurczewski and Andrzej A. Czynczyk (eds.), *Family, Gender and Body in Law and Society Today*, Warsaw: ZSOiP ISNS UW.

Kurczewski, Jacek (1993) *The Resurrection of Rights in Poland*, Oxford: Clarendon Press.

Kurczewski, Jacek (1993a) 'Notes on Lustration', in *Res Publica Nowa* 3 (in Polish).

Kurczewski, Jacek (1993b) 'Democracy Under the Rule of Law. Review of Experiences', in J. Kurczewski (ed.), 1993 *Democracy Under the Rule of Law*, Warsaw: ISSP PAN (in Polish).

Kurczewski, J. (1994) 'Privatizing the Polish Family after Communism', in Mavis Maclean and Jacek Kurczewski, *Families, Politics, and the Law: Perspectives for East and West Europe*, Oxford: Clarendon Press.

Kurczewski, Jacek (1994a) 'Democracy Under the Rule of Law: Institutional Opportunities and Social Strains', paper presented at ISA World Congress, Bielefeld 1994, RC Sociology of Law, copyright by Sociological Abstracts.

Laband, L. (1876–82) *Das Staatsrecht des Deutschen Reiches*, Vol. 2.

Lamentowicz, Wojtek (1993) 'Nationale Interessen und Europäische Integration', *Europäische Rundschau*, 2.

Lane, David (1984) 'Human Rights under State Socialism', 32, *Political Studies*, 357.

Laqueur, W. 'Russian Nationalism', 71(5) *Foreign Affairs* 114.

Larin, A. (1993) 'Procuror Protiv Suda Prisjazhnyh' ('The Procurator is Against Trial by Jury'), *Izvestija*, 12 May.

Lawyers' Committee for Human Rights (1993) *Human Rights and Legal Reform in the Russian Federation*.

Lebedev, P. (1988) 'Konstitutsionny nadzor: Kakim yemu byt' ('Constitutional Supervision: What should it be?'), *Izvestiya*, 13 November.

Lehne, Stefan (1991) *The Vienna Meeting of the Conference on Security and Cooperation in Europe, 1986–1989: A Turning Point in East-West Relations*, Boulder, Colorado: Westview Press.

Lemay, Joanne (1994) *The Legal Status of Aliens and Refugees in the Czech and Slovak Republics, Hungary and Poland*, MA thesis, Budapest Institute for Graduate International and Diplomatic Studies, Budapest University of Economic Sciences.

Lenin, V. 'Polnoye Sobraniye Sochinenij' ('Complete Works'), *Politizdat*, Moscow, Vol. 41.

Lenin, Vladimir (1964) 'How the SRs Sum Up the Revolution and How the Revolution has Summed Them Up' (7 January 1909), *Collected Works*, Moscow 1966, Vol. 15.

Letters of the CSCE High Commissioner on National Minorities to the Estonian and Latvian Foreign Ministers of 6 April 1993. Reference Nos. 206/93/L/Rev. and 238/93/L/Rev.

Lewis, P. (1993) 'Democracy and its Future in Eastern Europe', in D. Held (ed.), *Prospects for Democracy*, Cambridge: Polity Press.

Lewis, P. (1993) 'History, Europe and the Politics of the East', in S. White, J. Batt and P. Lewis (eds), *Developments in East European Politics*, Basingstoke: Macmillan Press.

Lieven, A. (1993) *The Baltic Revolution*, New Haven and London: Yale University Press.

Lieven, Dominic (1994) 'Western Scholarship on the Rise and Fall of the Soviet Regime: The View from 1993', in *Journal of Contemporary History*, Vol. 29, No. 2, April.

Lijphart, Arend (1982) 'Consociation: The Model and its Application in Divided Societies', in Desmond Rea (ed.), *Political Co-operation in Divided Societies*, Dublin: Gill and Macmillan.

Lind, Michael (1994) 'In Defense of Liberal Nationalism', *Foreign Affairs*, 3 (73).

Lindholm, Tore (1991) 'Are Collective Human Rights for Minorities Legitimate and Feasible?', in Helen Krag and Natalia Yukhneva (eds), *The Leningrad Minority Rights Conference*, Copenhagen: Minority Rights Group Denmark.

Llorente, Francisco Rubio (1988) 'The Writing of the Constitution of Spain', in Robert A. Goldwin and Art Kaufman (eds), *Constitution Makers on Constitution Making: The Experience of Eight Nations*, Washington, D.C.: American Enterprise Institute.

Loescher, Gil (1992) *Refugee Movements and International Security*, Adelphi Papers, No. 268, London: International Institute for Strategic Studies.

Longman Illustrated Encyclopedia of World History, 1991 London: Ivy Leaf.

Luhmann, N. (1983) *Rechtssoziologie,* Opladen: Westdeutscher Verlag.

Lukacs, John (1993) *The End of the Twentieth Century and the End of the Modern Age*, New York: Ticknor and Fields.

Lukacs, John (1994) *A XX. század és az újkor vége* (*The End of the Twentieth Century and the End of the Modern Age*), Budapest: Európa.

MacCormick, D.N. (1978) *Legal Reasoning and Legal Theory*, Oxford: Clarendon Press.

Mahbubani, K. (1992) 'The West and the Rest', 28, *The National Interest*, 8.

Maine, Henry (1897, 5th edn) *Popular Government*, John Murray.

Maitland F.W. (1931) *The Constitutional History of England*, Cambridge: Cambridge University Press.

Mansergh, Nicholas, (1975, 3rd edn) *The Irish Question 1840–1921*, Toronto: University of Toronto Press, citing Lansing, Robert (1921) 'The Peace Negotiations'.

Marx, K. and F. Engels 'Sobraniye Sochinenij' ('Selected Works'), *Politizdat*, Moscow, Vol. 3.

Mathernova, K. (1993) 'Czecho?Slovakia: Constitutional Disappointments', in A. Howard (ed.), *Constitution Making in Eastern Europe*, Washington D.C.: Woodrow Wilson Center Press.

Maynes, Charles William (1993) 'Containing Ethnic Conflict', *Foreign Policy*, No. 90.

Mearsheimer, John J. (1990) 'Back to the Future: Instability in Europe After the Cold War', *International Security*, 1 (15).

Miall, Hugh (1994) Introduction in Hugh Miall (ed.), *Minority Rights in Europe: The Scope for a Transnational Regime*, London: Pinter for RIIA.

Mitterrand, François (1982) *The Wheat and the Chaff* (Translation of *La Paille et Le Grain*), London: Weidenfeld and Nicolson.

Murphy, W. (1993) 'Constitutions, Constitutionalism and Democracy', in Greenberg et al, *Constitutionalism and Democracy*, Oxford: Oxford University Press.

Nagy, Boldizsár (1991) 'Before or After the Wave: Thoughts about the Adequacy of the Hungarian Refugee Law', *International Journal of Refugee Law*, Special Issue, Vol. 3, No. 3.

Nagy, Boldizsár (1992) 'Asylum Seekers and Refugees: Hungarian Dilemmas', *Acta Juridica Hungarica*, Vol. 34, No. 1–2.

Nagy, Boldizsár (1994a) 'Hungarian Refugee Law', in H. Adelman, E. Sik and G. Tessényi (eds.), *The Genesis of a Domestic regime: The Case of Hungary*, Toronto: York Lanes Press.

Nagy, Boldizsár (1994b) 'The Refugee Situation in Hungary: Where now?', *AWR Bulletin*, Vol 32 (41) 3.

de Nevers Renée (1993) 'Democratization and Ethnic Conflict', *Survival*, 2 (35).

Norrie, Allan (ed.) (1993) *Closure or Critique*, Edinburgh: Edinburgh University Press.

Nowak, Manfred (1989) 'UNO-Pakt über bürgerliche und politische Rechte und Fakultativprotokoll', Kohl: N.P. Engel Verlag.

Ogata, Sadako (1993) 'Refugees and asylum seekers: a challenge to European immigration policy', in *Towards a European Immigration Policy*, The Philip Morris Institute for Public Policy Research.

Ogonowski, Zbigniew (1993) 'Idea of Freedom and Legal State in Political Thought of XVIIth Century Poland', in J. Kurczewski (ed.), *Democracy Under the Rule of Law*, Warsaw: ISSP PAN (In Polish).

Okey, R. (1986, 2nd edn) *Eastern Europe 1740-1985*, London: Harper Collins Academic.

Okolski, Marek (1992) 'Migratory Movements from countries of Central and Eastern Europe', in *People on the move: New migration flows in Europe*, Strasbourg: Council of Europe Press.

Osiatynski, Wiktor (1992) 'A Bill of Rights for Poland', in *East European Constitutional Law Review*, Vol. 1, No. 3.

Paczolay, P. (1993) 'The New Hungarian Constitutional State: Challenges and Perspectives', in A. Howard (ed.), *Constitution Making in Eastern Europe*, Washington D.C.: Woodrow Wilson Center Press.

Pankratov, V. (1992) 'Deklaratsia prav cheloveka i grazhdanina: kak yiyo pretvorit v zhizn?' ('The Declaration of the Rights of the Person and Citizen: How to Bring it to Life?'), 2, *Sovetskaya Yustitsia*.

Parekh, Bhikhu (1993) 'The Cultural Particularity of Liberal Democracy', in D. Held (ed.), *Prospects for Democracy*, Cambridge: Polity Press.

Pashin, S.A. (1992) 'Konstitutsionni Sud Rossii: obrashchatsya mogut vsye' ('The Russian Constitutional Court etc.'), *Sovyetskaya Iustitsiya*, 2 January.

Pashin, S.A. (1992a) *Kak obratitsya v konstitutsioni sud Rossii* (How to Bring a Case to the Russian Constitutional Court), Moscow: Paritet.

Pashin, S. (1993) 'The Trial by Jury is Returning to Russia', *Pravozachitnik*, No. 1.

Pashukanis, Y. (1978) *Law and Marxism: A General Theory*, edited by Chris Arthur, translated by Barbara Einhorn, London: Inklinks.

Peaslee, A.J. (1968, 3rd edn) *Constitutions of Nations*, Vol. III Rev., The Netherlands: Martinus Nijhoff.

Pehe, Jiri (1994) 'Immigrants in the Czech Republic', *RFE/RL Research Report*, Vol. 3, No. 24.

People on the move. New migration flows in Europe, Strasbourg: Council of Europe Press, 1992.

Petö, I. and S. Szakács (1985) *A Hazai Gazdaság Négy Évtizedének Története 1945-1985*, Vol. I, Budapest: Közgazdasági és Jogi Könyvkiadó.

Pivovarov, Yu and A. Salmin (1994) 'Zametki na polyakh rossiskoi Konstityutsii' ('Notes on the new Constitution'), *Oktyabr* No. 1.

Plender, Richard (1988) *Basic Documents on International Migration Law*, Second, revised edition, Dordrecht: Nijhoff.

Pogany, I. (1993) 'Constitutional Reform in Central and Eastern Europe: Hungary's Transition to Democracy', 42, *International and Comparative Law Quarterly*.

Pogany, I. (1996) *Righting Wrongs in Eastern Europe*, Manchester: Manchester University Press (forthcoming).

Polonsky, A. (1975) *The Little Dictators*, London: Routledge & Kegan Paul.

Posner, Richard (1992) *East European Constitutional Review*, Vol. 1, No. 3, Fall.

Pravda (1989) 'Vedomosti Verhovnogo Sovieta RSFSR', 11 April, No. 37.

Pzreworski, Adam (1986) 'Some Problems in the Study of the Transition to Democracy', in Guillermo O'Donnell, Philippe C. Schmitter and Laurence Whitehead (eds), *Transitions from Authoritarian Rule: Prospects for Democracy*, Part III, Baltimore: Johns Hopkins University Press.

Rapaczynski, A. (1993) 'Constitutional Politics in Poland: A Report on the Constitutional Committee of the Polish Parliament', in A. Howard (ed.), *Constitution Making in Eastern Europe*, Washington D.C.: Woodrow Wilson Center Press.

Report on the Tatarstan Referendum on Sovereignty, 21 March 1992. Prepared by the Staff of the US Commission on Security and Cooperation in Europe, 14 April 1992.

Réti, T. (1990) 'A Román Tervgazdaság Kialakulása 1944-1956', in G. Hunya (ed.), *Románia 1944-1990*, Budapest: Atlantisz Medvetánc.

Rittersporn, G. (1993) 'Buying Intellectual Pre-Fabs', 96 *Telos*.

Rothschild, J. (1974) *East Central Europe Between the Two World Wars*, Seattle and London: University of Washington Press.

Rothschild, J. (1993, 2nd edn) *Return to Diversity*, Oxford: Oxford University Press.

Rudden, B. (1994) 'Civil Law, Civil Society and the Russian Constitution', 110 *LQR*.

Rupeshinge, Kumar (1987) 'Theories of Conflict Resolution and Their Applicability to Protracted Ethnic Conflicts', *Bulletin of Peace Proposals*, 4 (18).

Sakwa, Richard (1993) *Russian Politics and Society*, London: Routledge.

Salt, John (1993) *Migration and Population Change in Europe*, New York: UNIDIR (United Nations Institute for Disarmament Research).

Salt, John, Anne Singleton and Jennifer Hogarth (1994) *Europe's International Migrants, Data, Sources, Patterns and Trends*, London: HMSO.

Savitsky, V. (1993) 'Will there be a judicial power in the new Russia?', 19, *Review of Central and East European Law*.

Schoch, Bruno (1992) *Nach Strassbourg oder nach Sarajewo? Zum Nationalismus in postkommunistischen Übergangsgesellschaften*, Frankfurt: HSFK Report 6.

Schöpflin, G. (1993) *Politics in Eastern Europe*, Oxford: Blackwell Publishers.

Schwartz, H. (1993a) 'The New Courts: An Overview', Vol. 2, No. 2, *East European Constitutional Review*.

Schwartz, H. (1993b) 'The New East European Constitutional Courts', in A. Howard (ed.), *Constitution Making in Eastern Europe*, Washington D.C.: Woodrow Wilson Center Press.

Schweisfurth, T. (1990) 'The Acceptance by the Soviet Union of the Compulsory Jurisdiction of the ICJ for Six Human Rights Conventions', 2, *EJIL*, 110.

'Secretary General's Address at University of Bordeaux', SG/SM/4560, 24 April 1991, p. 6.

Selbourne, D. (1994) *The Principle of Duty*, London: Sinclair-Stevenson.

Semler, D. (1993) 'The End of the First Russian Republic', *EECR*, 107.

Seton-Watson, R.W. (1943) *A History of the Czechs and Slovaks*, London: Hutchinson Publishers.

Shafir, Michael and Alfred A. Reisch (1993) *Roundtable: Transylvania's Past and Future*, 24 (2).
Sharlet, R. (1993) 'Russia: Chief Justice as Judicial Politician', *EECR*, 32.
Shehadi, Kamal S. (1993) *Ethnic Self-determination and the Break-up of States*, London: IISS/Brassey's Adelphi Paper 283.
Shestakov, L.N. (1990) *Prava cheloveka: sbornik universalnikh i regionalnikh mezhdunarodnikh dokumentov* (*Human Rights: Collected Universal and Regional International Documents*), Moscow: Moscow University Press.
Sieghart, Paul (1983) *The International Law of Human Rights*, Oxford: Clarendon Press.
Sík, Endre (1992) 'Transylvanian Refugees in Hungary and the Emergence of Policy Networks to cope with the Crisis', *Journal of Refugee Studies*, Vol. 5, No. 1.
Skubiszewski, Krzysztof (1993) 'Nationalism in Europe Today', *The Polish Quarterly of International Affairs*, 3 (2).
Smith, Anthony D. (1993) 'A Europe of Nations – or the Nation of Europe', *Journal of Peace Research*, 2 (30).
Snyder, Jack (1993) 'Nationalism and the Crisis of the Post-Soviet State', *Survival*, 1 (35).
Sokolov, Maksim (1993) 'Timeo Romanos et Dona Ferentes: Valerii Zorkin - triumf mirotvortsa' ('The Triumph of the Peace-Maker'), *Stolitsa*, No. 3.
Steele, Jonathan (1994) *Eternal Russia. Yeltsin, Gorbachev and the Mirage of Democracy*, London: Faber.
Stokes, G. (1989) 'The Social Origins of East European Politics', in D. Chirot (ed.), *The Origins of Backwardness in Eastern Europe*, Berkeley, Los Angeles, Oxford: University of California Press.
Study on the Rights of Persons Belonging to Ethnic, Religious and Linguistic Minorities (1991), New York: United Nations.
Sunstein, Cass (1993) 'Against Positive Rights: Why social and economic rights don't belong in the new constitutions', 2, *East European Constitutional Review*, 35.
Swain, G. and N. Swain, (1993) *Eastern Europe Since 1945*, London: Macmillan.
Sword, K. (ed.), (1991) *The Times Guide to Eastern Europe*, London: Times Books, revised edition.
Szücs, Jenő (1993) 'Three Historical Regions of Europe: An Outline', in John Keane (ed.), *Civil Society and the State*, London: Verso.
Takada, Bin (1985) Die Auseinandersetzung um 'Rechtsstaat und rule of law', in Japan nach dem zweiten Weltkrieg (1945–1955). Österreichische Zeitschrift für Öffentliches Recht und Völkerrecht, 36, 9–32.
Teubner, G. (1991) *Law as an Autopoietic System*, Oxford: B. Blackwell.
Thornberry, P. (1991) *International Law and the Rights of Minorities*, Oxford: Clarendon Press.
Thornberry, Patrick (1993) 'The UN Declaration: Background, Analyses and Observations', in Alan Philips and Allan Rosas (eds), *The UN Minority Rights Declaration*, Turku: Institute for Human Rights Åbo Akademi University.
de Tocqueville, Alexis (1874) *De la démocratie en Américque*, Paris.
Tóth, Judit (1994) *Menedékjog – kérdőjelekkel*, Budapest: Közgazdasági és Jogi Könyvkiadó.
Trends in International Migration (1992) SOPEMI (Continuous Reporting System on Migration, Paris: OECD.
Trends in International Migration, Annual Report on Migration, 1993 SOPEMI (Continuous Reporting System on Migration), Paris: OECD, 1994.
Triggs, Gillian (1988) 'The Rights of "Peoples" and Individual Rights: Conflict or Harmony?', in James Crawford (ed.), *The Rights of Peoples*, Oxford: Clarendon Press.

UNHCR (United Nations High Commissioner for Refugees) (1993a) *The State of the World's Refugees; The Challenge of Protection*, New York: Penguin.

UNHCR (United Nations High Commissioner for Refugees) (1993b) *Legal Factsheet on Asylum Procedures in Central and Eastern Europe*, Prepared by the Regional Bureau for Europe of the UNHCR.

UNHCR (United Nations High Commissioner for Refugees) (1994a) *UNHCR Activities Financed by Voluntary Funds: Report for 1992–1993 and Proposed Programmes and Budget for 1994, Part III. Europe*, UN, A/AC.96/808 (Part III).

UNHCR (United Nations High Commissioner for Refugees) (1994b) *An Overview of Protection Issues in Western Europe:Legislative Trends and Positions taken by the UNHCR*, mimeo, June 1994.

Vaksberg, Arkady (1990) 'Legal Reforms and Basic Principles', in Brumberg (ed.), *Chronicle of a Revolution: A Western-Soviet Inquiry into Perestroika*, London: Pantheon.

Vaksberg, Arkady (1990a) *The Prosecutor and the Prey: Vyshinsky and the 1930s Moscow Show Trials*, London: Weidenfeld.

Van den Berg, G. (1989) 'The Conflict of Civil and Administrative Law in the USSR: Right to Housing and Freedom of Choice of Residence in Soviet Law and Practice', in Ginsburgs (ed.), *Soviet Administrative Law: Theory and Practice*, Amsterdam: Kluwer.

Van den Berg, G. (1992) 'Human Rights in the Legislation and the Draft Constitution of the Russian Federation', 18, *Review of Central and East European Law*, 197.

van der Stoel, Max, (1994) 'Preventing Conflict and Building Peace: A Challenge for the CSCE', *NATO Review*, 4 (42).

Várady, Tibor (1993) *Keynote Address on the First Regional Conference of the ILA* Budapest, October 2.

Vyshinsky, A. (1948) *The Law of the Soviet State*, New York: Macmillan.

Walicki, Andrzej (1987) *Legal Philosophies of Russian Liberalism*, Oxford: Clarendon Press.

Walter, R. (1994) 'Central European Constitutional Courts and Pure Jurisprudence', in *Právník 2*, CXXXIII.

Weber, M. (1921) *Wirtschaft und Gesellschaft*, Tubingen: J.C.B. Mohr.

Weitz, Richard (1992) 'The CSCE and the Yugoslav conflict', *RFE/RL Research Report*, 5 (1).

Wettig, Gerhard (1992) *Nation und Konflikt in Osteuropa nach dem Zusammenbruch des Kommunismus*, Cologne: Berichte des BIOst 28.

Weydenthal Jan B. (1994) 'Immigration into Poland', *RFE/RL Research Report* Vol. 3, No. 24.

Whyte, J.H., Letter to Clerk Assistant to the Northern Ireland Assembly, 16th September 1984, reproduced in *Second Report* from the Devolution Report Committee, Vol. II (Northern Ireland Assembly, 19th February 1985).8

Widgren, Jonas (1994) *A Comparative Analysis of Entry and Asylum Policies in Selected Western Countries*, Draft Version, Vienna: International Centre for Migration Policy Development.

Williams and Reuten (1993) 'After the rectifying revolution: the contradictions of the mixed economy? The political-economic transformations in central and eastern Europe', 49, *Capital & Class*, 77.

World Refugee Survey (1993) Washington D.C.: U.S. Committee for Refugees.

Yakovlev, A. (1988) 'The Political Philosophy of Perestroika', in Aganbegyan (ed.), *Perestroika Annual*, London: Futura.

Zaagman, Rob (1994) 'Minority Questions, Human Rights and Regional Instability: The Prevention of Conflict', in Robert L. Pfaltzgraff, Jr. and Richard H. Shultz, Jr. (eds),

Ethnic Conflict and Regional Instability: Implications for US Policy and Army Roles and Missions, Washington D.C.: Strategic Studies Institute, US Army War College.

Zaslavsky, V. (1993) 'Russia and the Problem of Democratic Transition', 96, *Telos*.

Zeman, Z. (1991, 2nd edn) *The Making and Breaking of Communist Europe*, Oxford: Basil Blackwell Ltd, Ch. 17.

Zile, L.Z. (1992) *Ideas and Forces in Soviet Legal History: A Reader on Soviet State and Law*, New York, Oxford: Oxford University Press.

Zoo, D. (1993) 'Democratic Citizenship in a Post-Communist Era', in D. Held (ed.), *Prospects for Democracy*, Cambridge: Polity Press.

Index